DAMPNESS I
Volumes 1 *&* 2 co

DAMPNESS IN BUILDINGS

VOLUME I & II Combined
Basement and ground floor conditions
   and
Condensation and penetration above ground

R. T. GRATWICK
B.E.M., A.I.O.B., F.R.S.H.

CROSBY LOCKWOOD & SON LTD
26 OLD BROMPTON ROAD, LONDON SW7

© *Copyright R. T. Gratwick 1966*

First published 1966
Reprinted with minor additions
and corrections 1968

SBN 258 96757 9

Printed in Great Britain by
Neill & Co. Ltd., of Edinburgh

Contents of Volume One

1	Problem and structure of materials	1
2	Physical interactions between materials	9
3	Interfacial reactions at material surfaces	16
4	Capillarity—Penetration of moisture into materials	25
5	Effect of surface treatments to porous materials	32
6	Condensation of vapour within pores	41
7	Examining damp walls and older remedies	49
8	Dealing with the cause, subsoil or land drains	56
9	Subsoil drains for running water and to assist tanking	65
10	Simple tanking to semi-basements	73
11	Encouraging evaporation from damp walls	80
12	Cutting and sawing in horizontal membranes	88
13	Examination of structural hazards prior to cutting in	95
14	Masking and lining treatments	103
15	Pore treatments, "linings and gels"	112
16	Proofing in depth, chemical infusion and injection	120
17	Tanking basements, injection and lining	130
18	Asphaltic linings, de-watering, loading, adhesion	138
19	Trees, plants and creepers; grouting structural fractures	146
20	Dealing with the cause electrically: electro-osmotic treatments	154

Contents of Volume Two

21	The processes of evaporation	179
22	Surfaces—Temperature and humidity	188
23	Diffusion of moisture vapour and heat through building constructions	195
24	Finding heat losses, surface and interstitial temperatures	202
25	Penetrating or condensational dampness	212
26	Occupational habits and dirty surfaces as a clue to condensational dampness	224
27	Use and placing of added vapour barriers and insulating layers	233
28	Ventilation—Convectional and fan-assisted; dehumidification	242
29	Condensation in domestic flues	253
30	Remedies for results of condensation in stacks and flues	264
31	Penetrating dampness in walls	279
32	Remedial measures for run-off penetration	290
33	Penetrative run-in not directly associated with weathered features	303
34	Jamb, sill, and isolated patches	317
35	External claddings and surface coatings	334
Appendix 1 Thomson weir		338
Appendix 2 Wet and dry bulb thermometers. Hygrometers.		340
Appendix 3 The Kata thermometer		345
Index		349

1: Problem and structure of materials

THAT the subject of dampness in buildings should continue to retain such interest, year after year, points to two conclusions; that moisture in the wrong places is a very real and continuing problem to many who build and maintain all kinds of buildings and that in many cases the inquirer does not really understand how, or why, the moisture got into the wrong place.

This state of affairs is not really surprising when one thinks of the variety of types of buildings, their location and their environment, the conditions under which they were built and by whom they were designed and built, quite apart from the materials used.

No other man-made product of similar magnitude, or complexity is subjected to the same degree of exposure, both climatic and occupational, as is a building. Furthermore, even with production line control or factory-built techniques or construction under cover, repair and maintenance work must needs be site work. One cannot return a defective building to the works for overhaul, repair or alteration. Such works, including perhaps the remedy for dampness, may have to be suited to a variety of environmental circumstances.

The builder sets a challenge to natural decomposition, for, after all, as far as material things are concerned, nature is a process of production, variation and decomposition. Even before the building is complete the "rot sets in." The elements, often aided by other influences, commence what will be the levelling process. Few people are unaware of the connection between dampness and decay in materials, even when the cause is a mystery to them.

Today, with ever rising costs and almost daily introduction of new materials, the industry is moving away from the traditional training systems. No longer is there time to learn only by our predecessors' successes or mistakes. We can profit by their, and indeed our own, experience. We can learn a tremendous amount from traditional building construction techniques, but sooner or later we come to the point when no one has met just this or that specific problem before. It may be dampness arising from a new type of construction or design, or affecting a new material. At this point sound traditional background knowledge, wide experience and good knowledge of the influences which affect materials in their surroundings, and of the material's characteristics, will be essential if a satisfactory solution is to be found.

We are today more able to find economic and satisfactory remedies to our predecessors' failures because our studies have included basic principles, building science if you wish, which, unless related to practice, may appear to be rather pointless. For instance, the study of evaporation of water and other liquids, or relative humidity of air, the solvency of water, all are of vital importance to the prevention or treatment of dampness, but unless we know what happens in practice, the knowledge alone is uninteresting. We do not all need to be experts in physics or chemistry, but a sound working knowledge of those principles which affect our business enables the approach to some, in fact very many, problems to become a matter of deduction and satisfactory solution, rather than guesswork.

It is quite obvious that many of the correspondents who reply to queries have this knowledge, and because of this often give the right answer. But the inquirer must at times be mystified by finding that two very different remedies are quoted to solve the same problem. Nor has he any idea why either remedy should solve the problem.

The omission of this full information, either from lack of space, or because the querist is usually satisfied without it, simply means that, given slightly different circumstances, another puzzled individual will either apply the same remedy and be disappointed or, as seems to be the case, send in another inquiry.

One realises that in a reply to a query it is not possible to give all the relevant information each time. Often such information is not needed, it might even confuse an individual inquirer. This book is written, therefore, with the object of supplying the relevant information. It commences with basic principles which may be repeated later should it appear helpful to an explanation.

The author appreciates that there can be more than one satisfactory answer to many problems and, further, that others may have found the information by experiment, research and study. He hopes, therefore, that readers will not hesitate to offer their comments to promote continued thought and discussion upon this important subject. It is only by such exchanges of information that progress is made.

He points out that some of the explanations, conclusions and diagrams are not in all respects exact in scientific detail, but they are sufficiently correct to present basic principles in simple form without falsifying them.

Before turning one's attention to the properties of individual materials about which it is necessary to have basic knowledge in relation to the problems of dampness, it will be useful to take a look at matters generally.

Material, be it water, brick, stone or steel, occupies space and is composed of tiny particles, each of which can have a separate existence in the particular substance of which it forms a part. Under a powerful microscope these particles are recognisable. Each piece will be identical to every other piece of that substance in all of its characteristics under the same conditions, temperature, environment, etc.

With simple substances, elements such as carbon, oxygen or copper, the smallest particle possible is called the atom. Those of more complicated substances, chalk, water or bronze, are called molecules. Molecules contain two or more, but not necessarily different atoms.

The space occupied by one atom or molecule of a substance

4 DAMPNESS IN BUILDINGS

cannot at any one time be occupied by any other atom or molecule of that same, or any other, substance (fig. 1). Nevertheless atoms and molecules are not themselves solid and, furthermore, are not each in contact physically with their fellows within the mass or piece of which they, individually, form part.

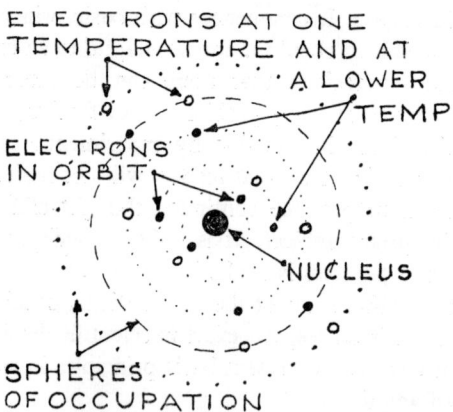

FIG. 1. *Matter; sphere of occupation. Electrons move constantly around a nucleus at high speed. Their relative station varies with heat content.*

The fact that we can have a piece of material larger than its smallest particle indicates that these smallest particles have the power to hold together despite the fact that they are not actually touching one another (fig. 2). Their ability to hold together is known to us as their strength. It will be seen that each and every different material has its own special characteristics in this important respect. Strength to resist being pulled apart, pushed together, twisted out of relative position, etc., but here again subject to temperature, environment, etc.

The effect of adding heat to, or subtracting heat from, materials does, in most instances, result respectively in expansion and contraction. Indicating movement within the mass or piece.

Since heat is a form of energy, it is not difficult to deduce that atoms and molecules do, or can, contain energy; that it is energy

DAMPNESS IN BUILDINGS 5

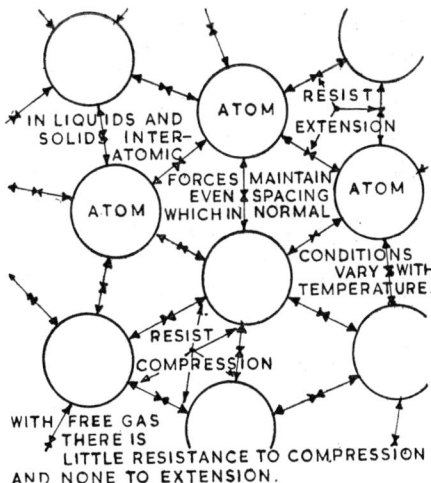

FIG. 2. *In solids the atoms vibrate, but normally do not change relative position even under temperature changes. Liquids and gas atoms change relative positions with such variations. As temperature rises interatomic forces weaken; with reduction they strengthen.*

in one form or another which gives them their strength in its various respects and that these characteristics will vary with alteration of that energy content. We have proof of this when a solid melts under added heat energy and the atoms or molecules are no longer able to hold together sufficiently well to retain shape. The resulting liquid needing to be retained within a vessel if it is not to run away. The liquid will have very little tensile strength or resistance to being pulled apart, whereas, as a solid the substance had considerable ability in this respect (fig. 3).

As it is not possible with our present knowledge to control the heat content of any material absolutely, then the atoms and molecules of every substance must be in a state of constant movement in relation to one another, either moving closer together or further apart. The exact position at any one moment being relative to the energy contained.

6 DAMPNESS IN BUILDINGS

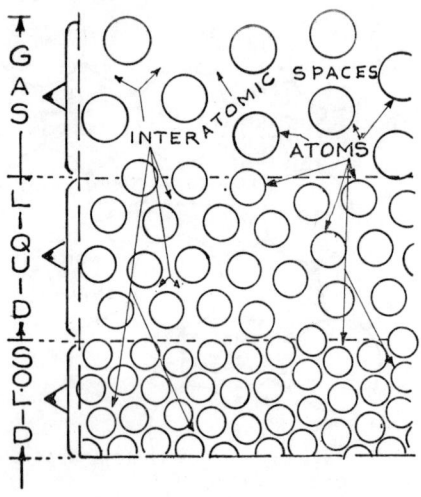

FIG. 3. *Symbolic representation of the three states of a substance. Increase in inter-atomic space occurs with increase in temperature and results in a change of state at certain levels. Heat absorption is energy intake.*

This is not the whole story, because the atoms themselves, not being solids, are also under the influence of energy, having constant motion within. Simply, an atom consists of a nucleus having positive electrical charge and electrons negatively charged. The composition of the nucleus and the number and disposition of electrons making up the atom varies with the substance.

It is when some form of applied energy, heat, electrical, chemical, or even light, disturbs the balance between the positive and negative electrical charges of the nucleus and the electrons, usually by causing alteration in the number of electrons under attraction to the nucleus, that the substance changes its characteristics. Part of it perhaps becoming another new and different substance and the remainder, or both parts, becoming parts of other substances. Alteration in the number of electrons associated with a nucleus does not necessarily change that element's essential characteristics. In some chemical combinations we find that when

Few atoms exist individually, even as element substances. When they are not individual then the unit particle of the substance is a molecule. Molecules have reactions to energy and combination, etc., in many respects similar to those of atoms.

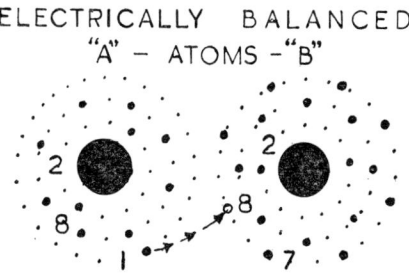

FIG. 4. *The odd electron with its negative charge leaves atom A and joins B. Atom B then has a positive charge and B is then negative. They will cohere to form a molecule of a new substance held together by electrical attraction. Salts are formed in this way. Where electron totals are even they will be shared and the atoms grafted together. Each of those in the new substance achieves electrical balance. Coherence can be broken electrically, but graft unions cannot be broken in this way though they may be broken by heat or chemical energy.*

two atoms have their electrical charges, nucleus to electron proportions disturbed (one positively rich due to the loss of electrons and another negatively rich due to the addition of electrons), they are held together by electrostatic attraction, whereby particles having unlike charges are attracted and those having like charges are repelled (fig. 4). This is so whether the particles are atoms or large visible pieces like dust. In other combinations the total number of electrons become shared by the two or more nuclei, each having an equal number in its attraction.

It will be seen from this that if three atoms combine under such conditions then the total number of electrons they contain must be divisible by three. Odd electrons being released entirely to some other atoms willing and able to receive them, either to become another individual substance, or to go into attracted combination with another of positive attraction, or be retained under the common influence of more than one positive attraction.

These properties of atoms and the characteristics of their combination into new substances can be the cause of dampness and can also be utilised for its cure and prevention. So too can those of inter-atomic and inter-molecular energies.

2: Physical interactions between materials

WE saw in chapter 1 that while no atom or molecule can occupy at a given moment, the same space as another, they can, in fact, pass between one another under certain conditions, the relative strengths of the inter-atomic or inter-molecular forces setting the condition. If this were not so then mixtures and combinations could not take place. Furthermore, it is also possible to understand that parts of these particles can pass into or out of attraction of others which again would not be possible if the internal attractive and repellant forces could not be influenced.

One further aspect of the reaction of inter-atomic and inter-molecular forces to the application or extraction of energy, which we should consider before proceeding, is that just as by applying or taking away heat we cause a substance to expand or contract, if we apply another form of energy to that substance which causes its inter-atomic or inter-molecular forces to alter in intensity one way or another, then it must take in or give up the balancing energy in some other form. Thus, if we exert mechanical pressure upon a substance and cause it to contract it must, if internal temperature stresses are to be relieved, give up heat or, vice versa, absorb it if we mechanically expand the substance (fig.5). Similarly, the release of absorption of electrical energy can be effected by applying the correct form of persuasion, chemical or mechanical.

Finally, in these respects we must bear in mind that no piece of material is independent of any other piece of material with which it is in inter-atomic or inter-molecular force reaction contact (as we usually express it). Solids may be in contact with other solids, or liquids, or gases. Within the gravitational attraction of this earth loss of contact between two pieces or surfaces of material is only possible if we provide a complete vacuum between them and then only in certain respects. Radiant energy would be able to have effect across a vacuum, but with this we are not basically concerned except where the effects of radiant heat would influence the warmth of a material and its behaviour in relation to moisture.

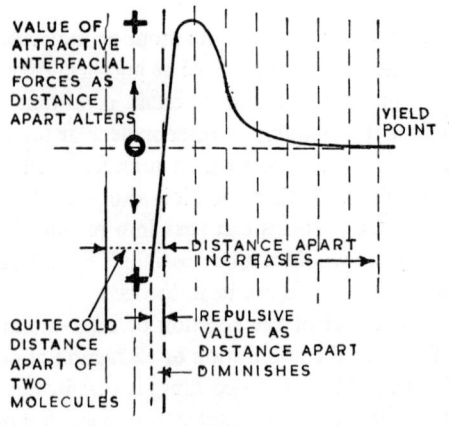

FIG. 5.

Few people today are surprised when a drip-dry shirt drips dry, and if you ask them why it does so they usually reply that it is siliconised. Further than that many are not interested, but we are; if a shirt can be made to drip dry so can a wall. In fact, the solution of the wall problem resulted in the shirt treatment. The problem is similar.

Similarly, few of us are surprised when dust adheres to a damp surface. But do we always show any surprise when it continues to adhere after the wall or surface dries off? Do we presume that in the damp state a form of glue is manufactured from the dust and that this glues the dust to the wall in its dry state? Then, if so in every case, why does perfectly dry dust stick to perfectly dry walls or ceilings; which also happens.

The first problem may be answered as follows: the wet wall provides the initial arresting power to the airborne dust by taking it into its mass when it touches the surface, the drag exerted by the water molecules being greater than that of the constituents of the air mixture. When the moisture evaporates or soaks into the surface of the wall, the dust particles are left in such close contact with the wall material molecules that, providing that too many dust atoms or molecules are not outside their influence, then the mutual attraction or inter-atomic or inter-molecular forces hold the dust particle to the wall in defiance of gravitational pull. It often only takes the influence of a draught of air or a feather duster to disturb the hold, but, nevertheless, it is there.

In the second instance the electrical charge of the surface has in some way become disturbed and so has the dust so that each has opposite tendency, electrical potential as it is called, to the other and when they are brought into reasonably close proximity seek contact with each other.

In this case we could separate them by adjusting the wall or dust charges, when as similar attractions they will repel one another. This process is followed in some air cleaning plants and in smoke and grit arrestment in chimneys. Surfaces vulnerable to such dry dust adhesion can be treated with "anti-static" compounds.

Why soakage occurs

Having now examined some of the characteristics of matter let us turn our attention to application of some of them to our problem, water, or moisture, in the wrong places.

Water gets into the wrong places either by running freely, normally downwards; being driven in in almost any direction by wind; or by standing pressure from some substance with which it is in contact; or by soakage, which also can occur in any direction. Often the circumstances permit one, two, or all methods to take effect in stages, or progressively.

The diagnosis of running water is not always as easy as might be supposed, the points of entry and those of effect often being some distance apart and apparently unrelated. Furthermore, running water may only show in effect after being driven or by subsequent soakage.

Similarly, driven water may drive so far and then run or soak before its effects become apparent. Thus this term soakage can be linked with much dampness.

We talk of a wall soaking up water like a sponge, when with reference to modern synthetic sponges we really mean like blotting paper; one must squeeze the air out of a modern sponge before it will take up water to any rapid extent. Even a real organic sponge takes up much of the water it can hold in the same way as the synthetic one, but it will, if left standing in water, become wet above the water line. If left in contact with water, blotting paper will become, without any squeezing, absolutely sodden.

Why does this occur, particularly in defiance of gravitational effects? To find the answer we must pursue our investigation into inter-atomic and inter-molecular forces.

If we are agreed that each atom or molecule is held in position relative to the others in a piece or mass, by forces which can both push and pull, then those beneath the surface will be acting in all directions because they are surrounded. Furthermore, those at a depth below a horizontal surface will, unless they are of some gases, be subject to additional pressures from the gravitational pull, or weight as we usually express it, from those above. The deeper they are the greater the pressure.

This is more apparent with liquids and we say that pressure at any depth is relative to that depth and equal in all directions: Note the equal in all directions, very alike to inter-atomic forces. That it occurs in solids is borne out by the fact that when a column of solid material fails under its own weight, it bursts near the bottom. Bursts because the inter-atomic forces are unable to hold the atoms together any longer because those at the sides have been stretched beyond the distance apart that they can hold one to the other any longer (see yield point, fig. 5). Those at the side give way because they have not got support from others in all directions. A liquid acts like this if the container is suddenly taken away and a gas bursts out, even in an upward direction under similar circumstances, unless it was a very heavy gas like bromine, which acts like a liquid in some respects.

You will note that with liquids and gases the container is important in retaining shape to all but one or all surfaces of a mass respectively, the solid mass being usually able to retain its shape in all directions, within limits, without container support. We shall probably have to consider the characteristics of "semi-solids" later when dealing with materials; pitches and bitumen being semi-solids.

Thus the surfaces of masses of material appear to have different characteristics to those of the body of the mass, and yet we saw earlier that every atom or molecule of any material is exactly alike in all respects at given temperatures, etc. One of these etc's, however, was environment and surface conditions differ because here two different substances are in contact. The difference is not chemical or of visual form, it is simply one of behaviour.

This characteristic behaviour of materials at their surfaces is called surface tension (fig. 6). It permits drops and globules of liquids to form in gases, and even one liquid within the mass or upon the surface of another and to remain upon solid surfaces, as we shall see later on. It also, although we do not usually consider this aspect, enables solids to retain their shape and recover it after distortion, providing, of course, that the elastic limit of the binding forces has not been passed. Indeed, some metals permit molecules or atoms to be driven about beneath the surface by the process of "bossing" so that intricate surface shaping enclosing the mass can be achieved.

The solid does not, however, naturally assume globular shape in the piece at ordinary temperatures, but it will do so as a liquid when molten, and if we cool the globules so formed they remain in that shape unless the molten liquid is contained within a shaped vessel or mould; even then it reacts like a liquid by filling the vessel to a "level" and also conforming to free to air surface characteristics as would a liquid.

Surface tensions of materials are important to our study of dampness. Most people are familiar today with the term capillary, meaning a fine tube, although we now refer to hair-like cracks or fine spaces between two surfaces as capillaries as well. Most people also understand the connection between such cavities and moisture penetration, capillary attraction, often and perhaps more correctly termed action, but it is worthwhile at this stage to look a little more closely at this phenomenon.

In chapter 1, fig. 3, we showed molecular particles in a solid closer together than those of the liquid and these in turn not so widely spaced as those of the gas. Also in that drawing we showed the planes where particles of two different substances or states of the same substance meet, as indented or irregular sections on the plane. This was because if a body is composed of globular pieces, and each of these pieces must be identical to all of the other particles in the mass, then, however dense the substance, they cannot pack to form other than a "pimply" indented surface.

If you put similar-sized steel balls into a glass box without packing them carefully, the nearest balls to any one side of the box will not all be actually touching the glass, and when we consider that with the atom or molecular "balls" these do not touch one another and are spacing themselves off in all directions from each other, it would appear extremely unlikely that any surface, particularly one that has been cut or manufactured to shape, could present a surface as uniform as the packed balls. Even if the particles do pack, the surface they present will still be a series of domes and intermediate valleys.

If now we indicate the inter-atomic or inter-molecular forces in the conventional way, radiating out in all directions from each particle, we find that at a surface there are some forces, those which are extending outwards, which are not balanced or counteracted by others of the same strength (fig. 6).

As each particle has (providing the temperatures are similar) the same potential force to repel and attract its neighbours and

Surface tension is contained only within a depth from surfaces equal to a few interfacial molecular distances, where the facial energy is not all balanced by counteracting forces from within the mass contained within the surfaces.

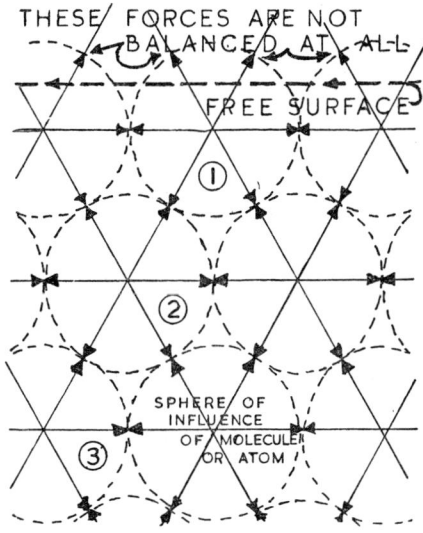

FIG. 6. *Layers of molecules in order 1-2-3 have less and less unbalanced potential energy to spare as the depth below the surface increases.*

also at a few atoms distance one from another, there can be only the most minute variation in a mass, then we could expect that those at the surface would want to utilise the potential not required to repel and attract neighbours of their own, to try to bring their forces into balance or equilibrium by counteracting those of other materials within range. If that effort is not sufficient to balance their forces, then one would expect these atoms to seek some other means such as forming stronger links with their neighbours in a similar state of unbalance.

3: Interfacial reactions at material surfaces

AS we have decided that the inter-molecular forces are in many respects relative to density in a material, it is logical to conclude that as a rule in its heavier state it should have the highest potential and, also, that their surfaces in any state should present particles with the highest amounts of forces unbalanced and available to form stronger links with its neighbours, attract and seek to balance those from meeting surfaces of other materials.

We can depict this state of affairs by force lines (fig. 7, a, b, c) to find, if we experiment with materials, particularly liquids having varying potentials, that providing gravitational forces do not overcome the upward effort of resistance of the lower plane the surfaces remain level, at a constant distance from the earth's centre, providing also that they are both of the same area. But if we introduce a third element or surface into the diagram (fig. 8)—which obviously must be at an angle to the other two, or the three cannot meet at any point—then the results must, if the three surfaces be of different substances, vary according to the relative potentials of the three surfaces.

In addition to these potentials, we must remember that at the same time that they are operative, so also is the earth's gravitational pull. Under this latter environmental effect, we must consider the fact that while liquid masses of relatively small dimensions, suspended in air or in another liquid, or a gas within a liquid, assume spherical shape (fig. 8), they cannot remain as spheres upon coming to rest against a surface beyond which they either cannot pass because it is too solid in a downwards direction

DAMPNESS IN BUILDINGS 17

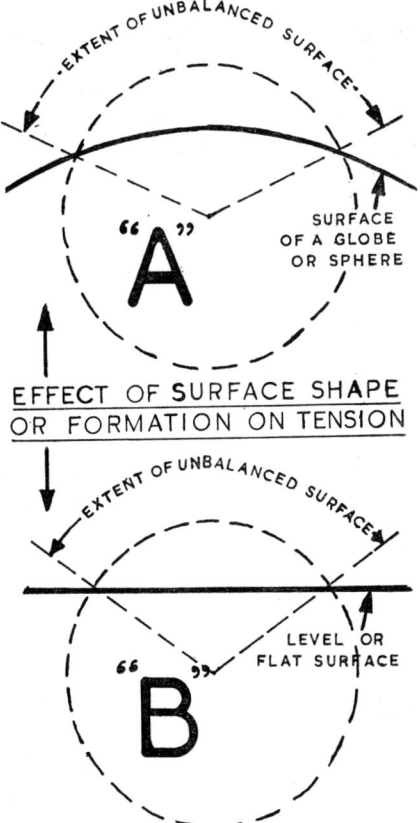

FIG. 7a. *Level surface B permits a smaller amount of energy to remain unbalanced than does that of a sphere A. Liquid or gas surfaces can hold the mass in one piece better as a sphere than as any other formation because more forces are available for division laterally.*

or pass upwards because the surface tension of the surface is too strong to be broken by their upward thrust.

This is evident when we put a drop of liquid upon a surface which it cannot wet or spread over. A flattened drop results, or

18 DAMPNESS IN BUILDINGS

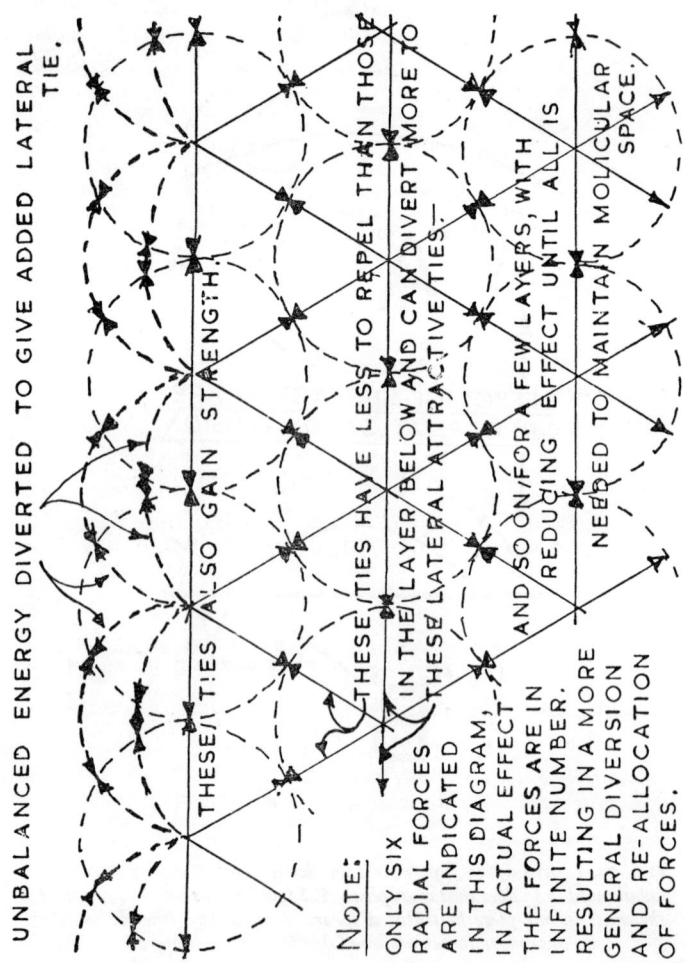

FIG. 7b. *As energy becomes surplus to balance requirements in any one direction, generally upwards, so it can be used to strengthen lateral ties and the surface layers develop surface tensions. Inward ties are also strengthened in these layers.*

DAMPNESS IN BUILDINGS 19

MULTIPLE FORCE LINES DIVERTED

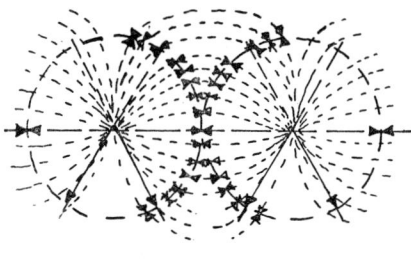

FIG. 7C.

beneath the surface of a liquid a flattened bubble lies. Furthermore, you will notice that the larger the drop then the flatter the formation. Gravity is the force trying to flatten the drop and surface tension is trying to maintain the sphere (fig. 8).

Since from your mathematical studies you will have learned that volume or weight is related to the cube of the linear dimension and surface or area only to the square of that dimension, then you will readily recognise that as the drop size increases so the difference between these two forces must also increase proportionally. With a small drop the surface tension can hold particles within the "skin" very nearly as a sphere, while the larger drops flatten until they have only spherical perimeters and top surfaces of upward curvature depending upon area covered, the smaller being visibly curved, the larger so much less that they appear to be flat (fig. 8).

It is supposed that liquids which "wet" surfaces spread out over those surfaces until they are little if any more than one molecule deep and the attractive forces of the surfaces have completely overcome the tensions of the liquid. This can happen not only on horizontal but also to a large extent with inclined and vertical solid surfaces. A tiny drop coming into contact with a vertical surface, or even the soffit or underside of a horizontal surface, first clings as a sphere, but then, providing that the surface is wettable, spreads out just as though it were a blot of ink upon blotting

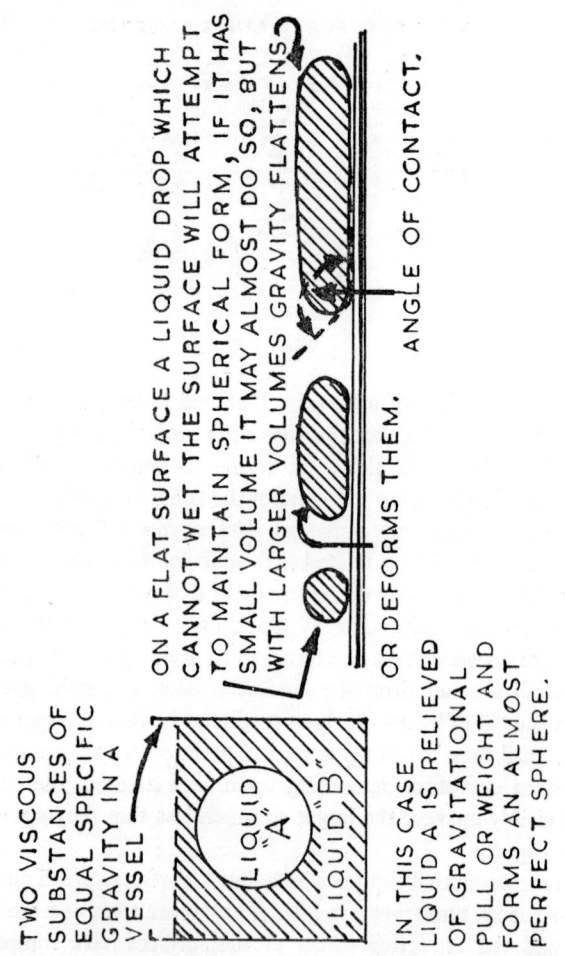

FIG. 8. *Surface tension together with gravitional pull (weight) control the shape or form of section which liquids assume.*

paper, but without necessarily soaking in, and vice versa on non-wettable surfaces. In fact, quite large liquid areas will retract to form drops within "skins" upon surfaces, apparently defying gravity (fig. 9). If this were not so then in the first

DAMPNESS IN BUILDINGS 21

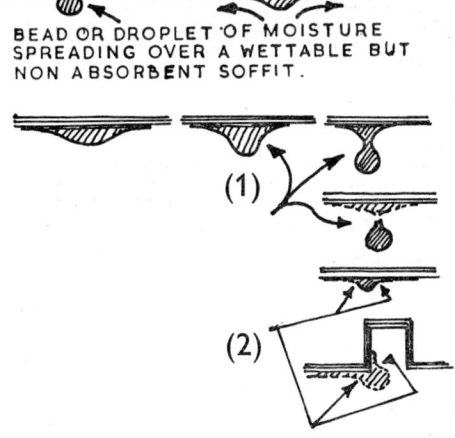

FIG. 9. (1) *Drips usually form where depth of the moisture film is increased where the creep meets a third plane—a speck of dust in a paint film or a drip or throat. It commences as two meniscuses.* (2). *If more moisture joins the spreading droplet, gravity will draw down the skin until it gives way and the droplet falls.*

instance there is no reason at all why circular wet patches—moist patches is perhaps more correct—should occur upon non-absorbent vertical of soffit surfaces, or indeed why drips should form and drop in the second.

Thus we see from this wetting of surfaces that drops of liquids can also hang from a surface to the extent of their surface tension's ability to counteract gravity or weight. When this occurs, part —note, part—of the liquid drips off and falls (fig. 9), or on the vertical or inclined plane the portion runs down the surface and in this latter case may, if it is not reinforced by joining with other similarly attracted quantities to form a stream, cease to continue its downward movement when the tensions and gravity regain equilibrium over larger areas.

The fact that the wetting liquids can creep up as well as sideways and downwards over the surfaces of solids puts our thoughts on to the first rung of the ladder in understanding capillary action.

The knowledge of the relative dimensions of the drop related to the gravitational pull upon it, particularly the reference to the area of the flattened drop and its perimeter and top surface shape, gives us a further rung or two progress.

It is possible to calculate the strength of surface tensions and the tangential angles (angles of contact) (fig. 8) which liquids will assume to solid surfaces or, in fact, liquid to liquid where they do not mix, but we do not need to be concerned with such complicated exercises for the purpose for which we are examining these properties.

The diagrams will, I hope, so far have shown simply, if the mutually attractive molecular unbalanced surface forces theory of surface tension is accepted, how surface tension comes into being from whence the forces are gathered and how the shape of the drop is influenced by gravity. Now let us try to depict the actions at these three-way junctions. If we can do this then we shall be able to understand fully why capillary action occurs and why it sometimes does not.

An alternative theory, with regard to which reference will be made in a later chapter and which is rather more difficult to understand and simply explain and illustrate, both as to the reasons for wetting or spread of liquids over solid surfaces and capillary effect in fine tubes, that surface tensions result from the inward pull of atoms or molecules without any assistance from "unbalanced" surface forces, in which case no "skin" is necessary or exists at a surface, which is now accepted by most authorities as the most reliable theory, would at this stage not assist readers generally in understanding capillary action any better than the mutually attractive theory so far here examined and for many years accepted in textbooks.

Let us therefore assume that we have a liquid which can wet solid surfaces. If we put a large drop of this upon a level surface it will flatten and begin to creep in all directions until such time as the vertical downward effects of gravity and the horizontal attraction to the solid surface particles around its perimeter can both be balanced by the liquid surface tension (fig. 10).

DAMPNESS IN BUILDINGS

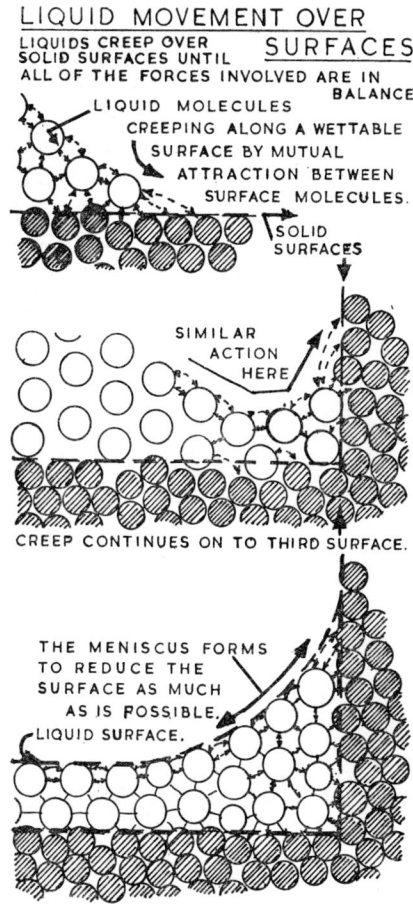

FIGS. 10 and 11.

Depending upon the weight of the liquid relative to the surface tension, so we will have a fully or less fully flattened drop. If, however, before the liquid can reach this state of balance of forces the perimeter should meet a third, shall we say a vertical, plane, then it is logical that it should want to continue to creep. In this case it creeps up the surface since the solid particles of the vertical surface immediately above the liquid surface are in exactly the same position relative to those at the perimeter of the liquid as if they were an extension of the level surface (fig. 11). This creates a situation where the liquid has to progressively overcome increasing gravitational forces resulting from increased depth of liquid. The liquid will attempt to conserve its tensional forces by reducing its surface area. It will try to form a sphere which is the only way in this case that the surface tension can be reduced and so release forces to permit continuation of the creep over the solid surface. The curvature of liquids at junctions like this is called the meniscus.

4: Capillarity–Penetration of moisture into materials

WE saw in the last chapter that with a large drop of water its upper surface became almost level away from its perimeter, but that as the drop became smaller this surface became increasingly convex. It does not take a great deal of thought to realise that surfaces of liquids between vertical surfaces will react similarly as though they were the surface to air half of the drop.

If, however, the drop surface has not achieved its balance with gravitational forces, then it would continue to draw up, or not slump down, so if the liquid surface is between vertical solid surfaces and cannot, owing to restricted width, complete the required reduction then there must be forces available, as seen in fig. 12, which can still engage those of the solid surfaces and the creep will continue until a balance is achieved.

With a restricted area or distance between vertical surfaces the only force which can bring those of the solid surface and the liquid surface into balance is gravity. As the depth of the liquid increases so does the gravitational pull and so when this increases sufficiently to balance the other two, creep, or in this case upward movement, ceases.

It will be seen from fig. 12 that in a wide gap the forces balance at gravity level, the meniscus being confined to a very small curvature immediately adjacent to the vertical surface, but that as the width decreases the "level" surface between these curves also decreases. Also that until the optimum width is reached, no actual upward creep of the liquid as a whole can occur, but further, that if very restricted widths are involved then as the width diminishes

26 DAMPNESS IN BUILDINGS

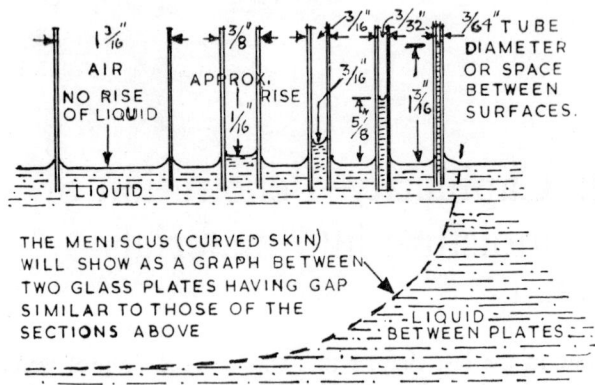

FIG. 12a.

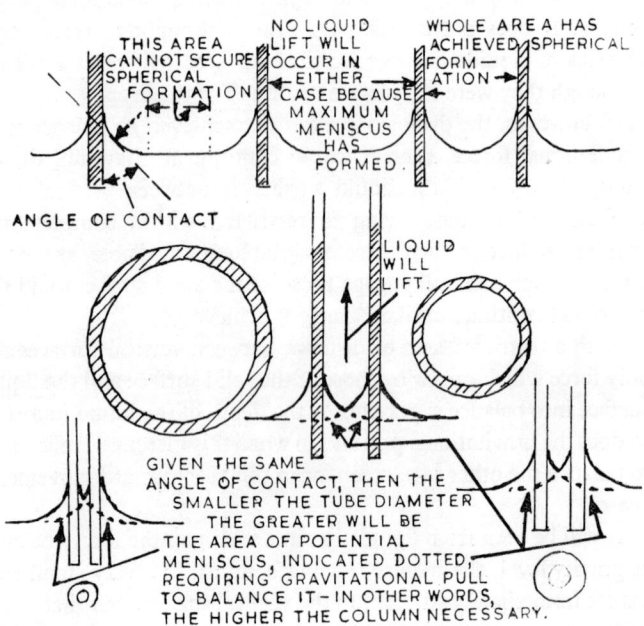

FIG. 12b.

FIGS. 12a and 12b. *Capillary action is most effective in fine tubes or spaces where the surfaces can be wetted.*

so too will the tendency for creep continue. Thus we find that capillarity is most effective in the finest tubes or cracks, always providing that environment is constant.

You will see that we take advantage of this knowledge when we introduce anti-capillary gaps in construction. They do in fact often occur as a natural "defect" in the tube or gap to give some materials limited porosity without permeability.

From the sketches it will be seen that it is not unnatural that some molecules should "pile up" at vertical abutments, as in doing so the molecule interaction between as many as is possible becomes more nearly balanced. Those packing into the meniscuses becoming more generally surrounded than if they were all adjacent to a flat surface.

We do find, however, that even when the surfaces are set sufficiently closely and the liquid is a wetting one capillarity may stop. The natural reaction to this train of thought is, why then does this process stop when there is still surface to climb. The answer may be one of several. The surface environment may alter when the liquid contacts warmer surfaces. If the solid is warmer then its attractive potential is lower than its cooler parts and, in its attempt to balance the heat energy content of the whole it warms the liquid and the gas. Then the whole balance is altered. Alternatively the gas alone may become warmer, sufficiently to be able to take up more liquid droplets into its mass, thus causing, if this process continues, continued loss of surface particles from the liquid, together with their potential. In fact if the process is sufficiently rapid then not only will the climbing process be halted, but the liquid surface will begin to fall. This is the process of evaporation.

Evaporation is taking place continually from liquid surfaces freely in contact with gases if those gases are not saturated already or under too great a pressure themselves. The ability of gases to hold liquid vapours, liquid particles so widely dispersed that they cannot be seen by the naked eye, but still not so widely separated as to have become the true gaseous form of the substance, varies with their temperature.

Most people relate evaporation to boiling but this is really accelerated evaporation. Even so this does demonstrate that this process can be speeded up if the liquid can gain added heat and the gas with which it is in contact can accept the liberated particles. When we see the vapour it indicates that the gas into which they are being forced by the violent surface expansions of the liquid is itself not sufficiently expanded, or warm as we say, to accommodate them individually. The liquid particles, therefore, form together into tiny drops contained within its surface tensioned forces.

If you look closely at a jet of steam emerging from a kettle spout or a steam outlet, you will notice that immediately outside the spout it is invisible. This is the true, or very nearly the true, gas of water, but within a very short distance the cooling influence of the air, although still quite hot, causes the inter-molecular forces of the water "gas" to reduce in intensity to an extent that the molecules (particles as we have been calling them) close together sufficiently to become a "mass" of the substance large enough to be seen, usually as a cloud of steam or mist.

The visible steam cloud, jet if you like, is all the time trying to return to its water state and is giving up heat energy as fast as possible to the air molecules, with which it can gain contact, but since in turn, as these gain warmth they open out, so then the process of evaporation, you note this time not boiling, recommences and if the air is sufficiently warmed, the steam cloud disappears again. This will continue until the whole of the air within warming range of the steam becomes saturated with water vapour. This means that the two gases have balanced their respective forces throughout their combined mass.

When this state has been achieved any further water "gas" will have to remain in droplets and so be visible unless it can find a means of releasing its surplus heat energy. This is a highly unnatural state for its environment and it will only remain suspended in the air if air movement exerts a persuasive effort upon its surfaces, the air molecules pushing and pulling it along and overcoming gravitational pull, just as they do to a piece of soot, dust or paper when it becomes windborne.

DAMPNESS IN BUILDINGS 29

You will note that if the material with which the steam or the air plus steam mixture can secure contact, can absorb some of its heat energy, then the loss of that heat enables the steam or the invisible vapour to revert to its normal state. If sufficient of these globules can get into attractive contact they will form pools, films and larger masses on surfaces or in air. Indeed, if the cooling stages are progressive at too rapid a rate the water droplets so formed in the air may become solid as ice.

I have extended this train of thought upon evaporation, particularly of water, because it is related to the prime material of dampness, in fact some of the sequences covered are at times the initial cause of moisture being in the wrong place; dampness.

If we continue and consider evaporation a little further, we will realise that since it is at liquid surfaces that this action takes place, then it is reasonable to suppose that the larger the surface a liquid exposes to a receptive gas, then the greater will be the total amount of the liquid evaporated, all other circumstances being equal. One of the equalising elements would, as we have seen, be temperature of the gas in contact and its relative humidity. But just as important, if the temperature and humidity balances are slight, is the ability of the gas to move over the liquid surface.

However little vapour from the liquid the gas can absorb there can be no further absorption once saturation level for the temperature has been reached and, furthermore, as this situation approaches the rate of absorption will decrease as it becomes more and more difficult for successive water gas particles to find gas particles still with potential unbalanced.

Therefore, the only way by which the evaporation process can continue at a non-decreasing rate is by means of gas movement over the surface. This should happen quite naturally if other influences do not prevent it. A mixture of gas and liquid vapour where the gas is air and the vapour is from water, is less dense than the air alone at any given temperature. This disparity in densities increases as relative humidity rises so that as a group of gas particles forms its association with vapour particles at the liquid surface the combined group become buoyant relative to the general gas mass and are displaced upwards by gas groups not yet associated with any or as many vapour particles. These movements are called convection currents.

The influences which might prevent such movement can and do often occur over large surfaces. A stream or large patch of cold, dry air can hold down warm, moist air for some time by its greater surface tension on its underside in just the same way as an air bubble can, if very gently formed beneath the surface of a liquid, remain submerged in contact with that surface and not break through, or a patch of heavy oil gently poured upon water float and not sink. The slightest ruffling disturbance at the surfaces, however, even if only initially causing a few particles of one of the surfaces to lose contact with one another, precipitates a wholesale breakthrough and natural stratification occurs quite rapidly.

Just as with capillary tubes the liquid surface tensions cannot equalise, and upward movement is induced, so in confined gas spaces these gas to gas tensions, if brought into effect gently, have this holding down effect within the gas mass. Furthermore, whereas over a wider area of surface the tension is more generally relatively weaker and liable to break up, so the reserve of potential at the surfaces in a capillary mitigate against breakthrough. The result being to prevent further evaporation, even when other conditions would permit its continuation.

Thus it is that only if this deadlock can be broken in the gas immediately above the liquid in a capillary, evaporation can continue and possibly assist in reducing the forward rate of movement of the liquid surface.

We have previously observed that surface tensions are weakened by increase in temperature of the particles involved. We can therefore reasonably suppose that if we can warm a capillary where it is in such a state of gaseous deadlock then the tensions will weaken and displacement within the gas mass could recommence, to permit continued evaporation. In fact if we only warmed the gas immediately above the deadlock level, we should reduce the tensions and, in addition, lower the relative humidity of the upper gas so that there would also be a strong tendency for vapour molecules, if abundant in the lower mass, to spread into the upper and so enlarge the buoyant bubble, thereby assisting its upward displacement simply by reason of the increased buoyancy bursting through any remaining tensioned surface above.

Similarly it is not difficult to understand that tensions in capillaries will be affected if air circulation can be induced near the area of a deadlock. This, however, is not at all easy. We should have to force in the air to cause movement in such fine tubes. We really want air circulation over the surface of the liquid. This can only be achieved without pressure if the tube can be cut very near to the point of deadlock, so that drier air passing over the cut end can induce movement sufficiently down the tube to disturb the air inside.

We see the effect of this where capillaries reach the surface of a material adjacent to drier air, particularly if that air is in motion. The surface will remain much drier than the general material mass, even if that mass is sodden, but only for a fractional depth inwards. With such surfaces we find that very slight air temperature or relative humidity change will make the surface appear damp or dry, often the change taking place quite rapidly. This is because of the very slight depth below the surface at which the tensions are balanced. Rarely do we find wet surfaces adjacent to well-ventilated areas.

At a later stage we shall have to consider ventilation and relative humidity in relation to dampness, but at this stage our next consideration ought to relate capillary to porosity.

5: Effect of surface treatments to porous materials

PORES are defined as fine tube-like spaces within otherwise solid material into which liquid can penetrate. We sometimes call them capillaries. The definition of "pore" states "... into which liquid can penetrate," but it does not say whether this is by running in or by capillary action. It does not really matter to us at this stage of our studies, but you will appreciate that water normally does not move uphill unless it is forced or drawn up by capillary forces. It is necessary to define pores so that we do not confuse these fine cavities with inter-molecular spaces, which, as we have previously seen, cannot be occupied by other matter as a separate, material mass.

The division of building materials into porous and non-porous groups is made basically upon the method of formation of the solid state. Non-porous materials are those which have cooled from a molten state. Metals, glass and granite are clear examples; bitumen and, in certain respects, plastics are others. It should, however, be noted that metal masses, however thick, resulting from electro-chemical deposition (or plating, as we call this process) are porous. This is why chromium plate upon steel "rusts." It is also the reason why hot-dip galvanising and molten zinc spraying give better protection to steel surfaces than plated or painted-on metal coatings.

On the other hand, porous materials such as timber, sedimentary stones of a softer nature, many kinds of bricks, ordinary concrete and plasters all form their solid states in the presence of liquids, usually water. The water carrying suspended particles, previously formed molecules of solid matter or materials in solution may either be squeezed out or evaporated out, or it may combine chemically, wholly or in part, with the other materials it acted as vehicle to, to form the solid mass. The removal of the liquid by any of these means results in a more open structure, particularly where surplus gasses result from the chemical combination or if evaporation occurs. In both these instances pores would be formed as the gases attempt to escape.

Having considered the relationship of surfaces to wetting by liquids it will be readily understood that, apart from those instances when the surface is wettable and water is forced into a pore by gravity or by the wind, liquids penetrate the pore and travel within it by capillary action. However, they cannot proceed until they have entered, and the entrance conditions of the pore are, therefore, most important. Potentially porous material need not necessarily be porous, and if penetration is rendered physically impossible the porosity does not become actual. Furthermore, porous materials need not be permeable, i.e., permit liquids to pass right through and exude from the opposite surface.

Proofing solutions

Thus, if quite a shallow depth of a capillary or pore has its surfaces rendered non-wettable to the liquid being considered, capillary action cannot commence because the liquid cannot get in. This is the property which many of the brush and spray-on proofing solutions impart to the pores when applied to building material surfaces such as brickwork, masonry and timber.

We find, however, that as a general rule the manufacturers of these solutions claim that in addition to proofing the surfaces their preparations permit the treated surface to breathe. In some circumstances this is a valuable property, permitting moisture-laden vapours to pass through the proofed structure, but in other circumstances it could bring complications. The important consideration from our point of view, that is, dampness in buildings is that these vapours should be able to pass "through" the structure and escape.

Since the treatment of a surface of a structure by this method is carried out to combat water penetration, the air in contact with the surface will be moist; in fact, it is quite likely to be saturated at times, if not constantly. Thus, the air "breathed" by the pores is carrying water vapour with it when it enters a pore. The non-wettable quality of the wall at the entrance of the pore will not prevent this vapour entering since wetting is unnecessary (fig. 13).

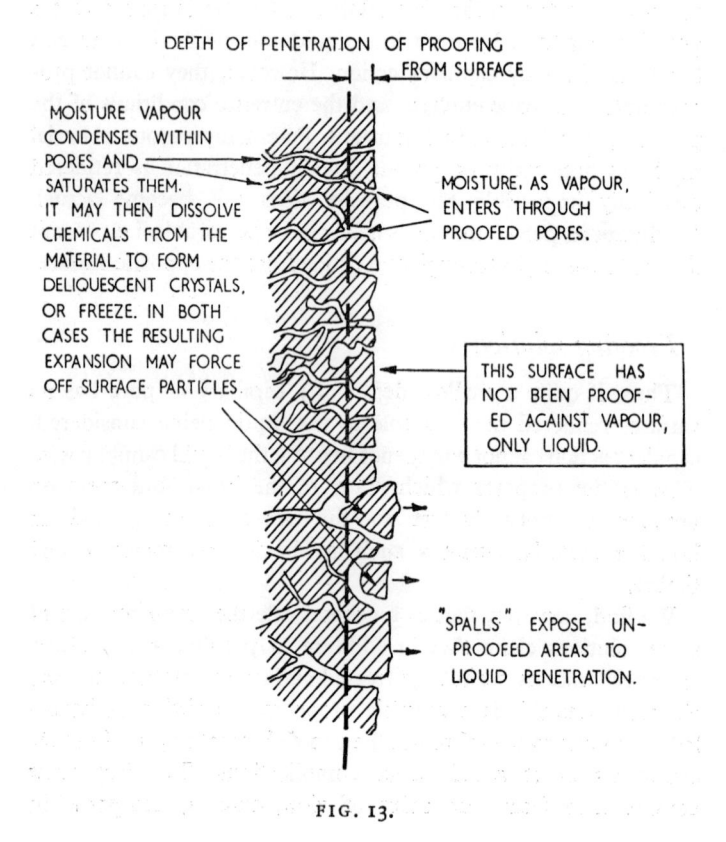

FIG. 13.

Having gained entrance its continued passage through and out from the other surface as a whole, air and vapour together, will depend upon, first, the relative humidity or percentage of moisture held by the air and, secondly, the temperatures of that air and of the solid mass in which the pores exist. If the air has high relative humidity it means that it is holding in invisible mixture almost as much vapour as it can at that temperature, and in the circumstances we are considering this is quite likely to be so. If the solid mass is cooler, condensation will occur as the solid extracts heat from the air in its attempt to equalise temperatures. This it must do if the natural laws of heat exchange are to operate. The conditions so created are known as "dew" conditions.

The moisture drops which form will first wet the untreated walls of the pores and then if the conditions continue, fill the pores. With non-wettable pore ends at the surfaces of the solid mass this water cannot run out or reach the surface by capillary action to re-evaporate and so it is trapped. Its only hope of escape is if the temperature of the solid mass is raised so that air in contact with the trapped water can take back heat from the solid and then can take up the water by evaporation and carry it out of the pore entrances as a vapour.

Trapped water

It is of little use raising the temperature of a proofed surface to attempt to draw out the trapped water because, as we saw earlier, evaporation is only effective to quite shallow depths into pores. Thus, if you proof surfaces by this method, you should at the same time take steps to prevent air of high humidity entering the pores, or, if it will still be able to enter, ensure its escape at the opposite surface by either not proofing that surface or maintaining the solid mass as a whole at a temperature high enough to prevent condensation within the pores. Fortunately, porous solids when dry do retain internally heat once gained better than when wet, but the drying out of the pores may be a very long process if surfaces are proofed while the solid is saturated.

So long as water is trapped within pores there is danger. Its presence facilitates the penetration of frost because wet porous solids lose almost all of their insulating powers. Also, the water may dissolve chemicals from the solid, which with others such as sulphuric acid already in the water can cause the formation of "salts" or crystals in the pores. This is especially true in the case of mortar joints. These reactions result in chemical expansion as crystallisation proceeds. Incidentally, you can see the effects of this quite clearly in isolated domestic chimney stacks, which bend over towards the south in the northern hemisphere as the northern joints swell with this "chemical expansion" more than those on the southern side due to their longer periods of saturation by rain.

In both cases expansion will take place just below the proofed surface and spalling of that surface will occur. This will open up unproofed deeper surfaces to direct wetting. In addition it is possible that where the material is strong enough to resist spalling the chemical salts which form in the pores will ease their expansion by exuding through the proofed entrance depth. This will show itself as efflorescence—a white powder staining the surface, and because this filling is of a deliquescent, water-attracting nature it may even draw in water through its crystalline structure and through larger proofed pores which it has filled. Wetting of the actual pore walls would not be necessary because the crystal pore-filling acts like blotting paper (fig. 13.).

So far as I am aware, none of the manufacturers of brush-on proofings claim longer life for the coating than five to seven years. This is not unnatural when one considers that these thin proofing membranes are subjected to all of the destructive tendencies of the weather—sun, wind, rain (often heavily polluted by acids, soot, etc.), frost and chemicals from the proofed material itself which is nearly always salt-laden before the application of the proofing. We tend to wait until things are at their worst until we proof so we cannot expect permanent remedial action or even long temporary life in all circumstances.

We must at a future date look into the question of treating solids with proofings throughout their thickness, but in the meantime

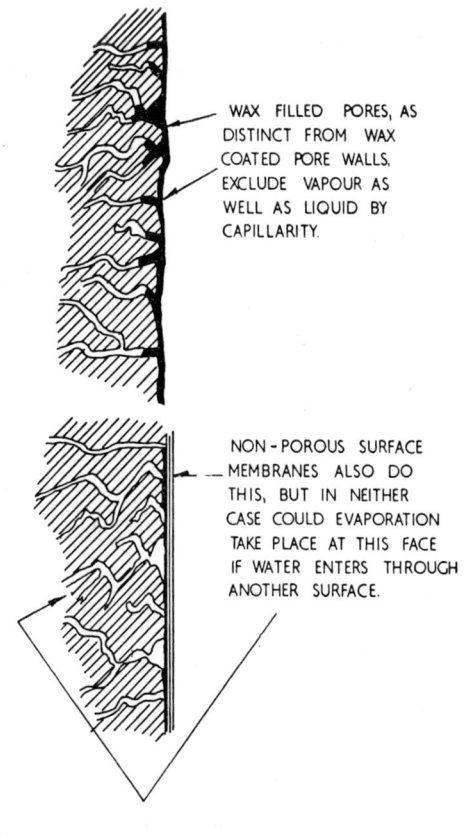

WAX FILLED PORES, AS DISTINCT FROM WAX COATED PORE WALLS, EXCLUDE VAPOUR AS WELL AS LIQUID BY CAPILLARITY.

NON-POROUS SURFACE MEMBRANES ALSO DO THIS, BUT IN NEITHER CASE COULD EVAPORATION TAKE PLACE AT THIS FACE IF WATER ENTERS THROUGH ANOTHER SURFACE.

FIG. 14.

note that if all of the pore ends are covered or filled with a non-porous membrane or filling, then capillary, soakage and condensation, within the pore, cannot occur (fig. 14). In this connection it should be noted that wax fillings are also subject to weather deterioration and are affected by sunlight in particular.

While we are considering this evaporation aspect of damp movement and deposition within porous solids, we can usefully look at the problem of a wall standing on its foundation in a wet soil.

38 DAMPNESS IN BUILDINGS

BETTER EVAPORATING CONDITIONS THIS SIDE RESULTS IN LOWER LEVELS OF BALANCE

WALL

GROUND LEVEL

WET EARTH

FOUNDATION

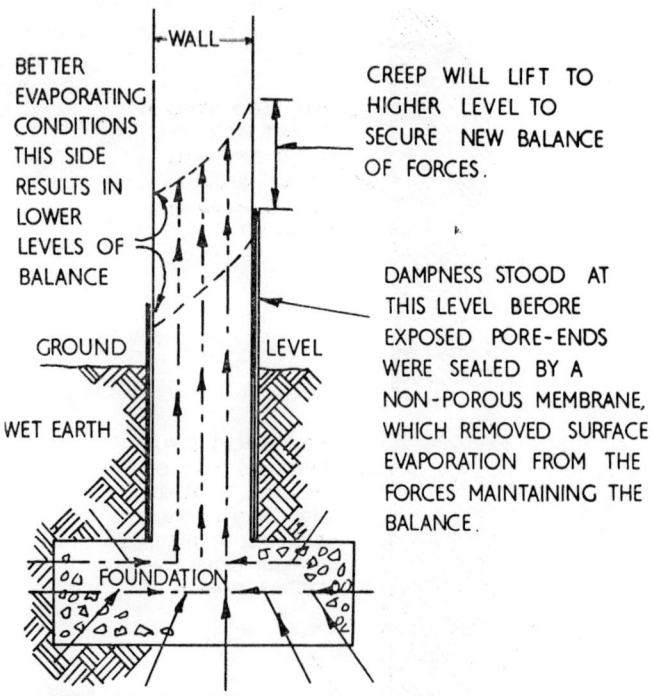

CREEP WILL LIFT TO HIGHER LEVEL TO SECURE NEW BALANCE OF FORCES.

DAMPNESS STOOD AT THIS LEVEL BEFORE EXPOSED PORE-ENDS WERE SEALED BY A NON-POROUS MEMBRANE, WHICH REMOVED SURFACE EVAPORATION FROM THE FORCES MAINTAINING THE BALANCE.

WATER GAINS ACCESS THROUGH PORE ENDS WHICH HAVE NOT BEEN PROOFED AND THEN CREEPS UPWARDS BY CAPILLARITY UNTIL ALL FORCES, GRAVITY, EVAPORATION AND CAPILLARY-CREEP SECURE A BALANCE, HOWEVER HIGH THIS MAY BE.

FIG. 15.

If we coat both sides of the wall itself, from the top of the foundation as is shown in fig. 15, then the sole result will be that the height to which the dampness rises will be increased. Capillary creep, gravity and evaporation must come into balance; if you reduce the effect of one of these forces then movement must recommence and continue until a new balance is achieved. In this case capillarity and gravity alone are seeking balance below the levels at which the proofing membranes terminate, the evaporating force having now been prevented from having its effect. Capillary action will lift the levels until either gravity alone halts its action or increased gravity effect plus renewed evaporation of lesser degree do so in combination.

Coating solutions, while having water repellent properties when applied and "dried", must in their liquid state have wetting powers in relation to the materials they are to proof. That this can be done shows that liquids, with proofings in solution or suspension can be designed to have specific tensions, enabling them not only to creep over or wet specified surfaces but also, if needs be, not to be able to do so over other surfaces. Proofing solutions and emulsions need to be designed for specific surfaces and most manufacturers have a range, each one suitable for one type of surface.

Proofing solutions

Until a few years ago proofing preparations were usually based upon paraffin wax or similar water repellents in solvent liquids other than water. Paraffin wax is still regarded as the most efficient repellent to water, the water having to its surfaces an angle of contact of about 106 degrees. Silicone liquid proofings in general use today give 90 degrees to 110 degrees. Neither paraffin wax nor silicones are soluble to any extent in water, but both can now be suspended in water as emulsions, tiny globules evenly distributed throughout, but not in solution with the vehicle suspending them. Each globule, although having lower or higher density than the vehicle liquid, is so tiny that it is unable to break through the liquid molecules and stratify. Being so tiny its own surface tensions are so strong that it retains almost perfect spherical shape, especially in a vehicle which cannot wet its surfaces.

The homogenisation of the insoluble butter fats in milk is an example of such suspension. The cream does not separate. Thus, today it is possible to use vehicles to carry or spread the proofing coat materials which will never the less mix with the water already in the pores, enabling pores already water filled or with wet surfaces to be treated and also achieving deep penetration by infusion. This is a valuable property when site treatment only is possible. Furthermore, the use of water as a vehicle in emulsions permits application to surfaces in contact with materials which would be damaged by spirit solvents, or where these might cause colours to run or greases to spread.

6: Condensation of vapour within pores

BEFORE leaving the consideration of condensation upon surfaces and within material thicknesses we ought to consider one other aspect. Flat roofs including those to vaults below footways, courtyards, etc, are nearly always covered on their outer side either mastic or as built-up "felts," sheet metal or perhaps a bitumen impregnated asbestos compound. Furthermore, such a roof, whether its base construction is timber or concrete, would be interlined between the watertight covering and the base with at least soft felting and most probably today with a depth of insulating material possibly of a porous nature.

Water vapour is less dense than air so that moisture-laden air will, under normal circumstances, rise within a room and come into contact with ceilings and soffits. Where the roof base is porous as is normal concrete or timber, then this moisture-laden air will pass through the pores and continue its upward passage through the base and porous insulation until it comes into contact with the underside of the covering. Here during cold weather, particularly at night when the sky is clear and heat losses by radiation to outer space are at their greatest, condensation will occur. This water will saturate the insulation and the felt (if present), rendering both of them useless for the purpose for which they were included in the construction, namely, to reduce heat loss and at the same time minimise heat gain from the sun.

Even the admission of solar heat does not help much to remedy this situation once it has occurred. It merely temporarily re-evaporates the upper water within the insulation which, being then warmer than the water-laden layers below, cannot escape downwards. It will merely push some of the liquid down in the pores, perhaps causing the appearance of sweat droplets on the soffit below. As soon as the sun sets the saturated situation will recur because the sweat, if it has not been evaporated into room atmosphere, will be drawn back into the pores. Where evaporation of sweat into room atmosphere has occurred, there is that much more room for vapour-laden air to re-enter when next it contacts the soffit.

If, however, we seal the underside of the insulation with a non-porous membrane such as thin sheet metal in foil form, a plastic film, or waxed or bitumen-treated paper, or use a non-porous insulator, expanded polystyrene or urathene for instance, then because the insulation remains dry and effective (see fig. 16) the concrete will also be kept at higher temperature and condensation will probably not occur at all.

Although this effect is most marked below roof surfaces, we find a similar problem where waterproof membranes are applied to the inside surfaces of damp external walls. Proofed cement and sand renderings, even an inch or so thick, must be classified in this case as membranes. The wall remains wet and cold because the membrane, being of dense material, is quite a good conductor and will present a cold surface to warm, moist air and surface condensation will occur. The effect will be seen as wet surfaces only where the rendering exists and not where softer and more absorbent surfaces present themselves. The wallpaper and decorations over the rendered areas will remain bleached even after the condensation has re-evaporated.

Damp walls

Where any form of non-porous membrane of dense material (even the now little used "pitch paper"), is applied to damp walls which will not subsequently dry out from other remedial action, then the membrane should be covered with a porous, absorbent layer of material such as soft plaster, expanded polystyrene, soft

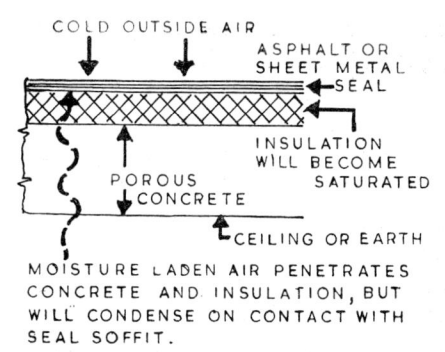

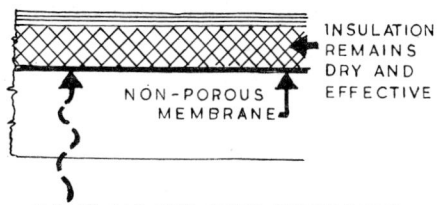

DAMPNESS IN BUILDINGS

[Diagram showing cold outside air penetrating asphalt or sheet metal seal, insulation, porous concrete, and ceiling or earth layers]

MOISTURE LADEN AIR PENETRATES CONCRETE AND INSULATION, BUT WILL CONDENSE ON CONTACT WITH SEAL SOFFIT.

[Diagram showing insulation remains dry and effective above a non-porous membrane]

MOIST AIR CAN ONLY PENETRATE THE CONCRETE AND AS THE DRY INSULATION KEEPS THE HEAT LOSS LOW, WATER VAPOUR IS LESS LIKELY TO CONDENSE INTO THE CONCRETE.

FIG. 16.

wall board. These materials will remain warm, and if condensation does occur on them they, expanded polystyrene excepted, will take the moisture up for the time being by absorption, but allow it to re-evaporate when air conditions within the room become less humid. There are, particularly in houses, periods of high and low humidity resulting from occupation or intermittent heating.

Whether condensation upon a surface will occur or not is decided within a very tiny temperature range if the air carrying the moisture vapour is at, or very nearly at, saturation point for its temperature. A degree or two can result in noticeable effects and several degrees in massive effects. Whether these are noticed, however, depends almost entirely upon the surface. If it is non-absorbent the droplets will be seen; if it is absorbent or can permit capillary flow, the vapour-laden air may penetrate and only condense inside, and if it does deposit its droplets on the surface they will be drawn in. In either case quite an amount can be accommodated before surface effects are noticed.

The manufacturers of such materials as expanded polystyrenes and insulation sheets and boards are aware of these properties of their products to the extent that they suggest that you place your hand on a surface of their materials and "feel the warmth." What they really mean is, experience the effect of your hand not losing heat to the surface, for that is what in fact happens. Normal heat losses from your hand (much of which by the way results from evaporation of body moisture or sweat through the skin pores), are carried away from the exposed skin by air circulating around it and by radiant effects. Insulators in contact with such a surface prevent, or at least considerably reduce, the possibility of both means of heat loss just as a glove on the hand would. Nevertheless this claim does show that "warm" surfaces, no matter how maintained, do assist in preventing condensation.

The problem of asphalted roofs has been tackled (in each case initially for other reasons), both by asphalt roofing manufacturers and by the Building Research Station. In both cases one of the remedies suggested was ventilating the roof cavities or insulating layer. The asphalt manufacturers used small copper tubes which were bent over to a half circle at the outside to prevent rain entering and were properly "flashed" to the covering. This system was called Parovents. The Research Station system put air bricks or similar ventilators at eaves which permitted air to enter the interconstructional roof spaces and leave, carrying evaporated moisture, through raised ridged ventilators at intervals over the roof's surface, or from chutes carried up within parapet or abutment walls to gratings above skirting or flashing levels (fig. 17).

Both systems achieve their designed purpose, to permit the extraction of trapped constructional moisture, or condensation, but they also permit air movement within the construction. This lowers the total insulating value of that construction because heat retention is not assisted by conventional air currents. However,

DAMPNESS IN BUILDINGS 45

THE PRINCIPLE OF 'PAROVENTS'

THE RESEARCH STN. PRINCIPLE

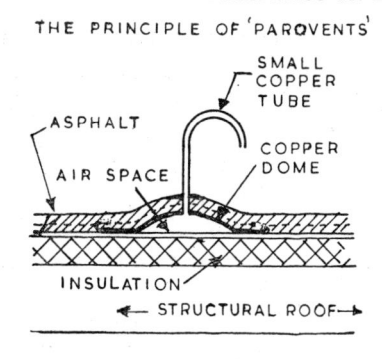

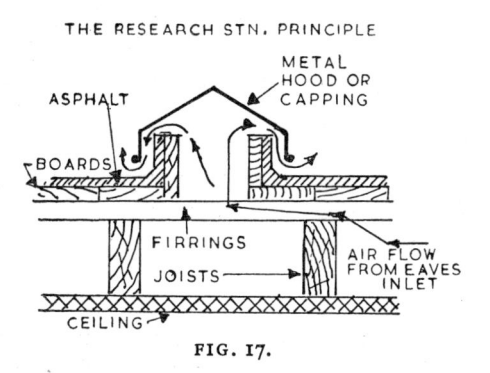

FIG. 17.

there would be heat loss if there was no ventilation and the air remained saturated, and the fact that these systems have been devised does illustrate the importance of keeping insulation dry, or allowing it to dry out before surfaces are sealed.

The fact that surfaces can be cooled or warmed by air which is brought into contact with them means that temperature differences exist between the surfaces and the air. Since surfaces do not exist without material thickness beneath them, then that material must itself be open, at some other surface, to a warming or cooling effect brought about by conduction or by radiation. Heat is passed from air to a solid by conduction. There will be no transference of heat from one mass to another by any means unless temperature differences exist between them. It should be noted here that all materials, however efficient they may be as insulators, do permit the passage of some heat, no matter how little.

It is worth spending a few moments considering this matter of heat transmittence through material, especially as we have already thought about warming the thickness of a wall beneath its surfaces. Many problems of dampness, particularly those where condensation occurs, be it upon or within a material, can be more readily diagnosed and a suitable remedy specified if thermal transmittence is properly understood.

Heat passes through solids (both porous and non-porous), by conduction where they are solid and by radiation where air spaces, pores or voids, however tiny, exist. Generally the more solid a material is, the better is its power to pass heat by conduction, providing, of course, that the heat can gain access through the surface. Some surfaces resist its entry and its emission, some do not resist so effectively (fig. 18).

Conduction is the passing of heat energy from one molecule of a mass to the next and to the next, and so on until the whole mass is at even temperature. This final state is never reached under practical conditions because if we apply heat to one point, then until all the other surfaces of the mass are at even temperature, heat will be passing from warmer points to cooler points within the mass. At the same time, however, other surfaces to which heat is not being applied will, if they are in contact with cooler masses or air, be losing heat. All of this action can be by conduction where molecules are in "contact".

When heat reaches a surface, whether it is an outer surface or that of a pore, capillary or void within the solid, and cannot continue its passage to a cooler mass by conduction, it will proceed by radiation, in the same way as the heat from the sun reaches the earth. That is always providing that the surface permits emission. This radiant heat energy will be reabsorbed into other solid or liquid surfaces which intercept its rays if the surface is such as will absorb and not reflect those rays. Radiant heat does not warm gasses through which it passes. Thus insulating materials which rely upon thickness to prevent the rapid passage of heat

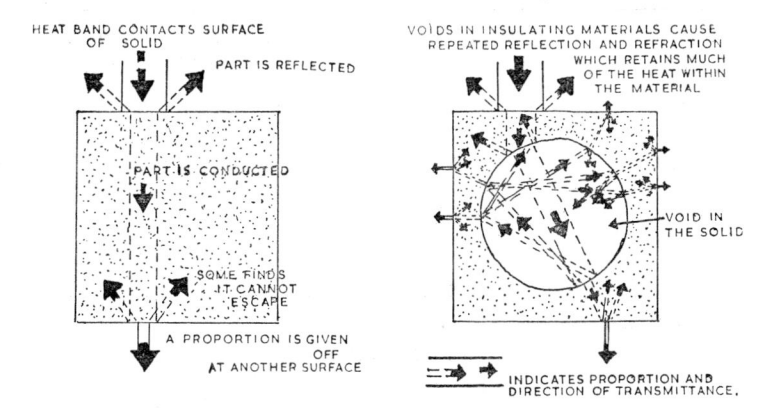

FIG. 18.

through them consist of as little solid as possible, which means there are as many enclosed air spaces as possible. Furthermore, those air spaces are surrounded by surfaces having low emissivity and high reflectivity so that heat reaching a surface has great difficulty in leaving that surface and, should it do so, experiences similar difficulty in re-entering at another point. In these conditions the heat energy largely becomes trapped within the material and the resulting rise in temperature reduces the temperature differences between the insulating mass and that from which the heat is trying to flow. One must remember that the insulation of cold stores is to keep the outside heat out, not as most people assume, to keep the cold in.

The full study of heat and heat transmission is very helpful to many aspects of practical building science, but the foregoing is sufficient, for the time being, for our study of dampness, *providing that it is clearly understood that a porous insulating material loses almost all of its heat accumulative power when its pores become waterlogged or filled with any other heat conducting substance.* Where it is not possible to prevent moisture vapour coming into contact with cooling absorbent surfaces or thicknesses of porous insulating material, and condensing we can, instead of sealing the porous surfaces of such insulators, use reflective type insulators of a non-porous character. Polished aluminium foil or a similar "surface" would do, but as we have previously seen, we must, in that case, be prepared to deal with surface condensation if the material backing the surface cannot also be kept warm.

Authors note to second edition.

The transfer of heat theory illustrated on page 47, (fig. 18), and amplified in the text on that page in italics has been criticised in a review, as misleading.

The author maintains that the illustration and the text give a practical picture of the differing physical reactions of solid conductors of heat and pored insulators having cell linings of high reflectivity.

The heat accumulative power of a porous insulator results in an earlier temperature rise of its near-to-heat contact surface material and trapped air or gas content, which provides its almost immediate insulating value beyond that resulting from actual reflectivity of its outer surface. Insulating value here being the inability to accept heat in quantity from the source of supply at a conducting rate. If the source temperature is maintained, then there will be a very gradual, continued intake of heat by the insulator as it very slowly passes its 'accumulated' surface heat into its whole mass, until that mass is at outside source temperature. This may take years, but as noted on pages 58-59, where there is a reference to insulators which are warmer than a 'source,' discharge of once accumulated heat to the 'source,' or surroundings, does occur similarly, very slowly.

All materials accumulate heat if they are able to accept it, it is the speed at which acceptance and internal transferance proceeds that decides whether or not the substance or material is an insulator or conductor of heat. The term 'heat accumulative power' is used here to indicate resistance of porous insulation to loss of accepted heat, when compared with that of solid material such as a saturated porous insulator.

7: Examining damp walls and older remedies

IT was not until 1875 that the first laws relating to the installation of damp-proof courses in houses were introduced, and rising dampness in buildings constructed before that date is usually due to the omission of an efficient damp-proof course. Dampness in buildings erected later is usually caused by either the breakdown of the damp-proof course provided or its circumvention.

Ordinary foundation construction is porous unless special precautions are taken, such as waterproofing mass concrete or building brickwork in impervious, engineering-type bricks, bedded and well flushed up in cement mortar. In the absence of these precautions water in the soil around the foundation will soak into the construction and then, by capillary action, penetrate in all directions until, as we have seen earlier, some state of balance occurs where gravity, capillarity and evaporation either mutually or singly halt further movement through the mass.

The usual methods of preventing dampness from rising above or penetrating below certain prescribed horizontal levels will be familiar to most readers.

Simply, they require that a non-porous barrier be inserted through the full thickness of the walls 6 in. above ground level at the outer face of the wall, and that it be below the level of any wookwork within the outer walls. Where rooms or floor levels occur below ground level, or floors are solid and resting upon the soil, then tanking by the insertion of a waterproof membrane around the portion below the damp-proof course is required. One has only to glance through the advertisements in a trade journal to find methods of satisfying these requirements in new construction. Some of the older methods, such as the dry area and the covered and ventilated external cavity, are still used, and often found in older buildings. They are interesting and worthy of consideration for new construction and for remedial work in certain cases (fig. 19). Indeed, the modern cavity wall is an adaptation of such construction.

Since our problem is "dampness in buildings" we must assume that something was omitted from the original construction or that what was done was, or has, become ineffective.

When one attempts to find a cause and specify a remedy to rising dampness, it is first necessary to carefully examine all the visible evidence upon and around surfaces. To find out what kind of protection was originally provided (if any) it may be necessary to probe deeper by perhaps taking up flooring, removing skirtings, hacking off a portion of an external plinth, or by probing joints in brickwork or masonry. Tracing and testing of water services and drainage and the use of electrical or chemical means of discovering the seat of the trouble could be necessary. Sound knowledge of traditional construction, local methods and materials and, above all, the matters dealt with in the previous articles will be of the greatest value.

The height and extent of visible dampness on wall surfaces tells us little than that there is no horizontal damp-proof course, or that if one exists it is completely ineffectual. The height to which dampness rises is controlled by other factors as we have seen. The full remedy will need variation according to height and other conditions. A level of no more than a few inches would indicate that existing evaporation is almost sufficient or that existing pores are of such a bore as to hold upward creep at that level by gravity, or that the means by which the water gains entry is restricted but continuous, or that there is possibly a narrow bridge through or around a damp-proof course (fig. 20). Where heights are great it suggests total absence or ineffectiveness of a d.p.c., the existence of fine pores (very porous material), lack of evaporation, or even hydroscopic or deliquescent conditions.

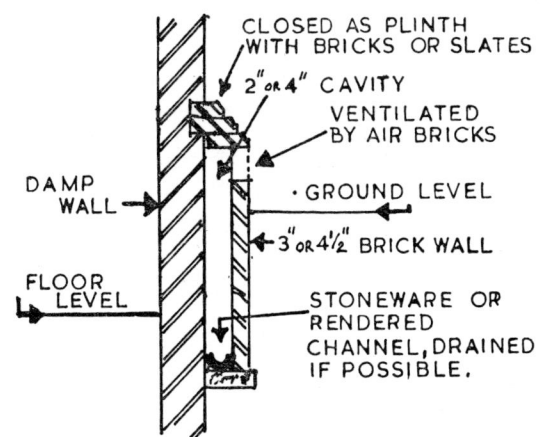

COVERED AND VENTILATED EXTERNAL CAVITY, ADDITION OR ORIGINAL CONSTRUCTION

PERMITS A DEGREE OF EVAPORATION AT EXTERNAL SURFACE OF WALL BELOW GROUND LEVEL.

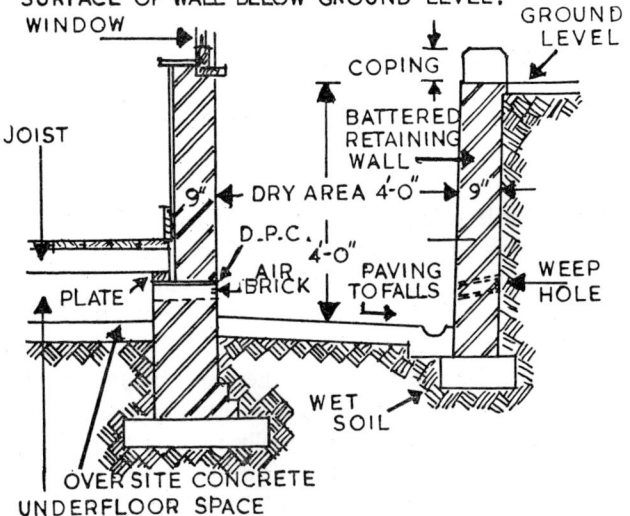

DRY AREA CONSTRUCTION

REPRODUCES GROUND LEVEL CONDITIONS AT AREA DEPTH LEVEL.

FIG. 19.

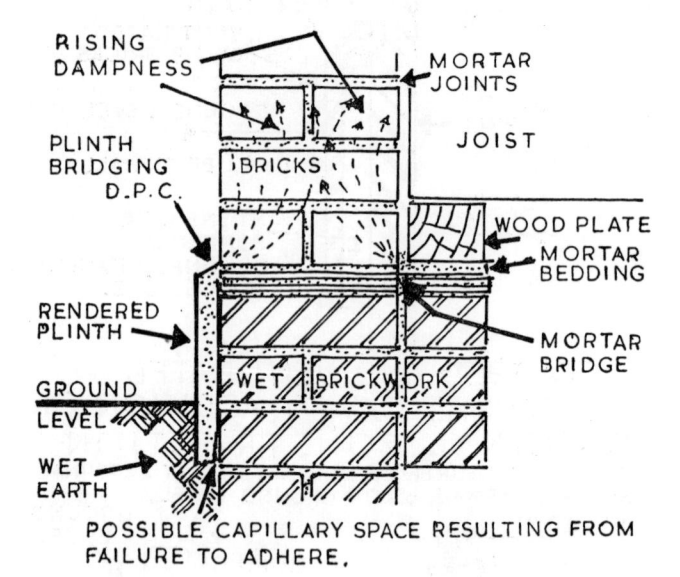

FIG. 20. *Bridging of damp proof courses.*

The water table level in the ground must, of course, be taken into account, since such forces as gravity, capillary creep and possibly evaporation will be affected by the level from which they begin to take effect. We should find that dry and wet season levels vary, and that taking measures outside the building, such as sub-soil drainage, might be the remedy if they lowered underground water table level sufficiently and permanently (fig. 21).

Isolated patches of dampness, usually roughly semi-circular, with their chord at the base, or fan-shaped patches in wall angles where internal walls meet external walls usually mean that there is a damp-proof course or its equivalent barrier protection, but that capillary-like gaps exist. These may simply be holes which are permitting limited capillary creep. The semi-circular or fan shape of the patch indicates the limits at which, from the point of entry, forces come into balance. The extent of such patches, too, will be in relation to the circumstances noted for whole lengths.

When examining the evidence one must never overlook the possibility that the effects present at that time could be wholly or partly the result of some previous attempt to combat the defect. For, as we saw earlier, it is possible to prevent the effects of rising dampness penetrating to the inside of an external wall and at the same time provide a new surface and wall condition which

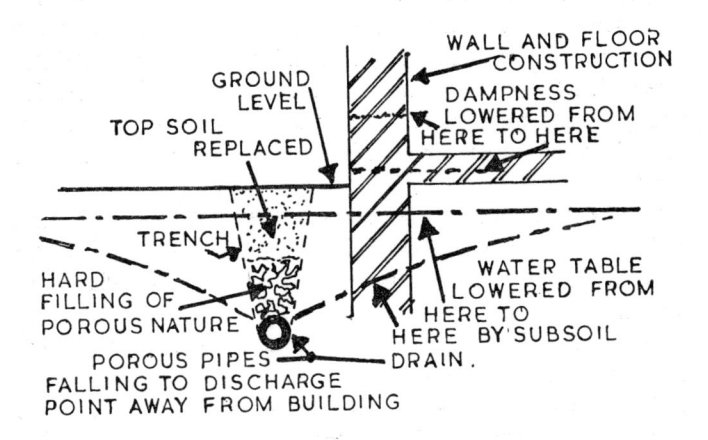

FIG. 21. *The effect of subsoil drain.*

will encourage condensation, perhaps producing surface effects worse than those which occurred from rising dampness alone. This as the result of the "remedy". Consideration of such possibilities will sometimes require prolonged examination, and perhaps the production of artificial or forced condensation.

This can be done by playing a steam jet from a kettle over areas of the wall suspected of having dense membrane surface treatment and, to give some comparison, over other parts not showing staining.

Quite often it is possible to ascertain whether such treatments have been used by probing with a pen-knife. In fact, the areas over which hard, dense membranes have been applied can often be defined by tapping over walls with a small, hard object, the dull ring or response indicating softer surfaces.

This operation can be assisted by the use of protimeters *— electrical instruments which record upon a dial the moisture content of materials. The instrument has test head needles which are used to probe the wall, and the degree of dampness is registered by small electrical currents whose strength is in direct proportion to the moisture content of the plaster or brickwork.

The needles will not penetrate hard surfaces, and if they are carrying surface moisture a good reading will still be obtained. Over softer areas (not treated with a hard membrane) the needles will penetrate more readily and these softer areas will, under conditions of equal air humidity, give lower transmittance readings.

Similar tests can be carried out with chemical adhesive plaster, which can be fixed to surfaces and will show, after a short time, the degree of moisture present in plastered surfaces by a change of colour.

Where examination shows that a damp-proof course does exist, efforts should be concentrated on tracing the bridging by which capillary flow by-passes the membrane. In most cases the effects from capillary bridging are usually confined to a few inches' rise above the d.p.c. That is, unless the bridge itself also rises to a greater height and is of a material that prevents evaporation in one or more directions, in which case considerable rise could result. Of course, if earth were piled up above the damp-proof course of an outside wall there would be enormous effects.

Other than where earth or some porous construction has been built touching the constructional wall above the d.p.c., the most common causes of bridging are cement-and-sand rendered plinths or mortar-filled cavities. The tendency is to carry plinths

* Details of the instruments mentioned here can be obtained from Protim Ltd., 356-358 Evelyn Street, London, S.E.8.
Details of the chemical indicators can be obtained from Sir John Gallwey and Partners Ltd., 13 Elvaston Mews, London, S.W.7. "The D.D.I. Protimeter."

up to just cover the joint in which the regulation horizontal d.p.c. is sandwiched. This produces a neater external appearance, particularly where the d.p.c. has, or gives need for, a thicker joint than the rest of the wall, slates in cement, or asphalt (fig. 20). If the rendered plinth mixture contains soft sand, or the mix for any reason is itself porous, no amount of surface trowelling will prevent it acting as a capillary path past the d.p.c. If its composition is waterproof and its thickness is dense and non-porous then its "key" or adhesion to the wall surface is of the utmost importance. Any patches where absolute adhesion is not secured means that a capillary space exists, and the thinner or narrower this is, the worse the effect, as we have seen. Any moisture in contact with its base will creep up past the d.p.c. where a capillary space bridges it. The wall at the level where plinths are usually applied is, at the time of application (scaffold striking and pointing down), usually dirty from splashing or dusty from dried droppings, and these conditions often lead to insufficient adhesion. Quite often moisture which has gained access to capillary spaces freezes and further loosens the rendering, sometimes breaking capillary tendency for a short while, but later opening the upper surface joint with the wall and permitting rain to run in. If this happens and it is trapped, further damage will occur, or if the rain fills the opened cracks with dirt a porous bridge is formed.

8: Dealing with the cause, subsoil or land drains

WHATEVER may be the cause of dampness in a building, there can be no doubt about its most satisfactory remedy. Eradication of the cause, if this is possible and practicable. Removal of the cause may, however, still leave changes in the material condition which need rectification if the position is to be restored to pre-damp conditions. Full treatment should thus include removal of the cause, remedy of effects and prevention of recurrence.

Where eradication of the cause is not possible we are left with containment and masking effects. Circumstances, the cost or the client may be deciding factors.

When a remedy is applied, consideration must be given to the effects which its application may cause, not only to the building being treated but to those adjoining. Generally, dampness over prolonged periods results in expansion or swelling, and softening and reduction of rigidity in absorbent materials. Softening and loss of rigidity means reduction in structural strength. However, concrete mixtures, providing the aggregate is non-absorbent, are exceptions. Drying out after treatment therefore results in shrinkage and hardening, but not always in recovery of strength, rigidity or former shape. Timber can take on a permanent set, and if dried too thoroughly lose structural strength. Mortars (particularly lime mortars) and some stone and plaster surfaces remain chemically changed. Bricks often show efflorescence from chemical salts carried to the surface by the escaping moisture and left at pore ends upon evaporation.

Thus it will be seen that remedial treatments must be conditioned to produce the state of moisture retention satisfactory to the material where its strength, or other qualities, would be impaired by too great a degree of drying. Similarly, where chemical change has occurred (particularly the formation of deliquescent material), action must be taken to prevent re-absorption of moisture from any source.

Most people who execute work designed to remedy dampness and many who advise upon these matters fail to consider its effect upon the adjoining premises, even when they are dealing with party walls. Quite often it is months later that the next-door neighbour notices dampness or the effects of dampness where hitherto it did not exist or was not apparent. This state of affairs can lead to trouble between neighbours, recourse to the public health inspector and the jeopardising of a builder's or surveyor's reputation.

Public health inspectors probably gain more experience of dampness in buildings than most other people associated with the building industry. This is because dampness can be regarded as a nuisance under public health legislation. It can thus be dealt with by notice to abate and may even be regarded (under Housing Acts) as rendering a building unfit for human habitation. In this latter case closing or demolition action may be instituted. But notices specifying remedial measures may be served where it is considered that such work would not involve unreasonable cost.

Additionally, the inspector is often consulted by owners whose premises are damp—often, one feels, in an attempt to transfer the responsibility next door, but at least because he is regarded as an authority upon its abatement.

Quite often he has, in the course of his duties, to reinspect premises where such work has been done, months or even years afterwards, and he is therefore in a position to check on any recurrence or other effects. He may even be called in next door to see the results of his specification upon those premises. This, too, can happen to the builder, surveyor or any other person carrying out, or supervising, works. Examples of cases from the author's experience where next-door causes or effects were a little out of the ordinary will illustrate this aspect of investigation and result.

An underground stream which had been causing severe dampness in the basement of a printer's and stationer's premises was diverted by laying sub-soil drains across the rear of the premises The water collected was discharged through a watertight drain beneath the basement floor into soakaway drains under the forecourt, the strata and ground sloping gently from rear to front.

This treatment effectively dried out the basement to the degree required, but some weeks later the licensee of the public house next door, and slightly downhill of the printer's, complained of the loss of his reputation for selling cool draught beers during the past few weeks of hot weather. His cellar, too, had been dried out! The stream actually flowed across his cellar floor in an open culvert and kept the floor damp. The continual evaporation of this moisture cooled the floor, which cooled the air, which cooled the beer casks. A branch from the watertight drain to the head of his open culvert restored the situation and still kept the printer happy.

A totally unsuspected side effect, robbing a chap of his dampness! One usually gets thanked for doing it. I always make tactful inquiries next door now as to whether or not they also have, and want, dampness before suggesting any remedy.

On another occasion we received a complaint of massive condensation upon a kitchen wall which was in contact with an adjoining factory wall. Inspection showed that not only was there massive condensation but that the plaster surfaces were beginning to crumble. Slight probing showed that moisture which had condensed upon the surface had been absorbed and was frozen in the plaster pores and that it was this which was causing pulverisation of the plaster. In this case there was no hesitation about going next door. There we found that a large cold store full of frozen salmon abutted the kitchen wall.

After some ten years not even lime plastering on a 9 in. stock brick wall in lime mortar, a 9 in. fletton brick wall in cement mortar, $\frac{3}{4}$ in. softwood tongued and grooved matchlining, and 8 in. of compressed cork insulation shielded on the cold store side with galvanised steel sheeting had prevented the cooling of the kitchen wall surface to a level where condensation would occur. Progressive absorption of moisture had occurred in the absence of sufficient warmth in the materials to re-evaporate the water in the plaster, brick walls, and the timber and cork insulators, which consequently became saturated. Once the cork became saturated its insulation qualities were considerably reduced and freezing occurred quite rapidly.

Here any attempt to contain or mask the dampness at the kitchen wall surface could only provide a temporary solution. The application of an impervious rendering, which by its nature is hard and dense, means that heat losses will continue and so too will the condensation. The most beneficial effect that might occur is that over the course of many years the walls might dry out. But if you remember, drying out requires means of evaporation at surfaces exposed to air and in this case very little existed. Masking (even with a porous insulating material) would be of little use since the new layer will quite rapidly cool in contact with the frozen wall. It would then permit condensation, absorb it and add to the frozen thickness.

Deep examination showed that the stock brickwork consisted simply of granules held together by ice. As a brick was thawed it crumbled to powder. The flettons, probably because they were set in cement mortar and were only some 10 years old, were in reasonable condition. The stock wall needed to be rebuilt and its plasterwork replaced. It was therefore demolished and rebuilt with a ventilated cavity separating it from the flettons, with no connecting metal ties. However, before it was rebuilt the fletton wall was warmed and dried by fanning warm, dried air over it. It was then covered with reflective insulation at its cavity surface. Polished aluminium sheets were used for this purpose.

Had the reflective waterproof membrane been inserted against the stock wall before the fletton wall was built, it is unlikely that the massive condensation would have ever occurred. Cooling would have occurred, but providing the cork kept dry, as it then would have done, this cooling rate would probably have been counteracted by the kitchen wall gaining heat from the warm kitchen air. If a little condensation was absorbed it would still re-evaporate when drier air conditions prevailed.

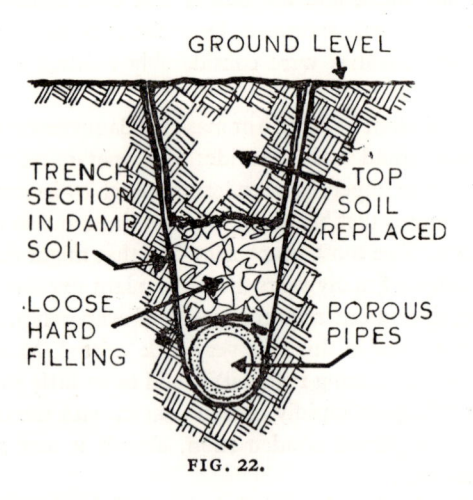

FIG. 22.

Waterlogged soil

These two, rather out of the ordinary cases, illustrate the connection between cause, remedy and effect upon adjoining premises.

Much rising dampness in older buildings results from foundations resting in saturated or waterlogged soils. When this is the case substantial improvement, and often complete and lasting cure, can be effected by carefully planned sub-soil or land drainage (Fig. 22). The open area mentioned earlier is land drainage in its visible form. Sub-soil drains may divert the flow of underground water or provide a means of carrying it away to a disposal source more rapidly than it can accumulate. Disposal may be to a natural watercourse or, where permitted, into public storm or foul sewers. Diversion can only be applied to water having a natural flow through the subsoil, while disposal can also deal with static water tables.

The object of designing such drains is to lower the level of the water table sufficiently to increase gravitational pull in the capillaries. This pull, together with any evaporation that takes place, can overcome the inter-molecular forces holding the water at an undesired level, and bring it down to the level required.

Where conditions permit, these drains are an economical method of dealing with dampness and they involve no cutting away or other work on the walls. Groups of buildings can be served, as was illustrated by the example of the printer's firm and the public house, quoted above.

When subsoil drains are proposed, trial holes should be dug uphill or, if the direction of flow is known, upstream of the building. The space available will dictate now far the hole must be dug from the wall. It should be between five and 15 feet away if possible.

Figs. 23, 24 and 25 show the effect produced by subsoil drain insertion. There is no set method or means of calculating the necessary depth or distance away the drain should be. The type of soil, its compactness or looseness, the water pressure or, where static levels are being dealt with, the table level, will all have varying effect. The trial holes will, of necessity, be part of the investigation.

Observation

As the digging proceeds pauses should be made so that the action of the water can be seen. First, the extent of saturation can be found. If actual waterlogging conditions exist, then the standing water level will be ascertained. If the water is moving, then careful observation, aided perhaps by the dropping of a matchstick, a small leaf, a drop of ink from your fountain pen or

62 DAMPNESS IN BUILDINGS

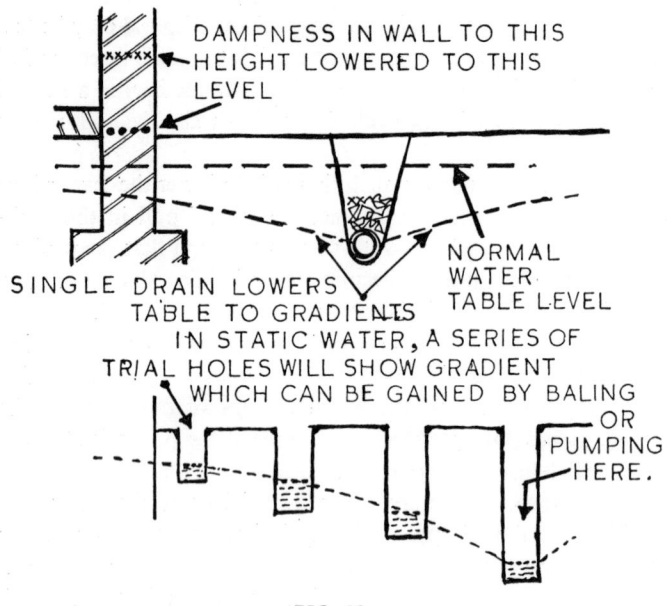

FIG. 23.

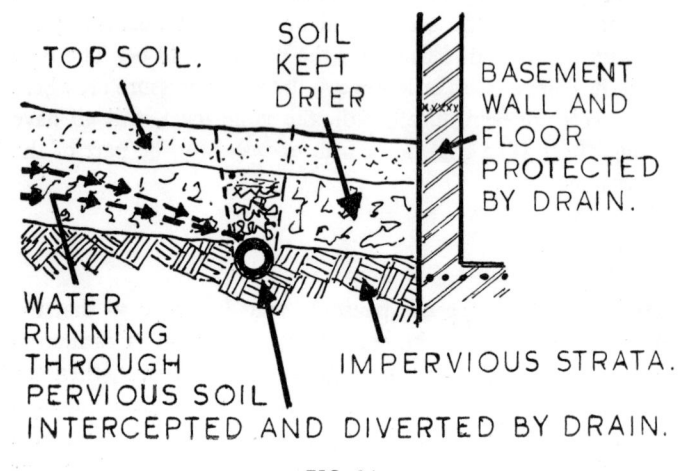

— DAMPNESS IN WALL TO THIS HEIGHT LOWERED TO THIS LEVEL

SINGLE DRAIN LOWERS TABLE TO GRADIENTS IN STATIC WATER, A SERIES OF TRIAL HOLES WILL SHOW GRADIENT WHICH CAN BE GAINED BY BALING OR PUMPING HERE.

NORMAL WATER TABLE LEVEL

FIG. 24.

TOP SOIL.
SOIL KEPT DRIER
BASEMENT WALL AND FLOOR PROTECTED BY DRAIN.
WATER RUNNING THROUGH PERVIOUS SOIL INTERCEPTED AND DIVERTED BY DRAIN.
IMPERVIOUS STRATA.

DAMPNESS IN BUILDINGS 63

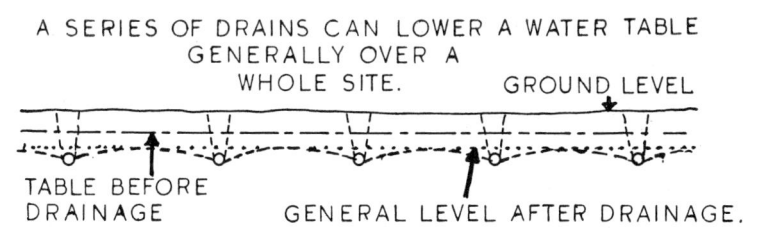

A SERIES OF DRAINS CAN LOWER A WATER TABLE
GENERALLY OVER A
WHOLE SITE.   GROUND LEVEL

TABLE BEFORE
DRAINAGE   GENERAL LEVEL AFTER DRAINAGE.

FIG. 25.

some dust or tobacco ash on the exposed water surface in the hole, will show the direction and speed of flow.

Where flowing or static conditions are discovered, one should dig the hole to a depth below water level at least equal to the height to which the dampness is apparent in the walls of the building, above ground level. Then dig a hole of similar depth immediately alongside, or as near to the wall as possible. Now bale out or pump out the first hole and watch the effect upon the other. This operation may have to be extended over some hours, or even days, and holes may have to be temporarily lined with pipes in loose soils. The closer together the two holes, the more rapid will be the observed result. In fact, if a line of holes is dug each, say, a yard apart and at right angles to the wall (fig. 23), they will indicate the gradient which can be achieved from the natural levels. The amount of baling or pumping necessary to secure the gradients can also be found.

This last information will enable one to decide whether the use of subsoil drains is feasible. There must be a means of disposal without recourse to mechanical pumping, or such a scheme becomes economically impractical unless large areas are involved or commercial considerations warrant such continued expense. Furthermore, estimation of the rate of flow required to get the surplus water away will decide the size of disposal drain necessary. There is plenty of published information available on carrying capacity of drains at varying gradients, so we need not dwell upon that here. Similarly, flow rates can be ascertained by the use of a simple notched "Thomson weir" (see page 338) placed across freely flowing water to form a temporary dam.

The aim in constructing the subsoil drainage system should be to lower the level of the water table by about half of the height to which the dampness rises at its worst on the walls of the building. This should allow the walls to dry out down to ground level providing reasonable means of evaporation are available to the walls as well. This would not happen if the damp wall material was encased in impervious skins or was otherwise out of contact with free air. Full drying may take quite a time. Much depends on the wall thickness and, of course, on the effect the damp condition has had upon the materials.

Where conditions warrant detailed investigation of subsoil water, "Wellpoint tubes" and pumps similar to those used to temporarily "de-water" building sites could be used to ascertain flow rates. If this technique was applied over a sufficiently long period and such lengthy pumping application was warranted by the circumstances, the possibilities of actual drying could be decided before any drains were actually inserted. Where adverse effects might result to adjoining premises, this method of investigation could save the abortive expense of actually inserting and later taking out drains. It would have saved the expense of laying the soakaway redistribution drains under the forecourt of the printers in the case quoted earlier.

9: Subsoil drains for running water and to assist tanking

SUB-SOIL drains designed to intercept running water should be sited a sufficient distance upstream of the building to be protected to bring down the water table beneath the building to the level required. This is where the trial hole investigation will pay dividends.

If it is intended to divert the flow, the redistribution (downstream of the building) should be from soakaways or a sub-soil) drain equal in capacity to the collecting system. The dispersal point should be at least as far from the building as was the interception.

Fig. 26 shows, in plan, the necessary arrangements, while fig. 27 shows a suitable arrangement for dealing with static, underground water.

Sub-soil or land drains must be connected to public sewers or private drains by means of a sealed water trap, ventilated into the open air on the inlet side, in the same way as waste or storm water is passed into a foul-water drain. It need be no more elaborate than that. Reverse-action intercepting traps with clearing arms are really meant for surface and storm water drain connections, not for sub-soil drains.

One should remember that these drains are laid with butt joints and that over the course of many years they will gradually silt up. When they do, a clearing arm at the outlet only is of little use, particularly where the diameter is 6 in. or less, because only a few feet could be raked clear. If the soil is fine, and liable to silt the drain quickly, it is best to provide top end access in the form of a rodding eye, so that periodic chaining can be carried out. If silting is not likely to occur for 20 to 30 years (in ground where fine particles do not exist) it would probably be more practicable to take up, clean and re-lay the drains if the system is not too extensive or deep. This is what the farmer does, and if this method is to be adopted a plan of the system (as actually laid, not as planned on paper beforehand) should be attached to the property deeds for future reference.

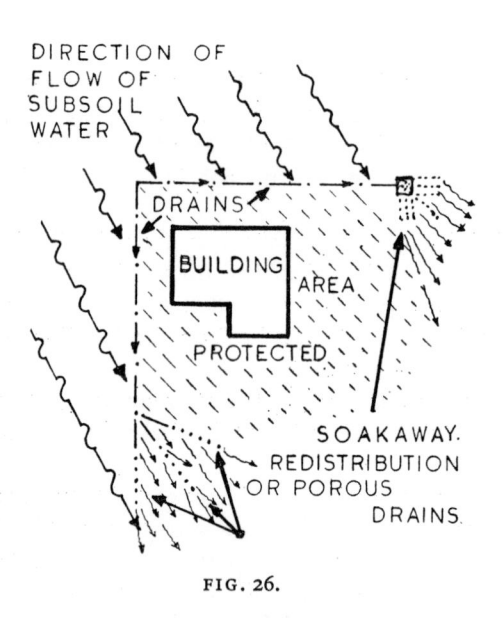

FIG. 26.

Sub-soil drains provide a remedy for dampness caused by waterlogged soils. Where the building has a basement and the water cannot be diverted and disposed of by these means (because the depth of the drain would have to be too great, or because there was no place for an outlet point or there was not sufficient space externally), then the builder must resort to "containment."

When buildings in waterlogged soils are under consideration, containment implies some form of tanking. In new buildings the

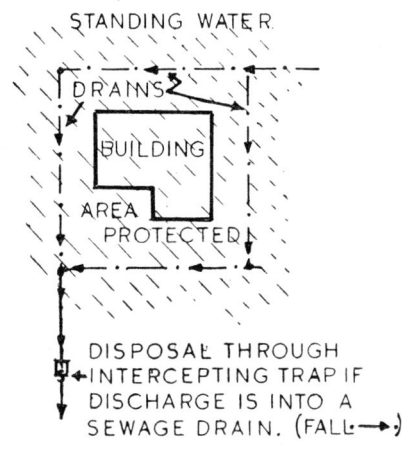

FIG. 27.

waterproof membrane, of whatever material, is best inserted below the structural floor and outside the retaining walls. This keeps the structural and finishing materials dry and consequently they retain their insulating properties. Thus, if there is reasonable ventilation there will not be undue condensation.

The floor and the retaining walls of the basement will have to be designed to support not only the weight of the building but also to resist the upward and inward thrust of the water pressure and the earth. The wetter the soil the greater these thrusts are (loose sand with critical water content is, however, an exception). A watertight ship floats, and its hull must be strong enough to resist the pressure of the water in which it floats. This calls for skill in the naval architect s design. He must produce the lightest structure that will still provide the required resistance. This explains the curved shapes.

Tanking

In the past, builders did not have to worry unduly about the weight of underground works, though some weight is needed to keep the building down. A tanked basement, although it is necessarily rectangular in shape, is like a ship's hull, particularly in waterlogged conditions. When the tanking membrane is applied to the new building, the structural floor and walls (strong enough to resist water pressure) support the membrane as well. The only additional material needed is a thin protective layer beneath the membrane to permit its insertion under the floor and outside the walls to protect it from damage during backfilling.

It is seldom possible to deal with dampness in a basement from the outside. Although one can sometimes patch asphalt, laminated bituminous sheeting, slates in cement, and waterproof renderings from the outside, this cannot be done where other buildings, without basements, adjoin. Sometimes it is possible to open up a floor in order to seal a patch, but these methods are of no use unless the building has been previously tanked. It is useless treating the outside of the walls and dealing with the floor unless one is prepared to envelop the foundation. This can only be done by underpinning the supporting walls or by using electro-osmotic treatments or a latex-siliconate infusion.

For this reason we are often forced to treat older basements from the inside by the more traditional and obvious methods. Seepage, resulting from capillary movement through the finer pores, takes place where damp basement walls are in contact with the earth. If the pores are large, percolation might even take place. But this happens only when the soil is saturated, whereas capillary movement can also occur in less wet soils.

Gravity, a reducing force in the case of rising damp, will not be effective in either of these methods of penetration. It will not operate at all in pores which are roughly horizontal, and it will assist the movement in pores which slope downwards. Furthermore, where saturation conditions exist, actual static water pressure helps penetration. This means that for every foot of vertical depth below the water level table the force increases by 0.43 lb. per sq. in. Thus, 10 ft. multiplied by 0.43 lb. would give a pressure of 4.3 lb. per sq. in., or 619 lb. (just over $\frac{1}{4}$ ton) per sq. ft. Imagine a floor constructed to carry a superimposed load of 620

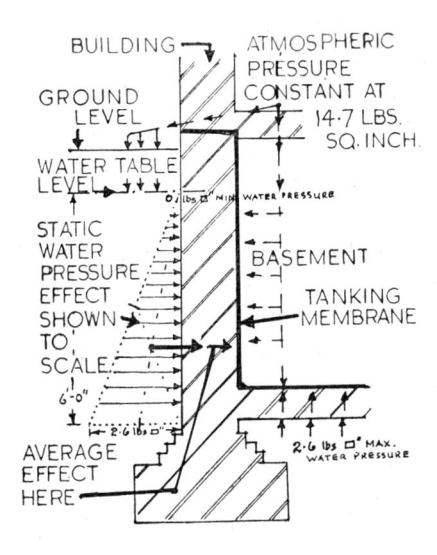

FIG. 28. *Forces involved in tanking.*

lb. per sq. ft., or a beam 1 ft. wide supporting ¼ ton per ft. of span, and you will understand the problem which this pressure imposes on tanking (fig. 28).

The membrane which we apply to the inside of the walls and floor must either have an adhesive grip greater than these pressures, or be adequately supported. The pressures are not apparent until we apply the membrane, and they do not become fully effective until the static conditions are set up with the sealing of the pore ends. Water flowing through a pipe has to overcome frictional resistance of the walls. Pores are tiny pipes, but although the frictional resistance in small pipes is relatively greater than that in large pipes, the whole question of friction ceases to be important under static conditions.

Thus, sub-soil drainage, even if it cannot solve the problem by itself, could, by lowering the table level of the external water, reduce head pressures and enable more economical methods to be used in tanking. That is, if it is at all practicable to put in a subsoil drain in the circumstances. One should always bear in mind the possibility of using combinations of remedies.

Obviously, the degree of dampness will decide the treatment required. Other influencing factors are the floor or wall materials to which the treatment has to be applied. If one relies on adhesion as the means of attaching the membrane, the surfaces must be sound and free of loose particles. If the membrane is to be retained by a supporting structure, however, the surface conditions are of less importance. Some membrane coatings will adhere better to damp or even wet porous surfaces than to dry, as the water in the pores assists tendrils of the membrane material applied in liquid or plastic state to penetrate. It then sets in the pores where the tendrils act as numerous root-like anchors. Examples of membrane coatings that behave in this way are ones that are cement-and-sand based, and tar and bitumen emulsions.

If the membrane is a mastic that cannot form tendrils to secure anchorage, a keyed or roughened surface will be required. The surface condition becomes relatively unimportant when stiff sheet membranes are attached to the surface by certain fixing devices.

Today, renderings and coatings can be anchored by bonding agents. These are preparations that have the effect of excluding air between the surface and the coatings. They can be mixed with the material to be applied or can be put on as a preliminary coat. Manufacturers often claim that their liquids or mastics will adhere successfully even to glazed tiles. The fact is, of course, that when this form of bond is desired, the harder and more airtight the surface is, the better the bond.

The supporting pressure holding coatings applied in this way is equal to atmospheric pressure, i.e., 14.7 lb. per sq. in. This is equal to the static water pressure of a 34 ft. head, or 2,000 lb. per sq. ft. It is important to realise that the exclusion of air from between the two surfaces is essential. It is equally important that the membrane preparation be airtight if full advantage is to be secured by these means. Nevertheless, some support is often provided even when air pressure behind the membrane is reduced. This may well be so once static water conditions occur and where the air outside the building cannot freely exert its full pressure on the water surfaces other than those in contact with the membrane. This can happen where water is contained in sub-soil strata underlying an airtight impervious top stratum (natural or artificial).

This may well explain why coatings sometimes remain attached to walls and surfaces even when the forces supporting them are less strong than the pressure of the water they are holding back. It also helps us to understand why impervious, nearly airtight, pavings often keep walls dry when put against them.

Apart from preventing surface water from soaking into the ground below (the primary purpose of their installation), they also prevent free air from exerting any pressure on the underground water, and allow normal air pressure within the building to push water in the pores back from the inner wall or floor surfaces.

Atmospheric pressure

When one considers the total pressure which is exerted by the atmosphere, it can be seen that if we can utilise even a small proportion of that force, considerable assistance is added to the supporting effort. Small airtight areas of a surface, if scattered over a larger area, provide sufficient key, or suction grip, to hold the whole membrane against low or reasonable static water pressures.

If one thinks of suction grip fittings, even small hooks attached to the kitchen wall by domed rubber suckers, it does not take much imagination to see that a number of these could provide very considerable support. In fact, one could roughly test the ability of surfaces to offer this type of attachment by fixing suckers to them and observing the length of time for which they remain attached (time being the controlling factor). This would be only a rough test, since on many surfaces the airtight areas are so small that both these and non-tight areas would occur under even the smallest sucker dome. But if it will stay attached for a few days there must be very restricted air movement through the non-tight patches beneath the sucker dome and an air-excluding membrane could find sufficient sucker effect to be held.

Quite obviously, surfaces which cannot provide sucker effect (soft, porous or other non-airtight surfaces) call for coatings which can tendrilise, are self-supporting or that can be given the necessary support, to retain them in effective position.

Air exclusion in some products is secured by entraining agents. Under normal wetting conditions tiny bubbles would remain attached to surfaces or in pore ends but would pass through the preparation being applied by forming into larger bubbles with greater buoyancy (rather like a reversal of the emulsifying process mentioned earlier). "Wetting"—which, in our case, really means liquids or mastics getting between a surface and air—is thus achieved.

10: Simple tanking to semi-basements

THE simplest form of tanking can be inserted where the floor level of a basement room is a foot or two below outside ground level and external treatment is either impracticable or not possible.

Quite often basement rooms are rather low from floor to ceiling and the substitution of a solid floor to replace a rotted wooden one enables a few inches to be added to its height. If this results in split levels, well we are familiar with them today. If it is desired to retain a suspended wood floor where dampness is bad enough in walls and underfloor space to warrant tanking means, that whatever its condition, it must be taken out completely, including sleeper walls, plates, etc., and then replaced after tanking is completed.

Preparation for tanking means clearing the walls of plaster facings, skirtings, grounds, and plugs. If these last items cannot be readily drawn then punch them in or cut them back half an inch or so, drive into them a couple of nails, leaving the heads projecting almost to wall surface level to key a cement mortar filling pointed off to surface level. You may meet gas or electric tubing, points, etc. These must be drawn off the wall and provision made for refixing by cutting out a suitable block depth behind, into which the tanking can be worked and a new fixing block inserted protected by the tanking. It is then good practice to wire brush the surfaces to remove loose material.

If you wish to tank with proofed cement rendering or similar treatment, it is advisable to mortar fill depressions which are more than about half an inch deep. This enables the rendering to be applied to a reasonable even thickness and the risk of uneven setting and cracking will be considerably reduced. Reasonable keying can be provided for in racked out joints or, if the surface is very tight and solid, by treating with a bonding solution, or the more traditional hacking with a scabbling hammer.

Careful preparation is important to the success of the job.

Where bitumastic or rubber based solutions or emulsions are to be used it is desirable to bring the surface to a rather smoother state, pointing in the joints roughly, filling all depressions similarly, so that bridging, particularly in sharp internal angles, does not occur. Where sheet membranes are used these must be of a type which can be "glued" to the wall and preparation will be as for solutions or emulsions.

Oversite concrete must be similarly prepared, but hacking or bonding is seldom necessary for shallow-tanking membranes. Cleanliness is, however, important. Dust, grit and debris must all be swept out immediately before laying the membrane.

If no oversite concrete exists, as may well be the case in older premises, then it should be put in. In fact the writer has got good results by putting in 3 in. of 8 to 1 mix ballast concrete on building paper, on rammed earth without hardcore or blinding and finished to a board screed, letting this set for a few days and then laying over it stout polythene sheeting from rolls of more than room width; or lapped generously at joints if of less width and then on this immediately laying a further 3 in. of concrete, with a light welded steel reinforcing fabric bedded at half that depth in it. In the latter case, the edges of the sheeting should be turned up against the walls about 9 in. and fixed with clout nails into a suitable joint, the corners being dog eared.

Where a suitable base already exists, such as over site concrete, stone flagstones or brick pavings, the membrane can be laid directly on to it, as can solutions and emulsions, one or more coats as recommended by the manufacturers. The membrane or waterproofing treatment should be covered as soon as is practicable with at least a couple of inches of fine concrete screed to protect it and provide a base for the floor finish. Water proofed cement and sand or concrete screeds are best laid at least two

DAMPNESS IN BUILDINGS 75

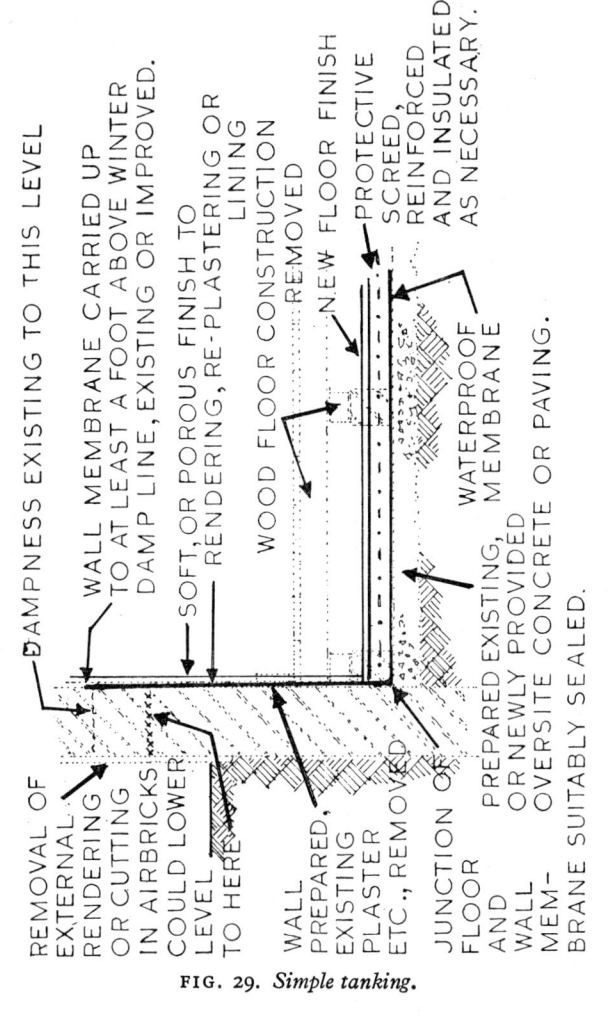

FIG. 29. *Simple tanking.*

inches thick, thicker if possible, particularly over large areas, but separated from the base with building paper to permit independent movement when setting and drying. If large areas are to be covered then joints, which will facilitate laying and permit expansion or shrinkage, should be made with keyed waterproof strips. Such large areas will of necessity be of thickness to permit this form of joint.

In thinner, 2 in., screeds I usually ask for some light wire netting type reinforcement bedded in. It is worth while remembering that all screeds put in for waterproofing purposes should be gauged with the minimum amount of water that will permit working. Over-wet mixes invariably crack, craze or dust off. A moist well mixed consistency, well tamped, will rule off and screed more easily and can, if required, be trowelled straight away to the smoothest finish necessary—not too much trowelling though.

If you propose to use the waterproofed layer as the surface on which to lay thin floor coverings which are not set in thick, depression-filling adhesives, or which are brittle, or are laid hot, tamp, then use rules, and float or trowel as little as is possible afterwards. Too many floor sub-surfaces today are left uneven; it does not notice until the coverings sink into the depressions, however slight, and polishing is done. Then see how the pools of light and shade show up, especially in long rooms with windows at the ends, or where there is artificial lighting at relatively low levels. Furthermore, where humps occur these pick up the dirt from traffic, take the wear of cleaning and break down before the rest of the covering wears out.

If bituminous felts are used as the membrane, two or even three thicknesses bonded together over the whole area or generously at joints, laid lapping, are usually specified; and there is no reason why they should not be "glued" to the base with hot or cold bitumen. In fact this brush applied bonding or dressing often envelopes small pieces of grit and prevents punctures in the first ply of the build up. This type of membrane can be carried up the walls if similarly "glued" on. If this is done, however, an angle fillet of mortar should be run at the floor wall junction before laying the first ply, as hard or sharp folding of felts is not recommended.

Wall treatment must be satisfactorily sealed to the floor membrane if it is of different material or where floor and walls cannot be covered as a whole. It is not practicable if plastering is to be replaced to use polythene type sheeting to walls, other than for a few inches of turn up from the floor; but if dry, self-supporting linings, or linings which can be fixed without puncturing the sheeting, are to be used, then this type of material becomes suitable.

Cement and sand wall renderings and solution and emulsion coatings can be bonded by sandwiching the sheeting between two coats for a few inches. The use of self adhesive polythene tape to retain the sheeting to the first coat is well worth while as a time saving factor.

The use of pitch treated dovetailed papers nailed to walls over a membrane riser as a base for plastering would be satisfactory, providing you are not dealing with very wet walls where the water is almost oozing through, in which case it would be difficult to secure a watertight joint at the base.

In simple shallow tanking it is not usually necessary to insert a horizontal damp-proof course if the external wall treatment can be carried to about a foot above the existing or improved damp line. One should have regard to evaporative possibilities. These are normally present or can be secured with external walls, but not with internal or party walls to other premises.

If it is not possible to provide an external surface which is free to the open air for a foot or so below the top level of your wall tanking membrane, then it will be necessary to provide a horizontal damp-proof course in the outside wall at the usual level above outside ground level but below plate level to internal walls.

It is always worth while to consider carefully what surface treatments exist to outside walls before deciding to tank, or to what height to carry the wall tanking.

The careful removal of external impervious renderings forming plinths, or even full height coverings such as painted stucco, pebble dash or roughcast, to leave the brick or stone wall free to air, can have a marked effect upon damp levels internally by permitting evaporation to take place. Cement plinths are often run simply for decorative effect, or with the mistaken idea that they prevent dampness.

If removal of these external surface treatments gives the required evaporative results during reasonably dry weather, but the walls so exposed absorb driven rain, they can be treated with a clear waterproofing solution "which can breathe"; this is their proper use. Similarly, if upon exposing the wall the appearance is poor, it could be restored by applying a porous covering, a rendering made up with porous aggregate and applying the solution to that.

Where such outside treatments are removed one should see that sills and projections are provided with throatings or drips. Often the rendering has been applied to prevent water running off these projections from soaking into the wall below. Also on stucco in particular, successive coats of paint may have filled in these grooves where they originally were provided.

Where the removal of outside surface treatments to limited height is not possible because it would spoil appearance, evaporation can be assisted by the insertion of weather louvred air bricks covering hollow pockets cut into the wall thickness to about half its thickness and at about 4 ft. centres about 6 in. above ground level. The Knapen atmospheric siphon is an efficient and unobtrusive form of providing this added evaporating power to walls.

The provision of added evaporating areas or facilities to walls which have been damp for prolonged periods sometimes has unexpected results. If deliquescent conditions have formed in the wall material and the premises are in a locality where periods of high humidity occur frequently, actual absorption of moisture from the air by means of these provisions may take place to more than offset any advantage gained during drier air periods. When tanking or alterations to a structure or surface are carried out regard must be had to "side effects" which may be produced. The substitution of a solid floor resting upon damp soil for a suspended wooden one can bring problems of condensation. If all of the materials used are dense, as they will be up to and including the membrane, then they are heat conductive and will, because they are in contact with underground water (which is usually quite cool compared with atmospheric temperatures), absorb heat from the air of the room, to pass to the soil, causing that air, if it is near to saturation point, to deposit some of its moisture upon the cooling floor surface.

The screed provided to protect the membrane and provide the base upon which the floor finish is to be laid should, if that finish is of thin hard material like thermoplastic tiles, have insulating quality either in itself or as an under or overlay.

Since hard finishes do not lie satisfactorily over soft underlays, the only practical insulation for a thin hard finish is lightweight concrete. There are several proprietary aggregates now on the market for making such concrete. They are often specified for roof screeds for the same purpose. It is usually better to put down a floor finish which is itself resistant to heat transmission, wood set in mastic, compressed cork similarly set, or such-like materials.

Walls, too, may become condensation surfaces and the membrane should be finished with a softer porous setting coat if it be rendered or, if it be sheeting, dry plaster lining, timber, etc. Some of the solutions and emulsions, the rubber based types, can provide a key for a cement mixed rendering coat for plastering, if clean sand is dashed over them while their surface is "wet." If this rendering coat is followed with a lime putty setting coat or a gypsum board finish not trowelled to a polish, the tendency to condense will be considerably reduced and, if it does occur, re-evaporation can later dry them out. Thin cellular plastic sheets instead of a setting coat will also provide an anti-condensation surface.

11: Encouraging evaporation from damp walls

IN the last chapter the use of air bricks and atmospheric siphons was mentioned as a means of providing additional evaporating power to a damp wall. We were thinking in terms of outside air absorbing the dampness from the pore ends so exposed as a means of lowering the damp level in a wall.

Where we find dampness in a basement which is not severe enough to warrant tanking, the provision of increased ventilation to that basement at the right levels will often improve conditions considerably. Ventilation means air movement and just as the air bricks or siphons mentioned earlier would be of little use unless air moved into and out of the cavities provided in the wall behind them, so too would the means we provide for increased ventilation to a room or basement as a whole, unless air moves in and, after absorbing moisture from the walls and perhaps the floor as well, moves out, taking that moisture with it.

A mixture of air and water vapour is, at any temperature, less dense or lighter in weight than dry or drier air at that same temperature. This means that if air takes up additional water vapour by evaporation it should be displaced upwards by drier air of the same mass, but it can only do this if its temperature is maintained. The cool damp walls and floor cool the air as it contacts them, and although it will still take up vapour, providing it is not then saturated with moisture vapour, it will have lost its tendency to be displaced upwards, because reduction in temperature means increase in density. Thus we must ensure that, either outlet levels are lower than inlets, or that the air is warmed after taking up the additional moisture, or is assisted in the required movement by natural draughts or mechanical means.

Readers will be familiar with the air bricks inserted in walls to ventilate underfloor spaces, and incidentally to keep them reasonably dry. They are usually at similar levels in two opposite walls of the building and the motive force is wind outside the building, assisted at times by warmth from the rooms above the floor. You will also have seen illustrations showing these air bricks connected by chutes in the walls, enabling them to ventilate underfloor spaces below outside ground levels.

The basement problem is similar. The beer cellars mentioned in an earlier chapter remained cool when damp because ventilation, or air movement, was restricted. But where a basement is occupied or is warmed by work going on within, a combination of outside wind movement pushing air into, or extracting air from, air bricks, occupational warming, and the opening and closing of doors and movements within, produce sufficient air movement to carry the moist air out and drier air in. Warmth added to incoming air by occupation also raises its moisture absorbing quality. Failing these possibilities, fans can be used to move air through the rooms.

Knapen atmospheric siphons (fig. 30) have been used to attract wall moisture in basement walls to points covered by exit grids. These are tiny air bricks, spaced about the internal surfaces of the walls of the rooms so that evaporation can take place at predetermined points and at a greater rate than the existing wall surfaces allow.

In one particular installation the damp walls had been rendered with cement and sand, probably waterproofed, and while this prevented the dampness entering the walls of the rooms from the earth from showing on the inside surfaces, it resulted in massive condensation when the basement was occupied. Additional ventilation was provided, but this was not sufficient to prevent the condensation, neither was the use of ordinary, intermittent room heating because the wet walls backing up the hard dense surfaces were always cool. Siphoning out the moisture from the

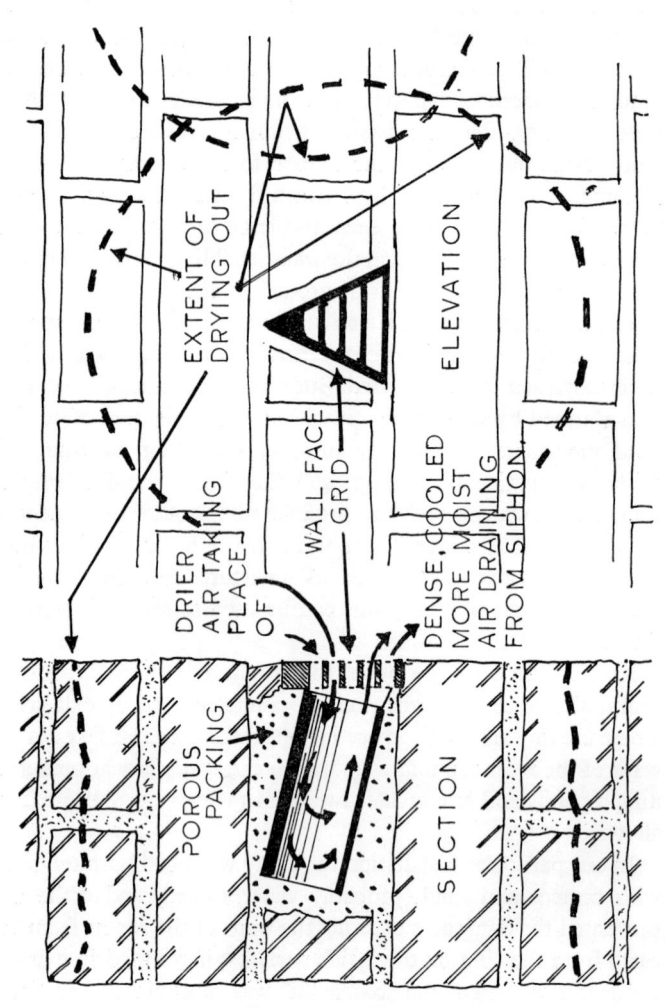

FIG. 30. *Knapen atmospheric siphon.*

wall thickness during periods of combined warmth and ventilation over a period, gradually lowered the cooling power of the walls by drying out areas of pores, and the condensation subsided.

Here we have an example of previous remedial work having to be supplemented in particular circumstances, by further work to overcome a side effect. The removal of external non-porous renderings from the bases of walls to afford additional evaporative surfaces should lead to the thought that this can be done in other ways too.

The lowering of ground levels against a damp wall, without actually forming a dry area, can sometimes result in the simplest of all cures for rising damp, particularly where the offending earth has been banked up higher than the general levels, either accidentally or be design. In outer urban and rural situations it is often possible to apply this remedy, but do not defeat your object by rendering the newly exposed wall, it if looks a little unsightly where natural ground levels are lowered. Builders often use materials of a non-facing type to construct walls below ground. If a satisfactory surface cannot be secured on the old wall it is better to build a false plinth a couple of inches away from the old wall (the ventilated and covered outside cavity referred to in an earlier chapter).

Later we shall be considering the provision of horizontal damp-proof courses to walls which are without them, but while we are removing causes of dampness at or near ground level, it is worth considering bridging, whether it be past an existing d.p.c. or assisting upward moisture movement in a wall by preventing evaporation.

A very common fault, particularly in terrace houses in towns, built 50 or more years ago, was to butt, if not bond, brick or masonry garden walls to the rear main wall. Today solid fence posts tightly placed in a similar position can also form a bridge when dust and dirt wedges in the restricted space. Thousands of damp patches at the junctions of rear and party walls, often in cupboards set in the breast side recess, result from such causes. Pointing the outside junctions and forming fillets or flashings at the top does not provide a cure, but making an inch space, between the wall of the building and the bridging wall or post will effect a simple, inexpensive one.

Fuel bunkers built or placed too near to walls, sheds, sun lounges and the like can all become offending items in this way. Another cause for complaint in many older terrace houses, built abutting streets without forecourts, arises from making up pavings of footpaths. In the course of years these pavings are laid, first where perhaps none previously existed, or where there was simply a raised kerb. Progressive relaying of pavings from one cause or another, may result in the pavement either bridging a d.p.c. where it existed, or covering an evaporative surface. In both cases dampness would begin to show on inside walls. Usually the raising process is very gradual and any one owner or occupier never really realises that the wall was ever free from dampness. Many an owner's representative has protested that this was a cause of dampness in a front wall when confronted with complaints or notices requiring abatement from local authority officers. Unfortunately for these owners' representatives, dampness to party and internal walls existing in the same house, can be used as a point to offset the allegation. But where it is noticeably higher in the outside wall than in the party or internal wall, where really all circumstances being equal, the reverse should be the case, or where definite bridging of an existing d.p.c. has occurred, the allegation ought to be maintained. Very often the train of thought which seems to lead to an attempted remedy for this is, that splashing of rain or drips from the paving has caused the dampness and a six-, nine- or 12 in. rendered plinth is applied. This does not cure, and for reasons with which you are now familiar, often results in worsening of the dampness.

Fig. 31 illustrates a simple and effective remedy applied where roughcast was forming a bridge past a d.p.c. for rising dampness. The 9 in. solid brick wall of local wire-cut bricks, in lime mortar, had a hessian based horizontal d.p.c. which although somewhat brittle with age and lime impregnation, could still serve its purpose. It was the statutory 6 in. above outside ground level

DAMPNESS IN BUILDINGS 85

but would not, it seemed, withstand much disturbance without breaking up. This condition is not unusual in such conditions. Bridging was suspected because the evidence of dampness (wallpaper stained, but not excessively damp at its surface), rose only to about 12 in. along the outside walls, and not at all on internal walls. The lime cement and sand roughcast was sound and ran down to about 3 in. below ground level.

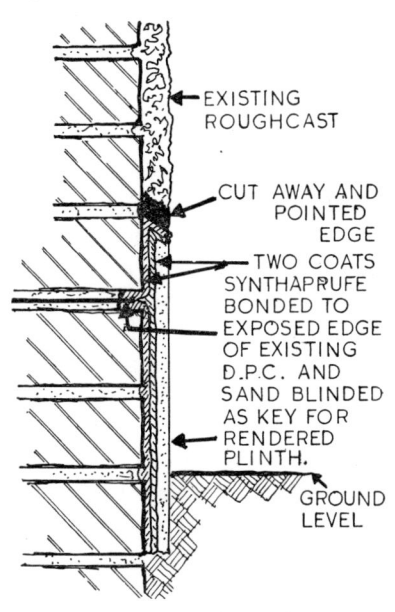

FIG. 31. *A remedy for bridging.*

Careful cutting away of a short length of roughcast from its base to 3 in. above d.p.c. level showed that adhesion was poor in places. As an exploratory measure, about 6 ft. run was cleared and left for three weeks, simply protected from driving rain, but exposed to air. Tests of degree of dampness internally using a protimeter, showed that considerable improvement had occurred during this time. There was no doubt that this treatment would have been complete if applied to all the affected walls, but to a detached house one cannot leave pale pink-white blotched wire-cut bricks exposed at the base of the walls, particularly those seen from the road.

The use of a cement rendered plinth with a waterproofing admixture was a first thought, but bearing in mind the condition of the d.p.c. and possible adhesive difficulties to very shiny brick faces (oil smeared from the extruding nozzle sides when formed), this was not proceeded with. Instead, the lower roughcast was carefully cut away to 4 in. above d.p.c. and trimmed to as straight a horizontal line as was possible. The underside of the remaining roughcast was slightly undercut, and carefully pointed with a 1 : 3 mix of cement and sifted, washed sand. Then the mortar joint sandwiching the d.p.c. was carefully scraped out until about an $\frac{1}{8}$ in. of the edge of the d.p.c. was exposed. Where it broke away, deeper scraping was done to expose a sound portion. A coat of Synthaprufe mastic was then brushed on to the exposed brickwork, making sure that at all points it linked with the d.p.c. and covered the undercut pointed edge of the cut roughcast.

Incidentally, poor partly unfilled vertical mortar joints were pointed in as the edge was treated. Two dwarf wing walls to a porch which were also bridging the d.p.c. and showing dampness to about three feet in the hall were cut clear of the wall face and the treatment extended to these areas. A second coat of proofing was applied to ensure complete coverage of pinholes in the first and while it was still wet, this coat was dusted with sharp, dry, sieved sand to give a key to a rendering.

Since it is not possible to match roughcast repairs to the original the rendering applied as a finish was floated to a plain face surface and then stippled with a chisel-shaped, tongued rubber brush to produce a not too severe contrast. After a period for drying out, a sample of plaster which had been damp was tested for deliquescence, but found to be unaffected. Since no efflorescence occurred upon drying out, redecoration was carried out without further treatment of internal surfaces, except normal stripping. A description of this treatment must of necessity be lengthy, whereas the application was relatively simple, requiring careful rather than costly work, coupled with an understanding of the principles involved. A jobbing builder's "handyman," paid at 5s. an hour, did the work. Costings showed that, including the builder's gross profit of 55 per cent on daywork costs and materials, to include overheads, supervision and the very small amount of plant necessary, the job came out at 6s. 10d. per foot run. This was considerably cheaper than renewing the d.p.c. initially suggested by the same builder.

There are circumstances where the insertion of a new horizontal d.p.c. is the only satisfactory solution to a problem, but it is worth a careful examination and a little thought about general principles before proceeding to that course. It is true that today with modern joint sawing equipment and other devices for inserting horizontal d.p.c.'s such insertions are not prohibitive in cost, that is providing that there are good straight runs and not too many obstructions.

12: Cutting and sawing in horizontal membranes

IN the last chapter the use of Knapen tubes to secure increased evaporating power was discussed. One must not forget, however, that evaporation can only take place if the moisture reaches or can be brought very near to the surface of the damp material exposed to free air. It is important therefore that capillary movement to those surfaces can proceed without interruption. Open cavities newly cut behind air bricks leave the capillaries of the actual damp material exposed, but where cavities for proprietary insertions are formed and partly filled with porous fillings to "attract" moisture to the evaporating point, then it is essential that the filling material provides an extension to the cut capillaries. This will not happen if the filling shrinks upon setting; in fact unless there is slight expansion one could not rely upon such extension. Similarly there must be no capillary severance between the filling and the tube. It is for these reasons that the materials and components used in the proprietary systems are not obtainable by builders. The company insist upon designing and installing the points themselves.

The actual insertion of a physical non-porous horizontal damp-proof course through the thickness of a wall, providing the wall is laid in reasonable courses, is not too thick and has lime mortar joints, is not the difficult job that many people imagine. That is, providing also that one understands what one is doing and why. The more even the courses and bed joints the better. Thus insertions into brick walls are usually easier than into stone and block walls, that is unless the bricklayer was running high and bedded his bricks frog down, leaving a horizontal joint $\frac{1}{8}$ in. thick.

These conditions will influence the method of insertion and to a lesser degree the choice of material for the membrane. Where it is necessary to take out a course or two of the wall components, then there is the widest choice of materials, whereas if it is possible to saw a joint, then only the thinner and relatively rigid materials which can be jointed or lapped sufficiently within the cut are suitable. If neither course is practical then infusional or osmotic treatments are indicated.

Perhaps, however, the level at which it is possible to make the insertion is the most important factor of all. Cutting out of courses requires man, hammer and chisel room at reasonable working level, kneeling being the lowest practical position. Hand operated sawing requires similar levels at least, and also clearance at the opposite side of the wall for saw to run through. Chain or circular machine sawing requires machine and man room for the operator and at least 3 in. must be left below saw level for handling. Furthermore all sawing calls for clear runs, free from attachments to the wall or vertical obstructions close to the operating surfaces, if economical operation is to be obtained.

Sawing is often of necessity a combination of hand and machine work supplemented by a bit of hammer and chisel work in awkward positions. Infusional treatments require room for operators and their drills and space adjacent to the wall where the containers and other apparatus of infusion application can be left undisturbed while penetration is secured.

The only reason for not operating from the inside of a building is usually to avoid disturbance of plaster, skirtings, etc., or the taking up and replacing of wooden floors. When the only level at which insertion is considered practical is "below the level of all the woodwork" operation from outside is generally more economical.

On the other hand, where plaster, skirtings and flooring, etc., have to be replaced as part of the treatment or where solid floors exist, or the wood floor is spaced off, the damp wall and only wall treatment is necessary, or where the inserted membrane is to link with tanking, then it is generally advantageous to work from the

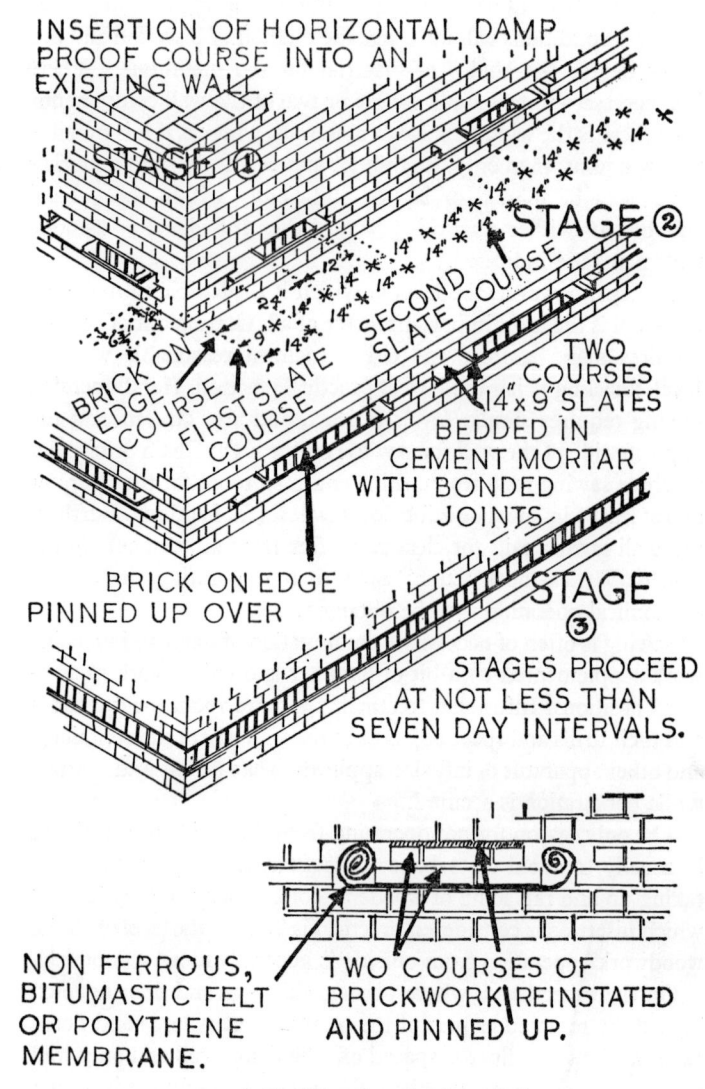

FIG. 32. *Traditional cutting-in methods.*

inside where apparatus can be left safely, and the job can proceed irrespective of weather conditions.

Osmotic treatment appears to be the only one requiring outside application unless the conductors can be concealed and earthing points made beneath the floors.

Even then it rather appears that the successful operation of this process can be jeopardised where earthing is only possible beneath the building. Osmotic apparatus is normally supplied by and the installation carried out by the operating company's own staff.

The builder who wishes to carry out insertions himself, without recourse to specialists, and who does not have regular employment for expensive equipment or the specialised labour required to operate it, is left with cutting-in as the method. Even hand-operated tungsten carbide tipped saws are very expensive and only repay their cost if used regularly. The author has on occasion used an old thick bladed single-handed cross cut saw, roughly sharpened and set several times during the operation, for sawing out lime joints where short lengths of insertion have been needed and where hammer and bolster work was not advisable or practical. In fact, any old carpenter's saw blade with its teeth well set will serve for a few feet of cutting. Narrow bladed compass and even pruning saws will cut lime joints but it is difficult to get a straight slot, without waviness, which is essential for the insertion of thin membrane material. If you have a selection of old saws for which no other use can be found, then the one having the least number of teeth to the inch will do this job fastest and be effective for a longer period.

Sawing, unless this is the method adopted to remove course material, indicates that the membrane insertion will result in slight settlement of the wall above. One specialist firm, F.L.S. Damproofing Ltd., of Kings Langley, Herts., say that they limit this to around 0.015, one sixty-fourth of an inch, which is extremely slight. This is only possible if pinning up over the membrane is done and indicates that the chain saw cut is in the region of one quarter to five sixteenths of an inch high, at least. Hand saws seldom cut this high and pinning up is not possible, so that settlements of the order of a sixteenth or three-thirty-seconds, or even $\frac{1}{8}$ in. must be expected when they are used.

Those who deal with d.p.c. insertions have come to accept settlements of this degree as unimportant, providing that they are even. But they look, as a general rule, only at the walls they treat. This does not mean that the building as a whole, together with its services, has similarly settled.

If the external walls only are treated, it is very unusual to find that services attached thereto have been correspondingly shortened. Where these are non-rigid and can concertina slightly, no damage is done, but what about a rigid soil pipe with its cement joint to a stoneware drain socket at its foot, the ceramic "P" trap pedestal pan directly connected to a stoneware or cast iron drain?

Think also of instances where outside walls only are treated and settle while partition walls at right angles to and attached to them do not. In such cases, a certain amount of stress must be induced at the junctions—the treated walls becoming cantilever loadings to the partitions. Similarly floors bearing over untreated partition walls parallel to treated walls will become slightly sprung and these in turn will have an altered relationship with attached items, such as gas, electric, water heating, services, etc., and also with such subsidiary structural features as hearths, partitions, stairs, door linings, etc.

It is true that in many instances such new relationships adjust themselves without ill effect, but in many cases the result is seen in cracks, locks and latches whose bolts no longer shoot the striking plates, doors which then rub floor finishes or bind, latent drain defects, or maybe only just slight creasing of wallpaper at affected wall junctions. You might say, "just minor inconveniences" and this may well be so, but if they can be avoided, especially those involving drainage services, by easing connections, joints, etc., so much the better.

In fact if no settlement occurs at all then it is a job well done. That should be the standard aimed at in underpinning.

This last thought brings out the essential consideration relative to d.p.c. insertions, that is that the operation is that of underpinning. Those experienced in such work know that short lengths of wall must be cut away and then securely pinned up and allowed to set before adjacent portions are cut away, each stage being secured before any adjoining is disturbed. This too, should be the procedure in d.p.c. insertion. With underpinning it is usual to proceed in maximum lengths around 5 ft.; with d.p.c. insertions 3 ft. is normally considered to be the limit.

If such lengths are treated where cutting out of courses is being done, and alternate lengths of wall are left intact until they have set, no shoring is normally required. Where sawing is done the process is, however, best carried out as a continuous one, starting at one point and leaving no gaps, but the membrane must be inserted immediately behind the saw or the resulting settlement may prevent its introduction. One cannot expect more than 3 ft. of wall in lime mortar to remain suspended, especially where the cut has been completed and settlement has occurred behind the portion being cut. The process thus becoming rather like a roller action with the wall settling as a slight wave behind the saw but over the membrane.

"Sawn-in" membranes

It is usual to insert "sawn in" thin membranes today in 3 ft. "maximum" lengths with 3 in. to 4 in. laps, one section over the next. At points where additional loads occur insertions should be of shorter length. Here your knowledge of construction and forces acting thereon will tell you that door jambs, piers and junctions with load bearing abutting walls are such points.

One should also remember that all loads are not downwards. Where aprons below window openings are of dwarf height there is often an upward thrust and closure of the cut will occur by lifting of the wall below rather than by settlement of that above. If you look carefully at window sill, or door sill for that matter, and there is a fracture at its centre, you can be fairly certain that upward thrusts have been or still are present, in fact upward course bulging as opposed to settlement is often apparent and can be seen. This indicates loading and strain in the opposite direction to that normally existing in walls at this level. Here one would be pinning down, not up.

Where chain saws are used it is usual to insert the length of membrane and then immediately force slips of slate in over it at about 12 in. intervals before settlement of the work above occurs, cement grouting being injected between the slips to complete the job. The settlement of one sixty-fourth of an inch which occurs results from the seating down of the membrane under the load as it is taken up. That greater settlement occurs where thinner saw cuts are used is because it is not practical even if pinning up with slips of hard material can be done to grout to wall thickness in the very restricted space left over membrane in such cases. Incidentally grouting as opposed to pointing should be done with neat Portland cement, not cement and sand. This has very little shrinkage; quite often, in fact, especially with very fresh cement, slight expansion occurs with neat cement. Sand in a mix absorbs any tendency to expansion to the point of slight shrinkage.

Pinning up, where there is sufficient room to do so must, if possible, be to the full wall thickness and length. This means forcing filling material in and unless a thin flat edged tool can be fairly easily inserted into the space, this cannot be done. You will see the difficulty of attempting to push filling material into a low gap from one face, where there is nothing blocking the opposite face—the material simply falls out the other side as you pack it in. The only satisfactory method is to push it sideways against that already in, or against uncut work. In practice a combination of diagonal sweeping movements and side thrusts appears to secure the best results. This is why, where two courses of 3 in. bricks are cut out and two courses of slates laid in cement, bonded as a membrane, are used, pinning up is best done with bricks on edge. Only 3 in. of side movement is then required for packing the pinning up joint and nearly $4\frac{1}{2}$ in. of hand and tool handle room is available closely alongside from which to do it. There is still a lot to be said for this very traditional method.

13: Examination of structural hazards prior to cutting in

WHEN we were thinking about horizontal d.p.c. insertions into walls of coursed materials, dwarf aprons below windows and doors were mentioned as a possible hazard. The need for underpinning should cause us to consider the structural condition of a building before attempting such work.

It is no good telling the building owner or an adjoining owner that this or that defect was present before you began work, when they draw attention to it during or while it is in progress or some time after completion. The time to examine the building and get the agreement of these people as to its condition is before you start; in fact, unless you do, your third party insurances may well be rendered void, or at least difficult for your insurers to settle reasonably.

Once a dispute arises as to the age or cause of a structural building defect, a fracture, settlement or even dampness making itself evident where previously it might not have been, or been noticed, expert examination by a neutral professional will be necessary. He will have to act as adviser to the insurers and possibly as an expert witness if the dispute goes to arbitration or law.

Where you intend to carry out work to a party wall, or where an adjoining property could be affected, you are under an obligation in law to notify the owner of that property of what you intend to do. This gives him time and opportunity to examine his building as to its existing state, call in his own expert if he wishes, incidentally at your expense, a point seldom allowed for in estimates, but most important of all to tell you in response that he does not object to the work being done, providing that you undertake to remedy any defects resulting from those works. This gives you the opportunity of examining his premises so that agreement as to existing condition can be reached. When this has been done only new or aggravated conditions can possibly be in dispute and your insurance company will be in a happier position. You too, providing that you have taken reasonable precautions, will stand in a happier position for future cover.

Any agreement with adjoining owners should of course be in writing and where necessary accompanied by sketches and measurements of defects, possibly good photographs, the negative being better evidence than a print. Where you cannot get agreement, such evidence, well authenticated by an independent professional, especially as to the date upon which it was examined or taken, will be very valuable if a dispute should arise later.

Where agreement is reached it is usual that the extent of existing defects is carefully noted; if necessary "tell-tales" are fixed, to structural fractures, plaster cracks, etc. (fig. 33), and protimeter reactions marked upon dampness, or its outline indelibly marked. In a technical book such as this one does not have to dwell unduly upon the need for extra care where structural defects exist in or adjacent to walls to be treated. It is, however, worthwhile to consider just for a moment or two the implications of material failure or displacement in walls. What is important is to realise where the stresses are likely to be present and what might result from undercutting, the release or aggravation of those stresses.

In masonry, this term being used in its widest sense, settlement in the length of a wall, if it is to the least degree uneven, is readily detectable. The extent, too, can be seen where some degree of horizontal coursing is present. It will be less apparent in uncoursed work, except where rectangular units, presumed to have been originally laid to level beds, show an out-of-level tendency. The experienced eye can often detect quite small settlements in even uncoursed rubble walling. Where the wall itself does not

DAMPNESS IN BUILDINGS 97

show the movement, the openings, or even the whole building, often do, if viewed from a distance.

Where such settlements exist one should suspect that along the line of "wave" troughs there could be a state of tension and therefore the tendency for units of unreinforced material to drop

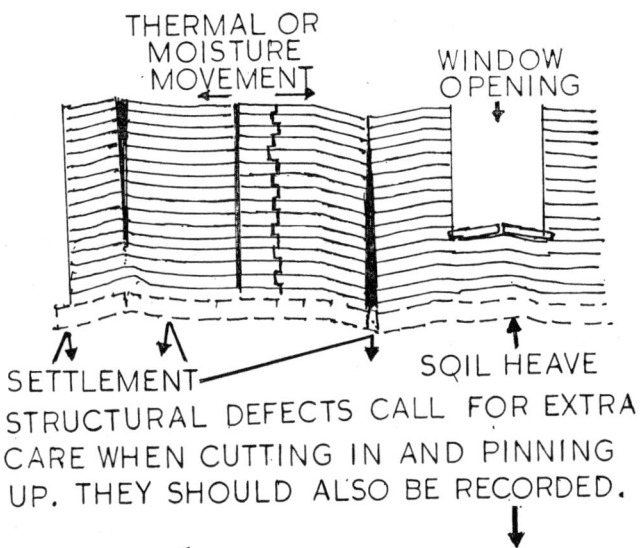

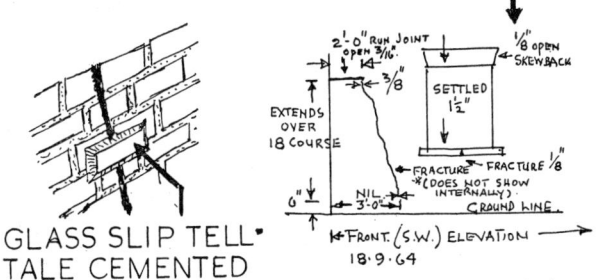

THERMAL OR MOISTURE MOVEMENT   WINDOW OPENING

SETTLEMENT   SOIL HEAVE
STRUCTURAL DEFECTS CALL FOR EXTRA CARE WHEN CUTTING IN AND PINNING UP. THEY SHOULD ALSO BE RECORDED.

2'-0" RUN JOINT OPEN 3/16"   1/8" OPEN SKEWBACK
EXTENDS OVER 18 COURSE   3/8"   SETTLED 1½"
FRACTURE (DOES NOT SHOW INTERNALLY)   FRACTURE 1/8"
0"   NIL 3'-0"   GROUND LINE
FRONT (S.W.) ELEVATION 18·9·64

GLASS SLIP TELL-TALE CEMENTED ACROSS AN EXISTING FRACTURE WILL ENSURE THAT SUBSEQUENT MOVEMENT, IF ANY, CAN BE DETECTED AND MEASURED.

FIG. 33.

out if undercutting is continued over too long a stretch without underpinning. At wave crests compressive forces may give an arch effect, and similar displacements are much less likely to occur. It will be realised that a few courses higher in the wall these tendencies are completely reversed, the tensions becoming compressions and vice versa. Thus the length opened at any one time must be judged and adjusted. Tight pinning up over the trough and less tight treatment to the crests will tend to ease the general condition back towards normal by releasing the stresses. At this juncture it should be clear that where no displacement exists in a wall being treated, uneven pinning up could cause stresses to arise and fractures, binding of doors and windows, etc., to occur later.

Vertical or diagonal fractures can indicate uneven settlement over the foundation. When fractures are of identical width throughout their length they can be taken to indicate thermal or moisture movement, but where they vary, they are more likely to be the result of foundation movement.

If the crack is wider at the top, then the settlement is at one side, or on both sides of the base and the closer the distance in either case then the greater will be the width variation at any given height, the degree of settlement being equal. Thus a quoin settlement will show a fracture having a wider variation where it is close to the quoin than if it is farther along the wall.

Fractures which are wider at their base than at their head indicate settlement beneath or very near to their base. Only sound knowledge of constructional forces together with wide experience can enable one to judge just where the maximum stresses and exact centres of settlements exist in such cases. Consideration of the foregoing notes will, however, provide a basis for determining where greater care should be exercised. If you take support away at a point of settlement, the tendency is for the fracture to open, while if support is removed at more distant points the tendency will be for the crack to close. One final point before leaving the consideration of fractures. Quite often debris, loose mortar, small pieces of broken material, etc., find their way into fractures and complicate the possibility of closure, whether from heat or moisture changes or from the swelling or shrinkage of foundation soils. This leads to variation in the shape of the fracture, the debris becoming a fulcrum about which the forces will then act. Wherever possible, therefore, fractures should be carefully examined to see whether they contain debris, and one's conclusions adjusted if necessary.

The removal of debris from sawn joints, and from the bed joint when cutting in, is also important where thin membrane material is being inserted. Sawn joints are best cleared with an air line from a compressor before inserting the membrane. Very pliable membranes such as polythene are more easily fed into thin saw cuts in walls thicker than a half brick, with less likelihood of

METAL CHANNEL FEEDING MEMBRANE INTO JOINT

RELEASING THE CHANNEL

UNFOLDING THE MEMBRANE EDGE

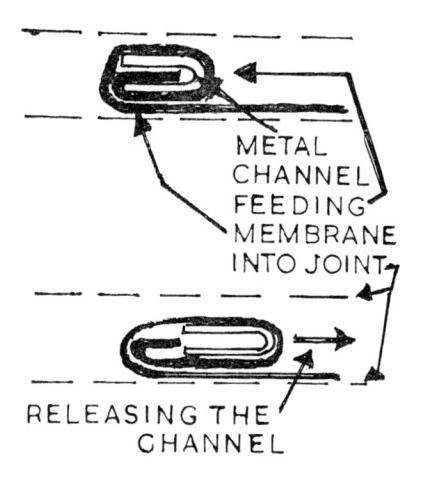

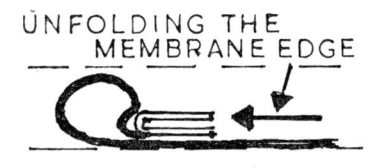

FIG. 34.

folding if the leading edge is folded into a channel (fig. 34) made from thin sheet copper or aluminium (by folding it over). This is drawn in over the last piece to be inserted using a quarter circle motion and then pulling it directly sideways until it is in the required position. A slight backward and forward movement of the channel will release the membrane so that the channel can be slid out and used to unfold the leading edge, using a combing action over the membrane.

The insertion of a horizontal d.p.c. above wood or solid floor levels, to avoid obstacles or to gain working room, was a complicated business when slates in cement was the accepted membrane material. Forming a junction between the horizontal and vertical aprons was impractical, and since sheet lead was costly, it was seldom used. The advent of mastic asphalt however, led to the introduction of this technique where cutting in could be done. Its adoption using 26 S.W.G. copper horizontally and 0.020 in. or 0.030 in. low density polythene for the aprons, as has been done by the specialist firm F. L. S. (Dampcourse Insertions) Damproofing Ltd., with the very limited degree of settlement mentioned in the last chapter (their sketches are reproduced here) is a natural extension now that polythene is an accepted membrane material. Bearing in mind their pinning up method, one presumes that the polythene is laid into the sawn joint beneath the copper, which would then protect it from damage during pinning up.

I have mentioned the difficulty of applying plaster type finishings over polythene vertical membranes, but in the insertions mentioned above, the few inches necessary could be covered where replacement of a skirting was not desired. In September, 1963, this company was quoting as normal charges for inserting copper/polythene horizontal and vertical membranes 20s. per foot run for 9 in. brickwork in lime sand mortars and 30s. for $13\frac{1}{2}$ in., while for all polythene their prices were $4\frac{1}{2}$ in. 10s., 9 in. 18s. 6d., and $13\frac{1}{2}$ in. 27s. These prices include for skirting removal but not for plaster removal or replacement, or in fact for any other incidental work, brickwork repairs or pointing other than to the joint sawn. Naturally such quotations apply where there is a reasonable amount of footage to be treated. They are useful as a guide to cost using specialised labour and equipment.

When one considers costs such as these, which by the way are competitive for this type of work, and adds to it the cost of cutting out defective plaster and making good where the dampness has risen to heights greater than can be covered by a drop apron membrane, it is not surprising that many people turn to internal lining and masking as their answer. Such answers can be completely satisfactory if all that is needed is to provide a surface upon which one can decorate, with the reasonable assurance that the wall dampness will not quickly spoil it.

If the choice is lining, or masking, then one must expect that deterioration of the wall material—into which the water can still permeate, and will probably permeate further on being denied internal surface evaporation or more restricted evaporation—will continue, perhaps affecting the outside surface finish, particularly in the case of painted stucco and the like. Severe blistering of painted plinths up to as much as five feet often occurs after internal surface damp-proofing.

Internal surface treatments alone must bear relation to the "life" required or expected from them and the internal air environment. In earlier chapters we have discussed the effect of providing a cooled impervious surface where air contacting it is likely to be humid.

The simplest surface treatments which are stuck, brushed or sprayed on merely hold back the moisture in the wall for a few thousandths, maybe an eighth, of an inch in depth. They do not alter other conditions very much. Those which are non-porous, such as non-ferrous metal foils, pitch or bitumen impregnated papers, metallic-based paints, wax in solution and wax and latex emulsions, do prevent evaporation of wall moisture into the room. They all, with the exception of the metal foils, have limited life, principally because of the effect of wall chemicals and light upon their organic origin material content. Nevertheless, they are cheap to buy and to apply, with lives varying from a year or two for pitch papers, a little more with the metal paints, to perhaps

102 DAMPNESS IN BUILDINGS

five or seven years at the most for the others. Foils have lives equal to the resistance of their adhesives to wall chemicals. Pretreatment of the surface with a petrifying or neutralising solution and the use of a non organic-based adhesive gives the best results.

Surface treatments, with the exception of some silicone compositions, are not suitable for loose or soft surfaces. The surface should at least be brushed with a stiff, preferably wire, brush and wallpaper and its paste completely cleaned off. Cracks, depressions, open joints and damaged areas should be filled sufficiently to permit the material to be used to form a complete close fitting skin. Foils and proofed papers can bridge small depressions and cracks but will be damaged when pressed on over sharp projections.

The finished membrane must be complete over the area to be protected. Sheet materials must be well lapped; brushed or sprayed on materials are usually applied as two coats, the second covering the defects of the first.

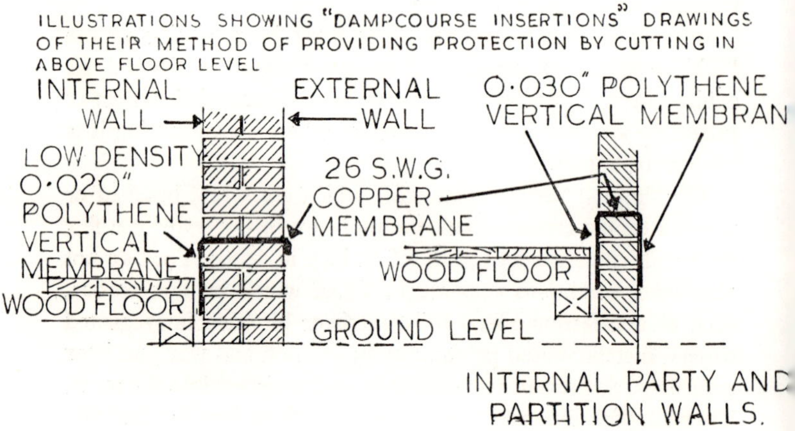

FIG. 35. (*Author's note: In neither case would the floor plate or floor be protected*).

14: Masking and lining treatments

SURFACE treatments which are applied to mask dampness, and which are preceded simply by stripping decorations can bring complications in their wake. Where a plaster surface is damp from rising moisture it may well be the case that, over the years, the moisture has carried into the material acids derived from the atmosphere or the soil. Upon reacting with substances in the material—the bricks, the mortar or the plaster itself—these acids can form new substances of a crystalline nature having deliquescent characteristics. These characteristics can be the cause of damp appearing at the surface with the result that a surface treatment is specified.

While deliquescent conditions are generally regarded as giving crystals the power to absorb moisture from the atmosphere and, therefore, show surface dampness in a humid atmosphere, it must not be forgotten that if this supply of moisture is prevented from reaching the crystals they will still absorb any moisture that can be obtained from other sources. They will gather it from the wall. But whereas this moisture can be given up when the surface is exposed to drying air, this drying action cannot take place through a masking membrane.

Some crystals which have deliquescent qualities are capable of taking up so much water that they become saturated solutions. Thus the condition in the material immediately behind the membrane can become much worse after treatment.

We must further remember that deliquescence is an ability to "attract" moisture and, where this type of dampness has been showing constantly to a level in a wall, saturation to that level will produce a new "water table" in the wall from which a further rise can commence, or spread. Masking can thus result in the spread of dampness to areas not previously affected.

Most people who have experience in this work will advise that an area some 6 in. to 12 in. higher and wider than the damp area should be covered with the masking membrane to allow for this spread. Where severe conditions exist, even this can prove insufficient and, over a period, more and more area needs to be treated.

Where the membrane does succeed in containing the dampness one is still not out of the wood. The moisture held immediately behind the membrane cools it and provides a surface favourable to condensation. This can be troublesome in an atmosphere where relatively high humidity was the initial cause of the surface condition. This is why so many masking jobs appear to break down so rapidly after application, and continue to show damp stained decorations.

We have mentioned the remedy for this in an earlier chapter viz., the application over the non-porous membrane but beneath the decoration of a porous layer, capable of taking up reasonable amounts of atmospheric moisture and holding it without becoming saturated, and permitting its re-evaporation when drier air conditions occur or, where the decoration is non-porous, preventing direct contact between the moist air and the cooling surface. Expanded polystyrene sheeting is such a material.

Use of Dadoes

These surface treatments, however, cannot be applied to a level, or to patches, without increasing the thickness of the wall and being noticeable (fig. 36). Quite often, therefore, a dado is built up, capped with a horizontal feature to disguise the projection. When surveying property, one is always suspicious that wall dampness exists when dadoes are present without the features, matching door and architrave formations and skirtings which are properly associated with the type of dado.

DAMPNESS IN BUILDINGS 105

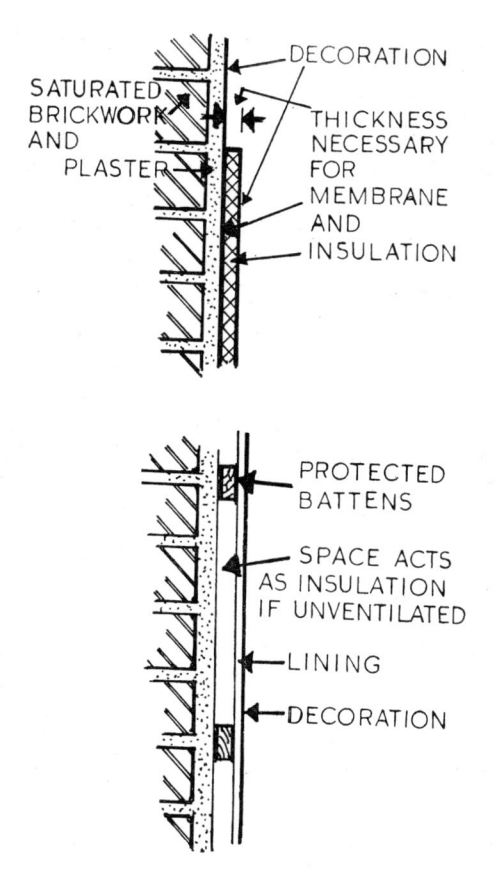

FIG. 36. *Surface treatments.*

It is because of the rather temporary nature of most masking treatments, and this need for anti-condensation overlays, that spaced-off dadoes are formed, or even whole wall linings used in this connection. However, we must not forget the possibility of damage occurring to surfaces which have been overlaid with anti-condensation materials as fragile as expanded polystyrene. Very light impact and even abrasive action will damage the decorations they support.

An example of an older attempt to overcome this problem is the use of lincrusta dado linings. Here, the dextrene adhesive, made from heat-treated starch and acid, was more resistant to breakdown by wall chemicals than the then normal flour paste. The thickness of the paper and its embossing provided insulation to a degree, and the varnish surface treatment gave some protection against impact and abrasive damage. That the plaster to which many such dadoes were applied was in poor condition from dampness before application, is evidenced from the fact that stripping very often brings the setting coat off with the paper, as also happens sometimes with varnished in situ papers, applied for similar reasons. This is quite apart from the constricting action upon a lime putty setting coat exerted by strong glue-like adhesives.

Spaced-off dadoes, or even whole wall linings, were often used in past years to cover damp areas. In the better class buildings, canvas stretched over battened framings carried the decorations, or timber panelling fixed to battens provided the base or was itself the base for decoration. In the meaner dwelling, the small shop, the workshop, etc., softwood matchlinings served the same purpose. This was not only cheap, but it served the double purpose of covering the damp surface and protecting the wall decoration from damage where impact or abrasion was most likely to occur, below waist height, particularly in narrow passages. Incidentally, it also saved many a Sunday suit, dress or topcoat from picking up efflorescent powder or the powdered colour from wallpaper which had dried during dry periods.

Such dadoes still exist in many thousands of older buildings, and many basement and semi-basement room walls are matchlined from floor to ceiling height to mask dampness. The author has seen it spreading to ceiling plaster where this was done. Evidence of the condition behind is, in many cases, apparent from the blistered paintwork on the wood surface and from the repairs, where short lengths of replacement lining have been inserted to replace decayed portions.

Today, resin-bonded plywood and hardboards, cedar and other imported matchings and fibreboard sheets have replaced the canvas, the panel and the softwood matchlining, but the battens remain and the purpose of application is the same. In past years, too, the use of ordinary cork or even hessian-based linoleum fixed to walls with nails through thin battens or mouldings was another dado material. Today, we have specially made dado height cork linoleum to stick on to walls with rubber solutions. This shows that consideration of the qualities of materials used as a makeshift in the past can lead to its re-use as a product specially prepared for a purpose.

With linoleum the fixative is in itself waterproof, but is unlikely to provide a complete membrane if brush applied to other than absolutely smooth surfaces, but it does no doubt protect much of the cork granules from getting damp. Cork itself has water-repellent qualities, which also gives some insulation and proofing against condensation, while the painted, varnished or oiled surface gives surface protection against damage. Furthermore, it can be cleaned and easily dried by wiping down with a cloth. One usually finds this material used where decoration material or plaster surfaces rub off, either when dry after dampness or when damp. As in the case of the foils, this covering is as long-lived as its adhesive.

This last material and enamelled and plastic-coated resin boards are also often applied to walls instead of ceramic or plastic tiling, both of which will also act as a damp-proof membrane providing that the joints are waterproof if fixed with spot adhesives or where their bed or screed is itself waterproof, as is cement and sand. You will not, however, be able to overlook the possibility of condensation upon these two surfaces.

If you decide to use spaced-off linings, then care should be exercised to protect battens with water-repellents which are also fungicides, and to ensure that nails or other fixings are resistant to corrosion by substances in the wall or the battens and linings.

There is little evidence that air movement or change, such as is required for evaporation and is necessary to dry walls or to keep damp levels down, takes place behind spaced-off linings where the lining is non-porous and relatively airtight. That is, unless special provision is made for air inlets and outlets at the bottom and top of the lining and through horizontal battens.

With wood floor construction there is seldom any problem of air entry at the floor to wall junction. Natural shrinkages, if not initial construction gaps between walls and the floorboards, provide a sufficient entry; but with solid floors holes to the room air or open air can be formed near floor level. The head of the spaced-off lining can be constructed as a dado rail or frieze rail with a concealed slot if it continues to that height. Even a false cornice may be used if it is carried to ceiling level, finishing a quarter of an inch or so below actual ceiling height.

Ventilation and Insulation

Where ventilation to spaced-off linings is permitted to take place into the room, room ventilation must be maintained or too humid conditions will build up, thus defeating one of the objects of treatment which is to create drier conditions in the room. Outlets, if provided to the outside air, need to be protected by air bricks, preferably of the louvred type, screened at the back of the louvres with copper gauze or perforated zinc before insertion to prevent insects gaining access and even nesting in the chutes or behind the linings.

As with most treatments "side effects" will occur if you ventilate lining spaces to the outside air. Most of the insulating value of the wall will be lost and your lining becomes the only real division between outside air and the warm room air. Fortunately, applied linings are often themselves reasonable insulators as, for example, matchlinings and soft fibreboards. But if thin, dense linings are used, then an insulating membrane, itself being waterproof, or protected at the wall side by a waterproof layer, should be fixed to the battens prior to fixing the linings. Hair felts protected by waterproof building paper would do this. Even a couple of layers of building paper can be quite efficient, forming a kind of quilted

SLOTTED BATTENS AND OPENINGS PERMIT VENTILATION OF SPACE

DOUBLE BUILDING PAPER QUILT INSULATES

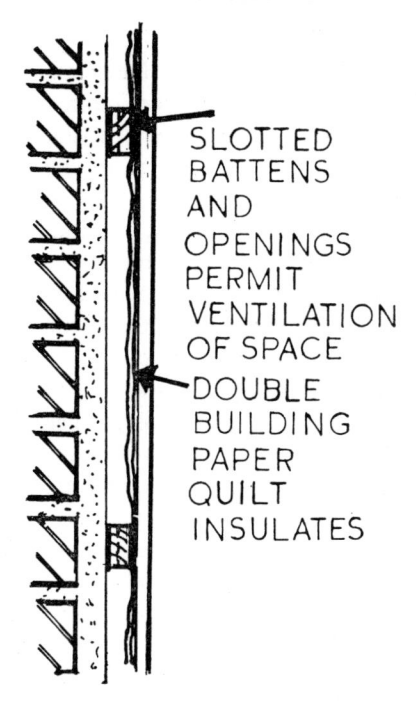

FIG. 37.

layer. The air trapped between the papers gives the main insulating value. In fact, if you "double line" over your wall battens to form a second cavity in which you trap air, then you have restored considerable insulating value to the wall (fig. 37).

If you insulate behind the lining in this way, you can use as hard and abrasion-resisting a finish to your dado as you wish. Expanded polystyrene, so used, is just as effective as an insulator no matter on which side of the lining it is placed.

We have looked at linings very thoroughly because this form of treatment is so often used, especially where either the decorator or the do-it-yourself renovator does not wish to cut out plasterwork or do any cutting in.

As we have seen, applied linings covering damp areas bring with them the problem of the projection of the area treated, however low or small in extent. Where this is not desired, then rendered type waterproofed membranes with a softer setting coat if they are inside, or with a decorative protective finish if outside, give the most economical answer.

It is true that if you have depth to play with, preformed thin membranes covered with plaster type finishings can also be used; but most of these, with perhaps the dovetailed pitch-impregnated sheeting as the only exception, present the problem of how to fix them to the structural wall and how to ensure adhesion of the plaster covering. Self-bonding emulsions, liquid and plastic coatings which also provide plaster bonds, can also be used.

If you have to make up thickness, however, why not waterproof and bring forward the surface to the required thickness with the filling? There may be reasons for and against.

Waterproofing agents mixed with renderings which set hard and brittle, such as cement and sand, only remain effective if the coating into which they are introduced remains intact throughout its depth and area. If any settlement or structural movement occurs, cracks defeat the object of the rendering. Where bondable emulsions, particularly of the rubber base type are used, a certain amount of elasticity remains after drying, and this will permit the structural element of the sandwich, or the plaster layer, to move very slightly, sufficiently in many cases, to prevent actual severance or parting of the waterproofed membrane. Where buildings are subject to slight movements from foundations, vibration, thermal or moisture causes, the sandwich type treatments appear to offer the most reliable remedy.

Nevertheless, the rendering waterproofed throughout its thickness has many applications, and can give long-term complete protection if properly applied, the manufacturers' instructions with regard to additives being of vital importance. Good concrete with well-proportioned coarse and fine aggregate, and the correct proportion of cement and water, will provide a waterproof solid if thoroughly mixed and then carefully tamped or vibrated into position, the object being to secure as dense a mixture as possible. Naturally, the ingredients must be non-porous themselves, or at least without through pores, so that if each pore is completely enclosed in a waterproof cement sac the whole will be non-porous.

Similarly, it is possible to secure watertightness in a thin cement and sand rendering if you choose hard (sharp) sand, use a two or three to one mix with cement, and then make sure that laying on, ruling off, floating or trowelling works out any air that might otherwise be trapped in the thickness.

Plain cement and sand renderings have long been used as waterproof coatings. A first-class plasterer and many bricklayers, given the right materials, simply clean sharp sand and Portland cement, render drain manholes and inspection chambers sufficiently watertight to satisfy stringent hydraulic tests. They can do so to walls. It has, however, become an established practice today that when waterproof membrane renderings are required, some proprietary proofing is added to these materials, a powder or liquid which either will block pores in the rendering, line any through pores with non-wetting linings or prevent pores from forming by expelling air before the mix has its initial set.

We all know that cork will float upon water for a considerable time despite the fact that it has pores and capillaries. Nor are we surprised when a wooden barrel holds liquids, including rainwater, and yet we know that timber will absorb water. We should not be surprised, therefore, that it is possible to render porous materials proof against the passage of water within certain limits, by adopting and applying the qualities which nature provides in such organic materials. We look into this in the next chapter.

15: Pore treatments, "linings and gels"

WE saw in chapter 4 that when water molecules collect at the surface of many solids they have the power of climbing in capillaries to considerable heights or, in a lesser degree, to travel in any direction over such a surface.

There is, however, no actual absorption of the water by the solid, or indeed any chemical combination. Thus the bond is purely physical. One would not therefore expect to find any increase in the volume of the solid to which the water is merely attached, however strong the physical attraction may be. The attachment is in the nature of a bond.

Later we discussed the chemical combination of substances, both where atomic of molecular electrons become distributed in the new substances formed and also where "odd" electrons are the cause of the combination between two electrically unbalanced structures. In both cases new substances were formed, some stable, some unstable. We also considered crystallisation and solution, wherein water is taken into solution as an evenly distributed part of the liquid or above saturation point of the solid so formed.

None of these processes fully explains the properties noted in timber or a hemp caulking, or indeed why some stones and concretes swell and shrink. There is a further way in which certain materials will hold together. This is by sorption, a very loose chemical attachment, in which water molecules produce expansion in combination with the solid without creating a crystalline or regular three-dimensional formation, simply (shall we say) causing swelling.

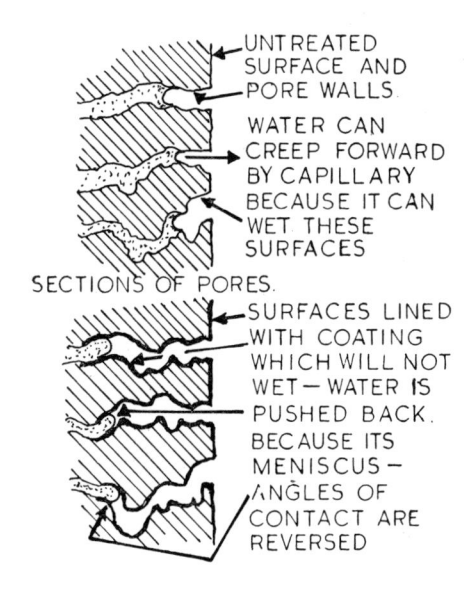

FIG. 38. *The effect of pore lining surface treatments.*

The substances which respond in this way to the presence of water are mainly of organic origin: gelatine, glues, saps, wools and animal and vegetable fibres. You have probably noticed that if you keep glue in cake form, or a household jelly for that matter, in a dry cupboard the glue will remain rock hard and would splinter if struck with a hammer, the jelly flexible but tough. If either, however, is exposed to humid air both become noticeably softer, more pliable and less tough. Something has entered their make-up, not only at the surface but through the thickness, and loosened up the structure. It has made movement of molecules within the mass easier, yet the piece remains solid and does not run in the manner of a semi-solid such as bitumen and wax which show marked reluctance to contact or combine with water in any way. This moisture-attracting process can in certain cases be continued until in fact a liquid or solution is formed which we can pour or stir, especially if it is warm. If, however, we cool it or cause it to come under evaporating influences, then it once again stiffens and in dry air will shrink back to the volume and to the hardness and toughness originally possessed before it gained contact with the water. These structures are called gels.

Gels are contained in the chain cells which form the fibres of timber. If the fibres are sufficiently open, or non-hardened by ageing, they permit moisture to re-enter the structure from which the natural moisture escaped in seasoning, to restore preseasoning volume, or very nearly so. (If we take the gels out of the timber or the animal fibres they do not lose this characteristic, as we see in the glue and in latex, the rubber tree sap.)

In timber and in vegetable fibres it is known that this swelling takes place almost entirely in the walls of the long fibres where chain cells exist, but not in the end cells which cannot be reached by the water. Swelling is thus in the width of timber and not in its length, while in twisted and spun ropes circumferential swelling must result in shortening in length and incidentally, as you have no doubt noticed, tightening of knots. In both cases drying out restores the position—not always, however, without permanent or semi-permanent effect, splits, shakes, distortions in timber, permanent knot shaping in ropes.

Where bricks, stones and concrete are affected, due to the presence of gel material, and the initial setting process of Portland cement is a gelling action in the presence of the water of mixing, the swelling in these materials is proportional in all directions to the size of the piece. The very substantial shrinkage which can occur in newly made concrete components is often the result of completion of full chemical reaction following initial gelling, many of the gels then having chemically combined with the water. Those which do not succeed in achieving this state are liable to swell and shrink when moisture can reach them to produce a degree of moisture movement.

We are thus presented with two methods of waterproofing

DAMPNESS IN BUILDINGS 115

porous materials. We can line the pores or capillary passages with water repellent "linings"* alone, or we can introduce into them gels which will swell and block the further passage of water. If we combine both methods we shall not only prevent water creeping in and through, but also bar the passage of vapour, the "linings" achieving the former and the gels the latter result but not, it will be noticed, preventing drying air from later picking up the "attached" moisture and carrying it out (fig. 39).

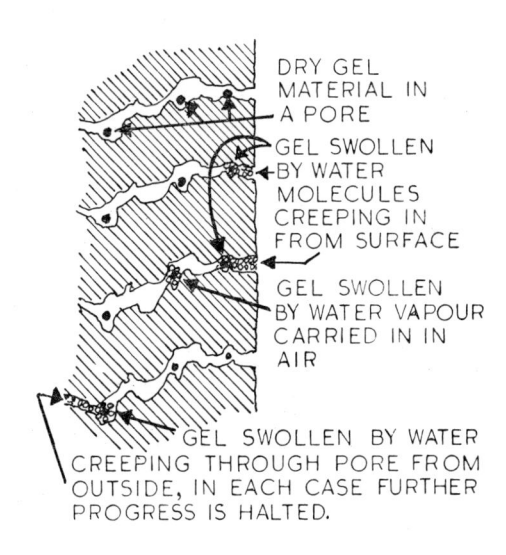

FIG. 39. *The effects of gel deposits in pores.*

An alternative method would appear to be to add to a mix a material which causes any trapped air or gases evolved in the chemical processes of setting to be readily released to a "free to air" surface, so producing a dense, pore-free material. We noted

* "Lining" in this context means an irregular deposit on the tube surfaces which is not and need not be smooth and continuous in order to serve its purpose.

such materials when considering the removal of air bubbles from surfaces to gain a bond thereto. With thin renderings, however, dense mixes are liable to craze, whereas less dense ones are less prone to this defect. Thus this method should only be applied to structural thicknesses. It is not suitable for applied membranes.

When gels are associated with water we have what is known as a colloid, other than liquid or gas molecules associated with but not chemically combined with the liquid or gas. Glue, a domestic jelly, even smoke, which consists of solid carbon particles suspended in air, are all colloids. Some waterproofing solutions are described as being "colloidal solutions" by their manufacturers.

The older pore or capillary lining repellents were silicic acids chemically combined with alcohol to form silicic acid ester. In this process the water portion of the silicic acid is removed, leaving the silica in the resulting solution. This can then be further diluted for application by adding to it a suitable volatile solvent which will, when applied to a material to waterproof it, evaporate in air leaving the silicic ester to hydrolyse with wall or atmospheric moisture to form a water-repellent coating. This process incidentally will also cement stone particles together and applications of this type can be used in restoration work where surfaces are becoming eroded.

It is interesting at this point to mention that silicic acid is prepared by adding acid to sodium silicate, and this acid readily decomposes into silica and water, its formula being H_2SiO_3 (silica, SiO_2 plus water, H_2O). This is why the ester is necessary for its application in this case. Sodium silicate, prepared by fusing powdered flint, which is a form of silica, with sodium carbonate, has long been known as "water glass" and was used for fireproofing inflammable materials, for stone protection and for egg preservation, a solution of this substance rendering their shells airtight. It is also used for concrete floor hardening.

Today silicones are available which require no reaction with water and separate from their solvents to form their repellent coatings simply upon evaporation. Water repellency does not actually become evident for about 24 hours after application with such materials, but it has a reasonably long life—in the region of 10 years near the surface, longer if deep within the material being proofed. These coatings are also effective in preventing efflorescence.

It will be seen from the foregoing notes that rendered membranes can be fortified against damp permeation by admixtures of such kinds and that they can also be used as a surface application. If such preparations are used internally in order to prevent moisture already in a wall thickness continuing to reach the inner surface, one must remember the considerations noted in the last chapter, that the protection is only skin deep and the wall will still remain cold, ready to condense room air moisture at the least sign of high humidity. The deeper the repellent penetrates the more dry material there is to act as "insulation." This is one of the reasons why outside surface treatment with a repellent solution can be so effective in the case of horizontal penetration. It permits the wall thickness to dry out and secure its original insulating qualities. But it cannot do so where rising damp exists. The Building Research Station Digest No. 90, entitled "Colourless Waterproofing Treatments for Damp Walls," gives some interesting details of these solutions and their uses.

These pore blocking methods which rely upon gels, or temporary chemical expansions of deposits therein could, in earlier days, be quite easily introduced into solid concretes and like materials at mixing and deposit stages, or they could be used in membrane treatments in the form of rendered surfaces. Air globule removal agents also were used to produce the dense concretes and renderings. They still are today. The admixture of five per cent to 10 per cent of hydrated lime to the Portland cement content of a concrete mix, as many plasterers still do today for floating coats in two-coat solid plastering to walls, will impart a considerable degree of waterproofing. A relatively small percentage of powdered alum together with soft soap will achieve similar results, the former producing a softer rendering less likely to craze, but the latter better able to be trowelled to a smooth finish without the consequent risk of surface crazing.

To any interested readers one formula used successfully was: Portland cement and sharp sand, 1 to 2 by volume, mixing with the cement through a sieve before adding to the sand ¾ lb. powdered alum and then adding a similar weight of soft soap to each gallon of mixing water used in the mix. Alum and soft soap can still be obtained from decorators' merchants. The author has used the old-fashioned "soap powders," Hudsons, to secure quite good results when "soft" was not available.

Readers will, of course, be well aware of the many proprietary proofing powders and liquids available today which rely upon gelling, temporary chemical expansion in the presence of moisture and pore lining repellent action which can be admixed, into renderings to damp walls or into solid work, or else applied to penetrate very slightly into work already in position.

With the proprietary materials the manufacturer's instructions should be followed carefully. He does not go to all the expense of publication and research unnecessarily. Good results are dependent upon correct application of a material. Quite a number of firms not only publish suggested treatments using their products, but will also send technical representatives to advise if the job is likely to be of reasonable size. One cannot expect expert advice gratis if the order will be for a half a gallon or pound of mixture and no possibility of repeat. The last condition is most important to the manufacturer, repeat orders after satisfactory initial use.

In this chapter I have not covered the application of latex-siliconate pore lining and gel blocking to either membranes or wall thickness because it is better to cover both aspects at once. Deep penetrations require solvents which do not encourage premature gelation, or solidification of the injected materials when water is present in the pores being treated as is the case in remedial work. Furthermore this material opens up a method of proofing gypsum plasters and even plasterboards for surface applications both to new and existing buildings. We have, however, covered the initial thinking about pore lining and gel blocking with the older materials, so that the principles involved in these more recent developments will not need repeating.

These recently developed treatments are particularly suitable where the minimum degree of disturbance to the existing surfaces is necessary, or where other treatments would be impracticable.

16: Proofing in depth, chemical infusion and injection

LATEX-SILICONATE or non-latex bearing silicone fluids can be infused or injected into walls to much greater depths than can be obtained by the process of absorption through brushing or spraying on the surface. However, as a much greater bulk of liquid is used, evaporation of the vehicle used to convey the essential chemicals must be carefully controlled. The pore wall coating and the gel blocking-off materials must not dry off or chemically combine with other components—or allow moisture already in the pores to cause swelling of the gels until they are in position within the wall material pores. The operation can be likened somewhat to inserting a model ship into a bottle.

Where incorporation of gel material either as a powder or in a colloidal solution is possible in the plastic membrane—or even in solid constructional concrete mixes before placing and setting—the only consideration necessary are that there is enough blocking material to serve all the pores and that it is evenly distributed. This is why powders are best batched into the cement according to weight and then mixed into the cement powder by passing the mixture through a sieve prior to adding cement to the aggregate. It is also essential to ensure that neither powder nor liquid gel material interferes with the gelation process necessary for the cement to set.

These additives often have the effect of assisting rapid setting by speeding up the process of gelation of the cement, and therefore any manufacturer's instructions with regards to maximum times between mixing and placing should be strictly observed.

DAMPNESS IN BUILDINGS 121

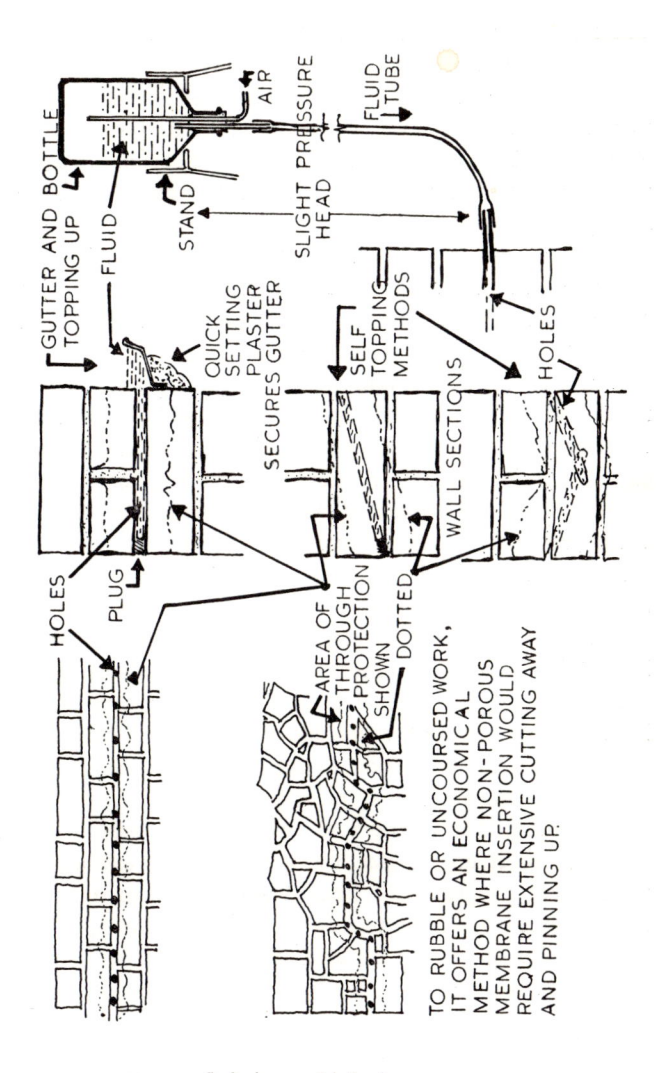

FIG. 40. *Infusion and injection treatments.*

The fact that water is necessary to set the cement in a mix also means that intimate contact must be gained between the cement and water molecules. Colloidal solutions (or any liquid admixtures), while being in a very convenient form for putting into wet mixes, must be so designed that they do not chemically combine with water in such a manner that it ceases to be available for setting (this means that it is either free or can readily separate from a combination) but that the additive is able to mix with the water in emulsion form for distribution throughout the mix, enabling setting to take place and the concrete to be "formed" before the pore coatings form or gels are released.

Recent advances in application techniques overcame the main reasons why infusional and injective deep penetration had not been introduced earlier, the possibilities of producing emulsions containing globules of very minute size being the key to the application of gel-containing admixes to existing pores, and coating materials into deep pores of very small diameter.

A further point with regards to the "combined operation" technique is that the good results of pore coating with non-wettable material, plus gel blocking, shows how recent research has also taken advantage of material properties known long ago in other fields but not applied to building. The means by which insects secure water repellent and retentional surfaces to their bodies led to the realisation that gel materials will cling more securely to non-wettable surfaces than to water wettable ones, thus ensuring that where water can exert a "washing out or flushing" effect upon pores, the gel material is not washed or pushed out progressively when without its maximum water adsorption it is too small to lodge in pore restrictions, or a sufficient number of gels are not able in combination to form a plug in one of even bore. Unless there is "defence in depth"—gels along lengths of pore, all having good anchorage to the walls—there is danger of displacement.

Dr. H. Hurst, BSc., Ph.D., F.R.E.S., of Cambridge Timberproofing Laboratories who developed the latex-siliconate process and whose researches into the means by which insects secure water repellency led to this development has protected the laboratories' rights of these researches and their application under British patent No. 848,352 and the registered trade mark "Actane" covering the manufacture and use of waterproofing fluids containing siliconate and latex as integral components in such fluids.

A dodge used by plumbers in the past, when lead pipework was almost the only material used for water services, also illustrates the above point. Where the stopcock could not be found, or it was inoperable, and some water continued to pass and a repair had to be made with wiped soldered joints, the "live" pipe would be cut and the ends plugged with wooden or cork plugs while the plumbers prepared for jointing. Then, when all was ready, the corks were removed and plugs of dried bread were pushed into the pipe ends. The ends were then quickly put together and the joint wiped. The bread, being a gel material, became swollen as water soaked into it, expanded and formed a reasonable plug. Progress of water through the pipe was delayed long enough for the joint to be wiped.

The "gel" plug ensured that water did not leak from the ends to be jointed, but also that the pipes were not "water cooled" for a short distance on either side of the joint. The slowly-swelling bread plug did this effectively, but furthermore—and this is the point of similar illustration—the wettable side of the jointed pipe did not give secure anchorage to the bread gels, with the result that in short time these particles began to wash through and were displaced at a progressively faster rate until all were washed out from an open tap.

Here we had advantage being taken of gel absorptive properties of a material and its inability to anchor to wettable surfaces for other than short periods when subject to water thrust. If the pipes had non-wettable surfaces inside, the bread plugs would have remained firmly in place after the repair, just as the corks would have done. With damp-proofing work we want our gels to stay put so we must assist them by coating the pores with water repellent.

This illustration also helps us to understand why gel materials can effectively penetrate more readily into wet pores than into dry, the still wettable walls preventing adherence until there are sufficient gel particles present deep in the pores to coalesce so that satisfactory plugs will form when subsequent moisture adsorption occurs after initial drying out.

Water expulsion

When the combined action of the latex and the siliconate is reaching completion, water present in the pores is actually expelled from the pores. The gels and coatings deepest inside the wall, reaching maturity of action before those entering the pore ends later have had time to mature, and so prevent water—pushed back from within—passing out, as would be the case if non-wettable wall coatings or gel blockages were present.

Thus, you will see that not only must the waterproofing injection itself be satisfactory in all the circumstances, but its application must be under correct control. For this reason The Cambridge Timberproofing Laboratories do not sell their fluids but carry out the whole "Actane process" themselves. On dry surfaces within dry pores the fluids rapidly cease to be able to act as the vehicle conveying the gel particles in and should the complete process of coalescence, or gathering of rubber particles, occur very near the surface together with formation of the non-wettable linings then further penetration becomes impossible, so that the formation of a damp-proof layer through the complete thickness of the wall (as required to form a horizontal damp-proof course) cannot be completed. The processes which occur within the pores cannot be reversed once they have reached a "drying-out" stage. If this were possible then they would not be as effective as they are.

The practical application of this method of waterproofing walls through their thickness must, as you will now have seen, be a complete process from start to finish and without any possibility of surface or shallow-depth drying off. This is why "infusional" and "injection" are the terms which describe it. Infuse means "to pour in, or steep," and inject, "to force in." The latter process is of less effect in this case if there is not a degree of resistance within the wall structure. Therefore, infusion is better suited to walls having both surfaces exposed to air, while injection could be more suitable where water pressure exists at the side opposite to that from which treatment can be applied.

Injection of fluids into material through which such forceful penetration might find relatively easy passage right through larger pores, without entering smaller ones, could result in certain areas only being proofed and not the whole, whereas the less forceful seepage resulting from infusion (in which capillarity assists) permits steady penetration throughout the mass. Where resistance to penetration is, however, present, then the force of injection will be spread over every possible passage through which a fluid could pass because, with fluids under pressure within a container, pressure imparted at any point is transmitted equally in all directions, no matter how tiny the area of connection between the main body of the fluid and any other part of the same mass. Furthermore, as the water existing in the pores is pushed in front of and out of the opposite side of the structure by injection pressure, the proper and progressive formation of coatings and gel accumulations may not occur throughout the mass.

When we were thinking about space alongside walls necessary for particular horizontal treatments, we noted the need for room to accommodate, and leave undisturbed, infusional and injection apparatus. You will now see why this is necessary.

The practical methods of application employed to date are as follows: First, holes about $\frac{3}{4}$ in., or of slightly larger diameter where possible, are drilled into the softer parts of the wall. Where remedial work is being done these parts usually are the lime mortar joints. The holes should be at quite close intervals, $1\frac{1}{2}$ to 2 in.* centre to centre for infusional processes but could be up to 6 in.

---

* Improved knowledge of the penetrative properties of infusional liquids and suspensions now suggests that holes can be at about treble these distances apart and of $\frac{1}{2}''$ and $\frac{5}{8}''$ diameter only.

for injection work. The holes should penetrate to the full thickness of the wall minus a little less than the distance apart to which they are spaced. In practice, where it is possible, it has been found more practicable and reliable to drill right through and then plug the ends from which it is not proposed to apply the fluid with mortar, to which some proofing fluid has been added, and let the plugs mature for 24 hours before commencing the infusion.

Where thick walls, such as in basements, are being treated from one side only, then drilling should be carried in as deeply as it is desired that proofing should extend, as it may not in such cases be necessary to treat the full depth, only enough to create dry conditions at the surface and sufficiently behind that surface to create a dry insulating layer which will prevent possibility of condensation upon the surface. Where thick walls can be treated from both sides then drilling from both sides, penetrating about half the thickness in each case, is the best method.

Latex-free fluids utilising silicone solutions can be bought from the manufacturers "by people who understand their use," this being the phrase used by Messrs. Midland Silicones Ltd., whilst Messrs. Peter Cox Ltd., who prepare a P.C.M. solution and have protected the inverted bottle technique of application, "supply the fluid and apparatus to selected nominated local contractors" in some areas.

Messrs. Richardson & Starling Ltd., of 21 Hyde Street, Winchester, Hants., manufacture a fluid for infusional dampproofing, known as Wykamit D.P.C. which they sell retail at 40s. half gallon, 70s. gallon, or in five gallon drums at 60s. per gallon, and in their leaflet "Product information sheet (2F)," dated April, 1968, give instructions for its use at one gallon per 10 feet run of half brick thick, 5 feet of 9 in. and 2 feet 6 in. of 14 in. wall.*

Infusional treatment appears to be best applied by first introducing into the holes drilled in the wall a tube through which the fluid can be fed to the far end of the hole under slight head or

---

* These amounts include additional materials for surface spraying of the infused band to ensure protection against penetrative bridging.

pump pressure and as the hole fills with fluid the tube is gradually withdrawn.

The hole is kept topped up with fluid until absorption slows down to an almost negligible rate. Since continuation of application to maintain wet conditions at and near the surface is essential, the initial tube injection should not be allowed to stop prematurely and then the infusion commence. Further, since there will be many holes requiring application progressively along a wall or over an area it has been found that the use of bottles connected by polythene tubes provides both the initial slight head pressure, and a means of measuring the amount of fluid necessary and then (if the tube is a snug fit just into the hole entrance) continuous topping up. Another method adopted by specialists is to use the tube injection method over a small gutter or trough secured to the wall so that if this is kept topped up from one container fluid will find its way into, and top up, a number of holes. The gutter or trough must, of course, be attached so as to be fluid-tight to the wall at its base. Escape of fluid can then only be into the prepared holes. In this case there must be a certain amount of fluid loss by evaporation whereas with the bottles this does not occur and, in addition, the slight head pressure is maintained.

Where it is not possible to provide bottles or gutters, holes drilled diagonally downwards into a wall can be used to retain their fill of fluids for seepage into surrounding material. But, unless topping up of each individual hole is done meticulously as required, drying-out may occur and defeat the attainment of complete protection.

Research has also shown that once the wall has taken up enough latex-siliconate to slow down absorption to a negligible amount, particularly where basements are being treated from inside only, evaporation by increased ventilation, together with gentle heat if possible, of surface mositure already on and in surface pores—together with that expelled to the surface by the maturing process—helps to dry out the wall and set the protection within. This could be most useful where flooded conditions outside a basement wall might tend to carry injected fluids out before they had time to "set." The tendency with applied heat is to draw water and fluids back into the wall by capillarity and retain the fluids within the pores long enough for them to set.

Since these treatments do not have any chemical after-effects upon the material into which they are injected almost any kind of building material can be treated. In fact, it is suggested that plasterboard could be factory-proofed in this manner for use as membranes. But, if this were done then only adhesive fixings could be used and joints would have to be made with plaster mixed with similar fluid. Other proofed preformed membrane materials may well evolve from such applications in the future.

Finally, with regards to treatments in depth, using latex-siliconate or even silicone alone, the full effect is to leave a material structure with silica gel coatings in its pores, which it appears can harden naturally, or be artificially hardened by chemical additions to the prepared fluids, the former in the course of time, the latter more quickly. Col. B. C. C. Shore, an authority on stone restoration and preservation has noted in his book "Stones of Britain," page 192, "I put much of the credit for this to the use of silicon ester as a toughener, after the work was finished" in referring to work at Ringmer, Sussex to greenstone masonry having withstood eighteen years of exposure without deterioration. In a later reference page 246, he states "the silicones have no binding effect whatever on weakening stones and must not be expected to do anything but act as water-repellants" but he adds later in the same paragraph, "I think that it is worth while soaking the stones in ethyl silicate before using the silicones, so that we can have the strongest surface and near background that we can safely achieve."

These opinions were written before infusion techniques were adopted and it is logical to assume that with deeper penetrations deeper strengthening can occur, this must reinforce the material treated and in addition to preventing further deterioration from absorbed moisture, add to the strength and durability of the structure as a whole. This indicates that damp-proofing treatment by these means serves two purposes and its cost should be related to reduction in possible future expense or after treatment to surfaces, or indeed blocks of material, when compared with treatments where a thin, non-porous membrane only is inserted and no such additional advantage is gained. The company whose figures of estimated cost I quoted for membrane insertions consider the cost of injection of their particular fluid to be 10s. per foot run for half-brick or similar thickness stone walls, 17s. 6d. for 9 in., 22s. 6d. for 14 in., 33s. for 18 in. and 40s. for 24 in. walls.

When infusional or injection treatments are complete, the holes should be filled with mortar mixed with similar additives to that used for the main treatment and well caulked in.

Where mortars or wall materials are too friable for holes to remain clear of debris for a sufficient time to permit infusional penetration to be drilled, then a preliminary injection of weak cement grout to stabilize the material, over the area to be infused will be necessary. This should be allowed time to set before infusional drilling is begun. Walls built of impervious stones but having loose rubble cores in weak mortars, where here is the cause of the rise of dampness, should be similarly grouted. This treatment reinforces the structure as well as assisting in its damp-proofing.

Grouting such as this is a modified form of that described on pages 150-151, with injection pressure adjusted downwards to just overcome resistance internally.

Where resistance to grouting is so low that leakage from the opposite side, or points distant from the injection point on the same side, of the wall occurs from the first injection, then raking out and pointing of the joints with reasonably impervious mortar of those areas should be completed before further injections are attempted. The procedure then being as for grouting noted on pages 150-151.

17: Tanking basements, injection and lining

AS we have noted, latex siliconate deep treatments can be applied to very irregular walls, even to uncoursed rubble. The sloping drilling technique also permits its application to walls which, in addition to being uncoursed, are curved or irregular as a result of settlement, or whose surfaces are rock faced. We found that even frail walls can be treated, providing that drilling does not cause undue vibration. Here, a reference back to careful structural examination of the wall before treatment is valuable.

One of the problems of deep drilling, especially at a slant, is the clearance of debris from the hole prior to feeding in the fluids. Where emulsive treatments which can penetrate damp and wet porous materials are to be used, as is the case with latex siliconates, flushing out of holes with water is possible after drilling to clear debris without interfering with the process. It also ensures better absorption of the fluids.

It is the usual practice to remove internal plasters from walls, at least over the area to be treated, particularly if they have become hydroscopic. Skirtings, too, should be removed so that drilling can be done at as low a level as is possible. Here downward-sloping drills enable the fluid to penetrate to below floor level without disturbing the floor. This ensures that the skirting, when replaced, is not exposed to dampness from behind and the need for a vertical membrane, in addition to the horizontal treatment, is removed.

Replacement plasters can be fortified in their rendering coats by using the fluid as an admix in the mixing water, in the region

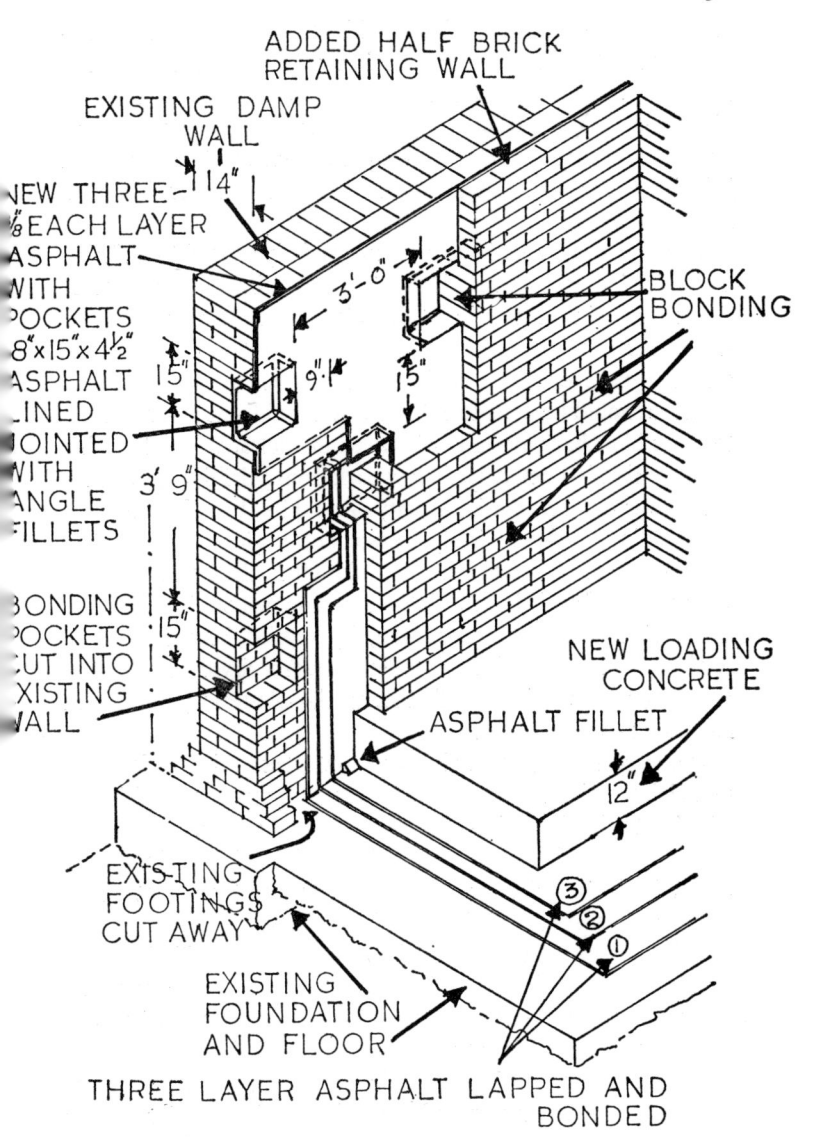

FIG. 41. *Mastic asphalt tanking in a basement.*

of one to 40 of water by volume. This will help to prevent penetration of water through any holes in the wall which are too large to retain sufficient gels from the fluids to effect their complete blockage, especially where they occur on the opposite side of the wall from which the treatment was introduced. It will also prevent bridging of the treated areas where replacement plaster rises from solid floor levels.

Wet basement walls have been successfully treated by infusion and injection techniques. Here, inclined drillings are done at about 4 to 6 in. centres in all directions over the area requiring treatment. Damp portions can be infused, but wet areas where actual seepage occurs need injection. Sufficient pump or head pressure should be used to introduce the fluid but not sufficient to cause blow back around or between the holes. When, by using pressure that has not caused blow back from a drilling into which about four times its cubic capacity of fluid has been injected, the surrounding surfaces visibly moisten or begin to sweat, then pressure should be stopped. Any fluid left in the hole should be allowed to infuse if it will. Some four hours should then elapse before forced surface evaporation, by applied heat, is used to retain fluids in wet walls and accelerate surface drying time so that plugging of the holes and further work—plastering, decoration and so on—can proceed.

It is suggested by some observers that latex in the fluids might materially assist in strengthening weak porous materials, in addition to the formation of the silica pore deposits. Its action is comparable to that of sap maturing and hardening in timber fibres. This is quite feasible when one considers that many modern adhesives are rubber based, as is latex.

A further interesting use of infusion of these fluids is where membranes have failed locally and patches of dampness recur. After removal of the plaster setting coat one or more holes as necessary are drilled into the damp patch and infused, sealing the patch and making cutting out and replacement of the membrane unnecessary. Replacement of the softer setting coat leaves no chance of patchy condensation. All holes drilled for infusion or injection in any work should be caulked with mortar mixed with fluid.

I have not heard of latex siliconate treatments being applied to solid floors, but I see no reason why it should not prove satisfactory. In fact, everything points in its favour, providing the floor is not unduly cracked or dirt-impregnated and is generally porous, or if the joints alone are porous and have sufficient depth to resist water pressure if rendered non-porous. Retention of the fluids in the holes would be no problem at all, and if it tended to drain away, then applied heat would retain it as in a wall.

Thus, it appears that given a basement structure that is porous, but not badly cracked and which is reasonably drillable, then it could be "tanked" by infusion treatment to floor and walls.

Alternatively, where the floor itself could not be infused, an overfloor proofed with a fluid admix coupled with wall infusion applied after this had been laid, taking care to grout it well to the floor-wall joint, could also prove successful. Successful latex siliconate injections have withstood head pressures equal to 27 ft. head of water, where the holes penetrated to a depth of 12 in. into the structure.

There is every reason to suppose that if these new treatments are able to resist natural deterioration within the materials into which they are injected for long periods—say 20 years, at least— —they will have an increasingly wide application as their possibilities and application techniques become known and appreciated. They certainly warrant application where limited additional life is required or a building must have the least structural disturbance.

In letters exchanged with Dr. Hurst of the Cambridge laboratories, after the initial publication of these articles in *The Illustrated Carpenter and Builder*, he wrote as follows, referring to them: "As you correctly point out, ordinary silicone fluids are unsuitable for treatments where static water pressures exist. With silicone-latex fluids, where the latex acts as a pore block component, this difficulty is overcome and a much wider scope of application results, including tanking basements by 'multiple injection' at selected points. We have treated many basements by this means, including those which were unfit for human habitation and subject to closing orders.

"The injection technique has recently been extended to underground vaults and lift shafts where seepage may occur under considerable hydrostatic pressure. The method is similar in some respects, to a grouting operation. At high pressure considerable spread or penetration of 'Actane' can occur into pores, cracks or discontinuities of existing bituminous membranes which have failed, resulting in the formation of flexible waterproof joints.

"Tests are at present in progress in an underground tunnel.* Cracked concrete floors can be waterproofed in this way and in preliminary trials using 'Actane' have proved successful for making good perished or cracked bituminous felt roofing, here again 'Actane' converts the sites of leakage in the felting and underlying concrete into waterproof joints.

"With regard to my technical comment I think it should be made clear that in a siliconate-latex fluid the siliconate component is a water-based material which becomes converted into a silicone in situ. A conventional 'silicone fluid' is usually a solution of a concentrated silicone in a fairly volatile oil base, such as a distillate; this would be incompatible with latex, which is an emulsion of fine rubber particles in an aqueous medium."

In commenting upon this additional information I wrote: "Dr. Hurst thus confirms my appreciation of his process wherein I suggested that 'tanking should be possible' and that floors could be treated. The tunnel, vault, lift shaft and roof treatments described are extremely interesting and one very interesting aspect of the roofing felt treatment, following the preliminary trials success, will be the continued protection afforded in the waterproofed joint so formed in a thin very exposed roofing felt, from the effect of sunlight which is often a cause of initial breakdown."

Since we have considered the application of tanking to basements using these materials, it would seem a convenient point to take a look at the more traditional tanking methods which can

* This and a railway overbridge have proved successful. (June 1968).

be applied to existing basements, cellars, etc., which are damp. However good new treatments prove themselves to be over the course of years, there will always be a use for traditional and already-proved methods.

Except for the application of hot tallow, tar or pitch, probably the oldest of methods is that of bedding two courses of good slates, bonded in both directions, in cement mortar, with the floor-wall junction reinforced by using an angled cement fillet on to which a third slate slip is bedded (or the incorporation into the angle, between the slate sandwich, of a sheet lead angle turned about 3 in. up the wall and loosely welted to the cement). Providing there is not too much static water pressure, this method is still very practicable and suitable for use over small areas where ordinary cement, clean sand and sound, even second-hand, slates are ready to hand. The size of the latter is immaterial, providing that they will bond and can be set with side joints of about $\frac{1}{4}$ in. width, less if possible.

After raking out the joints, or hacking over the surfaces to be treated to give a clean, freshly-exposed area of about 25 per cent of the total area and then wire-brushing down, the wall or floor should be wetted (if it is not damp enough already). Then an area equal to just over three slate widths and one high can be rendered about $\frac{1}{4}$ in. to $\frac{3}{4}$ in. thick with a cement and clean, sharp sand mix, one to two, and roughly ruled off. A fairly stiff consistency is best, to avoid slump.

The wetted slates should then immediately be pressed and slid into position, the water on the slates being sufficient to float them easily. Once a slate is in position do not disturb it.

To floors or walls it is best to run courses along complete bays and then return to the starting end and repeat the process to form the next course. About 12 to 15 ft. run of one course at a time if the bays are long is sufficient, but with shorter bays, each course is best left until the cement bedding has stiffened but not set before adding the course above. To floors, timing delay is not of great importance.

When three courses are complete the first should be sufficiently set to repeat the process over it, but this time using for the first course half-height slates and also bonding sideways by starting with a half slate, so as to secure half lapping in both directions. The wetting and sliding-on process is the same as for course one. The slates of the outer leaf of the sandwich are left exposed, the joints being pointed off when stiff. There is no good reason for covering them, and they do not readily hold rendering over their surface. If the wall is to be left like this (and today it could be as a decorative finish), good-quality coloured slates should be used for the exposed layer. Slate floors are, I understand, the very latest fashion—and, incidentally, very hard wearing and easily kept clean. They take quite a nice wax polish.

In the case of a floor, one could, of course, use thicker sawn slates, but these are expensive and would need a thicker, waterproofed screed and bedding. Ordinary slates which will not laminate can, however, give good and very durable results. In either case, however, the surface will be cold. In the case of a wall this need not be troublesome if the slate is confined to a dado with softer plaster above and reasonable room temperature and ventilation maintained.

If it is not wished to leave the slates exposed, then their covering, if of plaster type, should not be applied until at least 24 hours after putting up the outer slates. A soft and fairly thick finish is preferable. There is no need to waterproof the mix with which the slates are bedded; in fact, any admix tends to encourage fattiness in the mix and the slates to slip.

I have drawn attention to the need for extra care at floor-wall junctions, and if tanking is your intention, similar methods are applicable, using fillets to vertical angles, and lead, copper or even polythene sheet to external angles. If the surface to which such tanking is to be applied cannot be roughened to give a key, then a bonding agent must be used to secure adhesion.

So much has been written about waterproofed cement renderings to floors and walls that any description of processes or mixes here would be superfluous. I would refer the reader to the various Ministry of Public Building and Works and Building Research Station leaflets, or to those available from the manufacturers of admix materials, where all the necessary information can be found. It will suffice to say that a mixture of clean, sharp sand, well graded, with cement up to about 33 per cent by volume, using just enough water to permit its working to the finish required will, if floated to a plain face or trowelled just sufficiently, produce a waterproof membrane. It should be at least $\frac{3}{4}$ in. in thickness, or if required thicker, then it should be in two coats with good key between them. To repeat what was said earlier, all "renderings" which are brittle by nature will not remain waterproof for very long if they crack or craze, whether due to vibration, movement or simply over-trowelling. If there is any suspicion that settlement or building movement will occur, however slight, then such renderings are not suitable as dampproof tankings, of even renderings which are not tankings but which need to remain waterproof.

A certain amount of additional strength can be given to renderings if wire mesh type or expanded steel reinforcement is nailed over the wall surface before applying the rendering. Where this becomes necessary, then one should seriously consider the use of an alternative treatment which can give without losing its non-porous qualities.

A combination of materials, such as a rubber-based liquid or mastic coating which will bond to the floor or wall and will provide a key for rendering or plaster-type finishings is, in my opinion, a better answer. I have referred to this type of membrane earlier.

The insertion of asphalt mastic or built-up sheet tanking to existing basements is best explained by first considering the process. An illustration is therefore given in this chapter and will be commented upon in the next.

18: Asphaltic linings, de-watering, loading, adhesion

WHERE the value of the additional dry accommodation gained warrants the treatment, or the treatment is necessary for other reasons—health for instance—then there can be no doubt that asphalt tanking, properly restrained, provides most reliable long term remedy to a damp basement.

Protected asphalt does not deteriorate, its layer construction and bitumen bonding permits slight, even reasonable building movement, without failure. The supporting linings and holding down loadings, where necessary, give dry material insulation and the base for finishings. The one drawback is cost, but providing that the principles of combating moisture movement and the behaviour of the material under the influences of heat and pressure are understood, then good organisation and skilled workmanship can offset its high potential cost.

First it should be remembered that one has to work by stages and that, while the job is incomplete, water deprived of outlets from the floor or walls at some points may move with increased effect elsewhere. Furthermore, if before you start there is free water upon the floor or oozing from walls, then measures must be taken to dry these surfaces down to no more than dampness before asphalting can be successfully done.

In severe cases, floor sumps, holes dug to about 18 in. below floor level, breaking through the existing floor and about 18 in. square, must be formed to facilitate pumping. It is good policy to line the hole with porous material, perforated metal sheet or elm or suchlike timber, even a perforated five gallon metal drum. This prevents any possibility of subsidence as the result of subsoil washing out when pumping commences.

Where linings are inserted into sumps one should terminate them a few inches above the existing floor level so the final sealing is not interfered with. Alternatively, where it is possible, a series of "well points" could be sunk to the required level around the outside of the basement. Where only some faces of the building can be so protected, sumps or other well points could also be used internally.

Well points

The use of well points externally will prove more effective in drying walls, while if used internally they are more easily sealed off and cause less interference with progress of the proofing work.

The actual strainer points and tubes below floor level can be sealed in to the existing floor immediately water extraction makes it possible to concrete around it. A screwed joint in the tube line just above that level, enables plugging off to be done to abandon the point at final stages of the work. Larger sumps, where more normal pumping strainers and hoses are used, may have to be adapted at sealing-off stages by inserting short lengths of pipe with screwed terminals to which the hoses can be attached so that similar sealing off procedure can be adopted.

Reference back is necessary here to the chapter calling for care with regard to structurally defective buildings and surveys of adjoining buildings. Before such pumping is commenced, careful examination of the building being treated and those likely to be effected should be completed, and where necessary the extent of existing defects agreed. The withdrawal of water particularly in substantial quantity, or in lesser quantity over lengthy periods, can cause subsidence. If mud or suspended solid matter, however little in quantity, appears in the water being extracted or diverted, one should take immediate steps to hold back the soil being carried with the water, because this is erosion and erosion is a first step to settlement. Wrapping strainers with gauze, either metal or linen, or in sacking, and plugging holes in boarded linings with sacking or linen gauze (plasterers' scrim) will often prove successful.

Having taken steps to dry down the surfaces, using portable space heaters if necessary, the next step is to secure a satisfactory surface to which mastic asphalt will adhere, or upon which sheet material can be applied without fear of perforation. Here I am of the opinion that where wall tanking is necessary and block bonding is needed for the supporting or retaining walls, then the use of preformed sheet asphalt to the walls is not an economical proposition unless the wall can be chased horizontally. Mastic work is better suited to pocket lining. But for floors and flat wall surfaces, where such bonding is not necessary, the sheet materials can be cheaper.

Adhesion of membrane

Adhesion of the waterproof membrane is necessary to some degree, even if support or loading coats are to be provided. The membrane must be capable of staying attached to the surface over a limited area while successive laminations are built up and the support applied and set.

Bond for asphalt type membranes is mainly by the absorption into pores of the material being coated, by what we might describe as capillary action. A degree of pneumatic atmospheric support may also occur. Naturally, this type of bonding can only take place with material which is sufficiently liquid to wet the surface to which it is being applied.

In its natural state, bitumen is semi-solid, and pure bitumens are not suitable for use on surfaces which are not level—other than as paint films—or indeed in any situation where even a thin layer might become loaded or compressed. Thus we use reinforced

DAMPNESS IN BUILDINGS 141

bitumen, impregnated hessian, or we stiffen it to make asphalt by adding powdered limestone.

Readers will also recall from earlier thoughts on surface tensions that if we raise the temperature of liquids, or even semi-solids, that ability to spread or creep over surfaces increases as tensions reduce. Thus hot bitumen appears to be a very suitable "primer" for bonding asphalt to solid structures, and laminations of asphalt or bituminous felts together.

Where hot application is not possible, then an emulsion or solution of bitumen can be used, the emulsion or solvent vehicle evaporating or being absorbed into the structure to leave a surface film of bitumen attached by capillary roots in the pores.

Where solutions of bitumen are used cold to seal layers of felt together, the solvent first takes the surface bitumen of the felt into stronger solution and then evaporates to give the "tacky" state recommended as necessary for bonding. This state is achieved by the solvent dispersing itself deeply into the felts so that the solution becomes so stiff as to resume or very nearly so, the nature of bitumen itself.

Adhesion is always better to roughened and clean surfaces, the former because more pore ends are exposed and leave their respective surfaces at varying angles, the latter because pore ends are not blocked by dirt or decoration. Hacking or otherwise roughening surfaces and stiff brushing afterwards is usually recommended. With brickwork, raking out of joints is good practice for mastic work. For built-up felts, reasonable pointing in and smoothing off of depressions with cement mortar should be carried out—even surface rendering if the wallface is rough.

If the surfaces can then be dried over a reasonable area by heat, either from a flame or by warm air so that the primer or the first layer of proofing can be applied before water resumes occupation of the surface pores, then this should be done and the primer and/or felt or mastic layer laid straight away to the floor, or applied to the wall. Where it is not possible to dry the surface sufficiently by these means, then hot primers are next best, that is providing that one realises that steam generated from water in the surface pores will blow holes in the coating. The primer in this case is simply the anchor for subsequent treatment. The action is that the water, in changing to steam and being subjected to pressure by the stiffening bitumen blockage at the entrance to the pore, pushes water back into the pore as far as this is possible and then bursts out through the bitumen, rewarming the bitumen as it does so, so that the bitumen closes over the hole to be then pushed into the pore by atmospheric pressure as the steam remaining trapped in the pore condenses.

There will, however, be holes too large for the bitumen to close over, but which it has reduced in area. These will be sealed by either a second coat of primer or the first layer of laminate, or maybe the second. The only reason for applying layers subsequent to the first is to deal with these larger blow holes.

Obviously the floor needs to be dealt with first. Progressive patches of bays should be primed and the requisite number of layers of mastic or felt spread and bonded together in both directions. The order of laying should be towards the sump or sumps from all directions, about a foot of "skirting" being incorporated at wall-floor junctions.

With mastic work, triangular fillets should be ironed in with a hot iron as the final layers are completed in order to bond and seal this junction. Sheeting calls for the formation of a cement and sand or fine concrete angle fillet foundation before priming, so that the felt can be eased around from floor to wall without a sharp angle.

If a loading coat is necessary then this must be applied before too great an area is left unloaded. It may be possible and economical to put down a thickness of plain concrete providing it has the weight necessary to counteract the upward thrust of the water pressure expected, plus about a 25 per cent addition if tailing down will not be applied by walls built thereon, or chasing in edges cannot be done to existing walls. (Concrete weighs around 140 lb. per cubic foot, water 62.5 lb. per cubic foot, but see the earlier notes upon this problem.)

Reinforcement "in reverse"

Where headroom is restricted, or when the thickness would need to be too great to be economical, then loadings can be designed as reinforced concrete floors "in reverse," the rods or steel mesh being near the top instead of near the soffit. A reasonable area should be left around the sumps for laying and bonding the membrane, and arrangements should be made for bonding the loading patch to the main loading slab. An undercut rebate or dove-tail should be provided for mass concrete and projecting rods or mesh where reinforced.

It is at this stage that arrangements for sealing off the tubes to the sumps should be checked to see that they will be well below finished loading coat surface if they are to be left in. But sealing off should not be done until the membrane and its supports have been applied to the walls and sufficient strength has been gained to withstand a return to pre-treatment water conditions.

Where support work to the wall membrane is not to be bonded to the existing wall, then a kerb upstand, about 6 in. high at least, suitably anchored with reinforcement to the floor slab, should be cast in with it, with starter reinforcement projecting above its top if it is to continue as reinforced work.

Where levels demand that the floor membrane is to be laid where brick footings project, then these are best cut back for mastic work, but could be roughened off or used as the base for the angle fillet recommended for bonded felts. Usually the number of courses found projecting from older thicker walls where this type of work is undertaken, renders their removal necessary if they are not to grin through the loading and make a watertight and structually satisfactory job impossible.

It is necessary to complete the laying of as much of the loading coat to the floor as possible and to cover any upstand before preparation of the walls is commenced, especially where pockets for bonding have to be cut out. Any attempt to do this work with the floor membrane exposed, or before it is laid, nearly always results in incorporation of pieces of broken brick into the asphalt or perforation of bonded felt layers.

Even so, there must be scrupulous regard to tidiness in such confined working space if the job is to be completed without unnecessary risk of puncture to the membrane—a defect which can cost a lot of money to remedy.

There will be cases where asphalt tanking is required but there is difficulty in drying off existing concrete floors, or steam may make the use of hot bitumen a problem and cold emulsions peel off. One is then forced to put down a waterproofed cement and sand screed, using as little water in the mix as possible. Usually a thickness of $1\frac{1}{2}$ in. will be required to prevent it from being floated off and the surface is just ruled off. Another method is to "hot prime" strips about 18 in. to 24 in. wide, leaving sufficient space between them to lay in and seal Parovent channels with the first mastic coat. The tube steam release pipes provided to these channels are flattened or otherwise sealed off into the loading coat after completion of the membrane. This is expensive, but may be the only practical answer in a difficult case.

Bonding pockets in existing walls may be large or small. I have seen 5 in. × 5 in. × 4 in. suggested, one per square yard, but for mastic work this makes cutting out by the bricklayer and lining, complete with ironed-in fillets, a fiddle of a job.

Once you have cut out the first half-header or a stretcher, the enlargement of the pocket to, say, 18 in. × 15 in. on elevation is easy to a half-brick depth. It also permits the lining to be done with normal tools, and if you start your supporting brickwork $1\frac{1}{2}$ in. in course height below or above that of the existing work then you can bond in four courses of all headers without undue cutting of bricks or thick jointing to mastic work.

If built up sheet work is demanded to walls, then 6 in. or 9 in. horizontal chases about every three feet up in height are more practical, with the supporting brickwork kept level with existing courses. A $\frac{3}{8}$ in. mortar joint can accommodate a three-layer build-up—three courses if you start right, permitting headers at the bottom and top of the built-in block. Two-course chases must be bonded all headers.

The larger pockets can be spaced 3 ft. apart horizontally and 15 in. vertically, giving two to every three square yards. All brickwork for block bonding should be in cement mortar and the pocket well grouted to give absolutely solid filling.

When the walls have been completely tanked and their supports are matured, the sumps can be sealed off. Here concrete grouting, laced with a gel or colloidal waterproofer, filled in around the pumping tube to existing floor level, will take its priming and mastic or bonded membrane patch in 24 hours. The loading patch can be put in immediately this is cool, after disconnecting the pump hose and sealing the tube with a watertight cap or plug.

19: Trees, plants and creepers; grouting structural fractures

WHEN considering the question of tanking many people are sceptical about the ability of a half-brick block or chase bonded supporting wall to provide the required strength, particularly as the pockets are not of dove-tail type. The general opinion is that there is no reason why the asphalt and the supporting wall should not be pushed off bodily from the existing wall. One should, however consider the forces trying to effect this result and the influences counteracting it.

First, the forces of water pressure through the wall. If we refer back to chapter 9, we can see that the effect of these forces is not equal throughout the height of the tank side, thus the tendency is not to produce a horizontal push of even intensity over the height, but a tendency to curve out at the base before the top (see fig. 42). Counteracting this will be the frictional resistance resulting from the locking of the block bond if it is tilted or twisted in its pocket. In any case the anchorage of the primer will require the shearing off of the capillary anchoring roots, as opposed to pulling out, before movement can take place. The primer gives the membrane a general grip over the whole surface area. Curvation is also resisted by the actual strength of the brickwork, to which must be added its frictional grip to the loading concrete and the support derived from cross wall bonding angles, etc. To all these factors we can couple the possible suction effect, due to unbalanced atmospheric pressures, mentioned in chapter 9. Where there is only dampness, and little or no static pressure, the asphalt and many "rendered on" membranes hold secure without such supporting work.

FIG. 42.

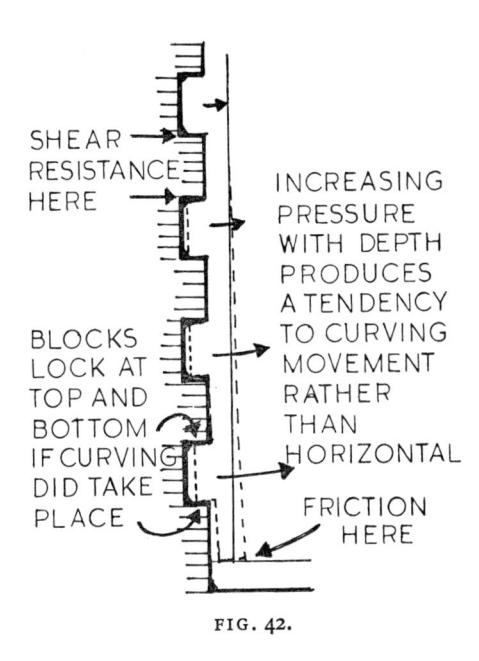

One final point with regard to pumping while work is in process. The rate of water extraction should never exceed that of natural seepage or flow into the sump. Careful watch should be maintained so that pumping rate is adjusted to inflow. Initial flow upon opening the sump is often far more rapid for a short while, than the rate to which it settles down once pressures have been relieved, but most likely it will fluctuate during progress of tanking. Excessive pumping can encourage erosion and increases the rate of clay shrinkage from or in surrounding soil.

Effects of trees and hedges

While we are considering the effects of the withdrawal of water from the soil surrounding buildings it is worth remembering that trees and, to a less vigorous degree, evergreen hedges, privets in particular, extract large quantities of water from solids and in their processes of growth, evaporate it.

The removal of an old established hedge alongside or within a few feet of a wall is counterpart to taking out a shallow sub-soil drain, while the removal of a large tree even at greater distance, particularly those of the poplar family, is like removing a soakaway. Not only will such removals cause noticeable increase in rising damp wall conditions already showing within buildings, but they may result in the evidence presenting itself for the first time, the tree or hedge having been a balancing factor in the capillary struggle.

Please, however, think twice before planting rapid growing evergreen or privet hedges close to walls, or trees near buildings as an attempt to cure or reduce the effects of rising dampness. You will probably achieve your objective in a few months or years according to how vigorous is the growth of what you plant, but if you are on clay beware—you may produce excessive shrinkage therein and subsidence of the building which you sought to protect.

These thoughts upon trees and hedges may answer a few problems in some instances as to why dampness occurred or diminished. Hedge planting is unlikely to produce subsidence, unless the building has very shallow foundations, but if you contemplate trees, then take a good look around your neighbourhood and note the incidence of subsidence where largish trees exist within say 30 ft. to 50 ft. of buildings. You will then be able to judge the likelihood of similar effects upon the building that you wish to protect.

One does feel, however, that a shrubbery, or well planted flower bed or herbaceous border alongside a wall could be a better protection against dampness rising than a paved path. That is of course, providing that the plants do not interfere too much with the sun warming the wall, or the movement of air which helps evaporation.

I would suggest, from observations of these effects, that walls with northern aspects benefit from plantings, but that those having southern aspects gain no greater protection than the sun and drying winds give.

Creepers

Wall climbing or trained plants and creepers may be useful as water shedding claddings, and ivy will actually attach itself by suckers to mortar joints and to brick and some stone surfaces.

Wall plants of the creeper type which shed their foliage during winter, when the wettest conditions exist cannot be of great help, either in shedding rain, or of extracting water from the soil or the wall while bare. In summer they tend to keep the wall cool and prevent evaporation by warmth or free air movement.

Ivy which is evergreen and which "grows" on the wall, does no doubt have a continual drying effect, but it can also have a disruptive effect when its strong growth bursts joints, causes spalling of surfaces. As it matures it may even pull whole blocks of stone out of place. Its removal may, however, explain the occurrence of damp effects internally.

Ivy can, however, if the slow growing varieties of dwarf habit only are planted, which are usually the more ornamental, be used as an external live dadoe to a north facing wall without danger of serious side effects.

One should, however, consult a horticulturalist about the growth habit of any proposed plantation remedy before adopting it, or be prepared to whip it out, not always so easily done as said, should there be effects other than those desired. This type of remedy can only be applied where continued observation is possible over the years. One must also not forget that roots, in their search for underground water, will penetrate into the tiniest of cracks or holes in drain pipes, inspection chambers stop cock boxes having leaking glands, and into or under foundation walls. Then as growth proceeds and swelling takes place the tentacles will split or lift the material if it has not the strength to resist. Even, therefore, if planting would serve to remedy a case of dampness, do not plant deep rooted trees or scrubs near stoneware drain lines, or strong root growths near boundary walls or other shallow foundationed or light brick, concrete or masonry structures.

Readers will, I trust, understand this diversion by a builder into horticulture. After all I did set out to explore with you the causes as well as the effects and remedies for dampness rising in walls. Too often we look for causes in the structure and overlook a very obvious natural cause, or in our efforts to "build" fail to adopt a natural remedy. In fact, in our efforts to remedy a situation one can often do things which thwart its natural repair.

Dampness is a natural phenomenon, but most of our remedies in the past were artificial. Today we take greater account of natural remedies, such as the use of rubber Latex and gel materials. We can learn quite a lot from the observation of natural effects. Experience of the effects of tree and scrub removal and planting shows we must take these things into consideration when investigating dampness in buildings.

But let us now return to the consideration of basements. Where otherwise watertight structures leak because of structural cracks then the remedy, if work can only conveniently be carried out from inside, is usually some form of grouting. The finer the crack the more difficult the repair. One usually has to open out fine cracks in order to deal with them at all near the surface and then the caulking of the widened gap is the answer, rather than grouting. In many such cases, particularly in concrete, hard engineering brickwork and masonry, a combination of surface caulking with a rapid setting proofed cement and sand, or a mixture of cement and asbestos fibres, gypsum and asbestos fibres or metallic lead rope, coupled with grouting, provides the answer.

Grouting

The type of grouting necessary to plug deep structural cracks requires pressure application, using cement pumps. The process is to caulk foot lengths of the crack to give watertight surface conditions. As this proceeds, insert screwed steel sockets between the caulked lengths, into which short lengths of screwed steel tubes can be inserted, each equipped with a plug type cock at its outer end and a coupling for connection of a pressure grouting hose.

The Ministry of Public Building and Works, who developed this process for grouting finer cracks, without cutting out, recommend the rinsing out of the cracks with detergents before commencing grouting. This assists "wetting" by the grout and enables deeper penetration to take place with minimum pressures. Their method of procedure is to drill holes for the screwed sockets, the depth of penetration being ensured by drilling a smaller hole on into the wall for about a foot beyond the socket. They also recommend the pumping of detergents into the cracks as a means of tracing the extent of the area over which grouting will be needed. These areas, as they show, require further drilling and preparation for grouting.

Whether dealing with open or finer cracks, as much water as possible should be extracted by suction. If it cannot be completely exhausted it should be driven back with compressed air before pressure grouting starts.

Grouting should continue into any one tube until increasing pressure is noticeably required. This is indicated by the effort needed at a hand pump or the labouring of mechanical ones. Where continuous cracks up the height of a wall are being treated, start from the bottom. A good idea of the progress of filling is given when grout appears at the next tube above, assuming no outward loss is taking place.

Where porous areas are being treated filling is assumed to be complete when no more grout can be forced in after stopping, clearing the tube and recommencing pumping. The plug cocks are then closed until the initial set has occurred. The tubes must then be uncoupled, unscrewed from the sockets and cleaned out.

Advice upon constructing watertight basements and pressure grouting leaking ones is given in Ministry of Works Advisory leaflets Nos. 51 and 52. There are several proprietary plugging compounds and admixes which can be used to progressively caulk wider or opened cracks for an inch or so deep and finally seal them against pressure. But this is not grouting. It is plugging leaks. The advantage of grouting is that the structure too is repaired and enabled to dry out in depth, so restoring insulation, whereas plugging simply stops the leak from coming to the surface, adds hardly any strength to the structure, and does nothing to prevent water continuing to lie in the material very near to the surface. Nevertheless, surface plugging would be considerably cheaper. As with latex-siliconate deep treatments as opposed to surface coatings, the strengthening of the structure and the gain in insulation value should be taken into account when comparing costs.

One source of difficulty in tanking is the sealing of services passing through the walls, joists and beams, bearer brackets, etc. Where asphalt tanking is done, pipes and other penetrations can be sleeved after priming with bitumen in the same way as they are treated when they pass through asphalted floors or roofs. Metal pipes can be given welded, screwed on or soldered flanges to interleave between membrane coats. Most other treatments applied to internal surfaces call for the provision of sleeves similarly jointed to the service, with a flange buried or sandwiched into a membrane depth if this will permit it, or into a shallow cut-out pocket filled in with proofed rendering behind the membrane it it does not.

The use of mastic sealings which remain plastic will often seal around such penetrations and at the same time allow for slight movements such as those which occur on heating and hot water service pipes, or the expansion of other metal pipes.

Where it is not possible to apply any of the tanking or leak sealing or caulking treatments for one reason or another, but the continued use of the basement is necessary, then the only possible answer is—no, not to wear bathing suits!... or turn it into a swimming pool, as was done in a Kensington house basement a few years back—but to construct a false floor above the existing, after providing sumps therein, together with false walls to produce a cavity effect. Unless the newly inserted walls and floor are themselves impervious the same care must be taken to avoid bridging the cavity as is used in conventional construction. An automatic float operated pump should be installed to clear the sumps when necessary. This form of construction can well prove cheaper than tanking, and it avoids the necessity of cutting into the existing structure. It is like putting the drained cavity inside. At least one of our road and several railway tunnels are maintained in usable condition in this way, where sealing has been unsatisfactory or where this method has been found cheaper and more reliable.

In buildings where very many penetrations of basement walls are necessary, for example boiler houses and telephone exchanges, this method can indeed be the only satisfactory one.

20: Dealing with the cause electrically; electro-osmotic treatments

IN early chapters of this book we studied the forces which give materials their characteristics, determine their strength in various respects and govern their reactions to other materials. Among these forces we noted the ability to respond to added energy or its withdrawal.

We noted later that an increase in heat energy results in increased activity, which, in almost every case, causes the atom or molecule to expand and, in doing so, repel its neighbours. We saw also that this effect causes weakening of surface tensions to the extent that if it is pursued to too high a temperature gain, then atoms or molecules are so weakly linked with the mass of a liquid, or even a liquefied solid, that many of them jump right out of the mass to become either the gas state of the material or, if they collect together again, globules of liquid material suspended in the surrounding gas—their behaviour entirely depending upon the amount of energy contained.

Electrical forces

We noted too that this attractive and repellent energy is largely if not entirely connected with electrical forces, the positive charge of the nuclei being balanced by that of the negative

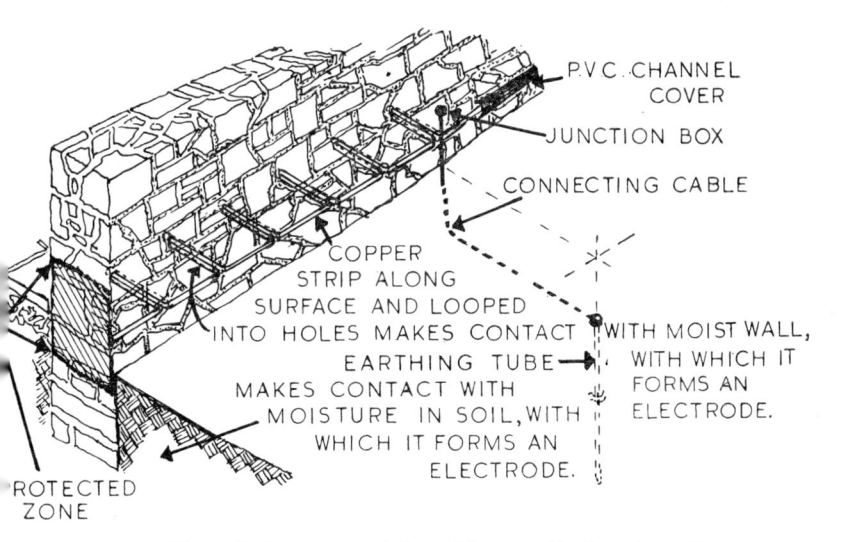

P.V.C. CHANNEL COVER
JUNCTION BOX
CONNECTING CABLE
COPPER STRIP ALONG SURFACE AND LOOPED INTO HOLES MAKES CONTACT WITH MOIST WALL, WITH WHICH IT FORMS AN ELECTRODE.
EARTHING TUBE MAKES CONTACT WITH MOISTURE IN SOIL, WITH WHICH IT FORMS AN ELECTRODE.
PROTECTED ZONE

FIG. 43. *The wall, the water and the soil form a cell, the strip, cable and tubes the circuit.*

electrons, providing that the particle is complete and of the type that can naturally exist alone. Some, you will remember, such as hydrogen atoms, cannot. Others, such as sodium, having an odd outer electron and chlorine, being short of an outer electron, will electrically link to secure a form of balance.

It is not surprising, therefore, that scientists and engineers have looked critically at liquids whose surface tensions permit them to defy gravity and whose powers of "creep" enable them to penetrate porous materials in any direction, suspecting that if it were possible to interfere with the electrical charges within their atoms or molecules, then they would behave differently.

It is a generally accepted theory that electric current as we know it means that electrons which are rather freer than others have been induced to transfer from one centre of attraction or nucleus, within the piece of material, to another and then to another throughout the entire piece, which we call a conductor.

They would do this in order to balance a potential unbalanced state of electrical charges.

Where there is no state of unbalance there can be no flow of current. The state of unbalance, electrical potential as it is called, can be induced by moving a coil of wire through a magnetic field, but it will not become evident until a conductor to a demand, a circuit, is provided through which it can secure balance.

Only as much current as is "demanded" will flow because, unless there is an excess of negative electrons of low potential at some part of the circuit, when compared with a higher at another point, there cannot be movement. If on the other hand the demand becomes too great, that is more movement than the conductor providing the circuit can accommodate, then the increased activity imparted to the atoms or molecules therein causes such massive expansion that the material state changes, metals fuse to liquid, or even to a gas, while other substances change so radically that chemical breakup occurs. Ceramic insulators, which are almost pure silica, will burst apart if they become internally overloaded. This fusing or breakdown is the natural reaction to overloading, because it reduces the demand upon the source of current to nil.

Electric batteries, from which electric current can be drawn, are of two main kinds. A primary cell produces current as the result of chemical reaction between its component parts, chosen because they have electrical potentials, one to another. A secondary cell, accumulator as we call it, will only have potentials and be able to respond to a demand if we have previously charged it. (This means pass a current through it so that its component parts are given potentials.)

Since we are attempting to apply this disturbance of electrical balance to deal with a liquid, our reference to electrical unbalance is related to cells or batteries, not to mechanical current generation.

A primary cell consists of two solid materials, each having different potentials to a liquid or moist granular solid, which itself is an electrical conductor. The solids, two different metals, or a metal and carbon (which is one of the few non-metallic elements), are called electrodes and the conductor into which they are immersed is called the electrolyte.

Directly a circuit is provided, by connecting a good conductor to both electrodes outside the electrolyte, current commences to flow and will continue until the chemical state of the components is so altered that either no potentials exist or, as is often the case particularly with two metal plates, one of them becomes "insulated" with gas bubbles clinging to it, formed as the result of the chemical changes, so that it is not in contact with the electrolyte.

The accumulator acts in a similar manner after being charged, but whereas the parts of the primary cell become exhausted when the potentials are balanced and must be replaced with fresh material, the accumulator materials can be re-charged.

Electro-osmotic application to damp walls means that advantage is taken of the fact that the components of a battery exist within the wall, the dampness and the earth. All that we need to do is to provide the outside electrolyte conductor, and a current will flow. The flow will be relative to the potentials.

Some materials have high potentials, some medium and some low. All that is needed is a difference between the wall, earth, and water. This being the case, one cannot imagine any building not having these characteristics, except perhaps a mud hut having exactly the same potential to its contained moisture as the earth upon which it stands. Even here there would be a difference due to exposure of the mud to a different environment, the freer air, which will very speedily effect alteration of its composition, particularly moisture content.

With a battery the strength of the current flow is relative to the strength of the electrolyte, that is up to an optimum level, weak solutions being relatively better than strong ones. Thus wall, earth and dampness current flow will vary from building to building and also with the amount of chemicals in solution with the water. Pure water is not an electrolyte, it is a very poor conductor, but with the slightest contamination it becomes a good conductor.

Thus a wall equipped with electrical contacts and conductors to the earth becomes a battery cell, and so long as potentials exist and electrolyte is present a current will flow. This will be the case so long as the wall and the earth are damp. If the earth dries out so will the wall (but not necessarily the reverse) and the action will stop. But it will resume immediately moistening recurs. In fact, all things being equal, the wetter the wall the better should be the drying action.

Here it will be helpful if further consideration is given to the theories relating to capillarity. An alternative to the attractive surface theory was noted in chapter 3.

First we accept the original conception that the atom or molecule have internal and interacting forces, just as before, but next we assume that a drop of liquid in seeking to remain intact in another media does so, first by re-packing, or adjusting its atoms or molecules by a process of inward concentration, each particle near the surface attempting to pull itself nearer to the centre and so compressing those nearer to that point with increasing intensity. In this process it would appear natural that a spherical "drop" should form, as in fact, in the absence of other disturbing forces does happen. If we now discard the previous theoretical assumption that "unbalanced surface forces" then "bend" to seek closer links with their surface fellows as depicted in figures 7, in an earlier chapter, then the "skin" conception of surface tension will also be discarded. We will be left however, with liquid whose surface particles hold the general mass within its surface.

This inward pull conception makes more feasible the processes of evaporation and condensation, accepted it removes the obstacle to molecule movement through the surface necessary for either to occur, that of penetration through side to side forces considerably stronger than those inwards.

Further it leaves "free" energy at surfaces and we saw earlier that free electrons mean potential electrical energy, which can induce atoms and molecules, even particles of matter, to link, attract or repel one another. The surfaces atoms become ions, incomplete or altered units and as we saw earlier unbalanced units can combine or seek changed form, if when in close relationship one with another their respective condition warrents. This does much to explain why some substances mix and others do not when their surfaces meet.

There is no need at this stage to persue this assumption of surface potential, or free energy further for our immediate purpose, the cause of capillary rise in tubes. All we need to do is to be satisfied that with inward pull at surfaces of liquids, densities will vary beneath them, greater deeper, less nearer the surface. Also that these conditions are related to the elctrical condition of the units. The accepted rules relating to ordinary static water pressures gives us similar density conditions.

If we now look at fig. 44a, this sort of surface and deeper condition is shown. If we now dip a capillary tube of material which the liquid can wet, into this surface, the "creep" of the liquid over the surfaces of the tube will form a meniscus. Beneath these concave surfaces, where the parallel to the surface interactions are interrupted or disturbed, the inwards pull of the liquid units nearest to the solid surfaces is weakened and displacement, to a relatively higher tilted position occurs. The dotted lines in fig. 44b depict this.

This disturbance results in reduced inward pull beneath the miniscus which, if it is semi-spherical or less, as in the narrower tubes shown in fig. 12b in an earlier chapter, will be reflected through units beneath those immediately at the surface and downwards to produce a generally lowered density within the tube. The density of the main body of the liquid mass outside the tube, except to a tiny area immediately under the outside meniscus, will not be altered. Thus in the mass we have unequal pressures or densities which will seek to come into balance. You would not be surprised if this situation occurred in static water, if water was forced up the tube and this is what happens with capillaries.

The wettable tube surfaces have little effect upon the rise of the liquid, except by not impeding it to any serious degree, a non-wettable surface in relation to the liquid would cause exactly the opposite as does murcury within a glass capillary.

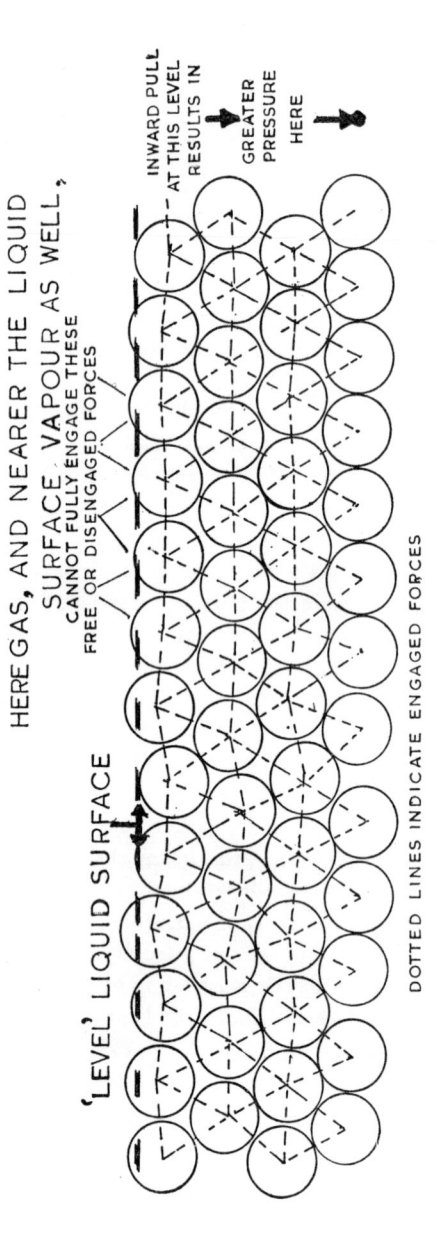

FIG. 44a

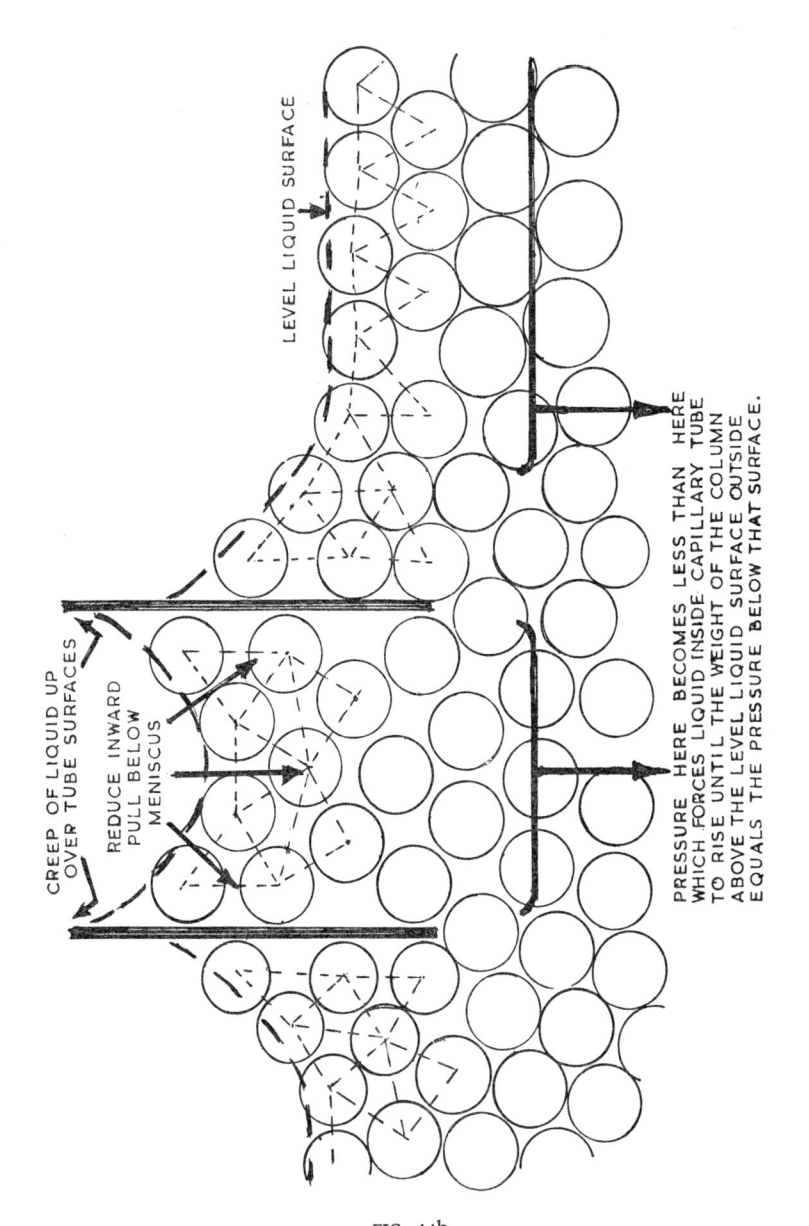

FIG. 44b

This theory too, explains why a drop picked up at the end of a capillary, or alighting thereon at a horizontal end rapidly deflates into the tube, the inward pull of the surfaces outside the tube end squeeze its contents in against the reduced effort of the meniscus, once wetting occurs. This is where surface silicone and wax treatments are valuable, they prevent wetting of the pore ends.

One would expect that gravity halts the rise as the column weight balances densities or pressures within the whole of the mass at the foot of the tube. All things being equal.

The root of the trouble

What really happens is that we electrically alter one of the forces seeking to gain equilibrium. You will be aware that "ions" move freely in electrolytes when a battery cell is discharging, all surfaces of the electrodes becoming reception or discharging points to them. Such activation must effect the pore surface/liquid activities within the wall and at the earth/liquid in the wet ground. Thus the forces within the electrolyte, "the dampness," render static or stabilised pressure variations within the mass and that in the tube such that lift up or into the tube is not induced. We did this before by aiding evaporation, or by treating the pore linings, now we deal with the water itself, the root cause of the trouble.

The treatment is preceded by tests of the wall and the soil, using apparatus similar to the Protimeter, inserting electrodes of similar metals, copper covered steel pins into the wall, rods into the soil. Readings of voltage flow are taken on the meter. From this information the spacing of wall contacts and the position and depth of earthing rods is calculated. Installations are at present in this country subject to patent rights held by the proprietary company, Rentokil Laboratories Ltd. They carry out the investigations, design and execute installations.

Attachment of the wall electrical contact is by drilling holes in a similar way to that employed for Latex-siliconate impregnation, but here the 1 in. diameter holes will be 14 in. apart plus or minus

DAMPNESS IN BUILDINGS 163

CONDUCTOR
ELECTRODES
ELECTROLYTE

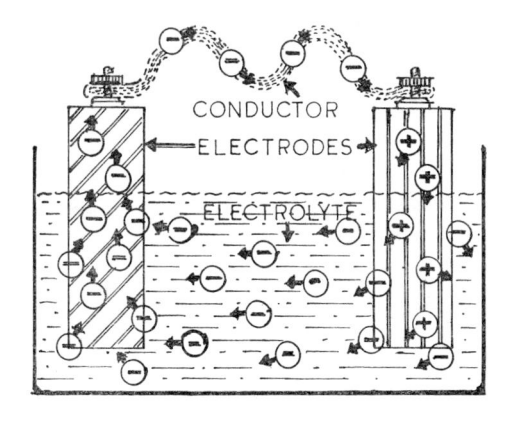

NEGATIVE RICH IONS TRAVEL FROM THE POSITIVE ELECTRODE THROUGH THE ELECTROLYTE TO THE NEGATIVE SO LONG AS THE CONDUCTOR PROVIDES A CIRCUIT.

THERE IS INTENSE ACTIVITY AT THE SURFACES OF BOTH ELECTRODES WHILST THE CIRCUIT IS COMPLETE, AND IS DISCHARGING THOUGH THE CONDUCTOR

FIG. 45. *The action of a primary cell with a conductor.*

50 per cent according to wall conditions. They can be horizontal or inclined, according to operating room and the levels required to be influenced. They can be from inside or outside, but since earthing is normally outside, through wall contacts would be necessary if they were inside and no below floor earthing possibilities were practicable.

Thus, Many kinds of wall can be dealt with, with minimum disturbance. When the holes have been drilled and cleaned of debris a continuous length of soft drawn copper strip about half an inch wide is placed along the wall surface and looped into the holes to their full depth, which is to within a few inches of the opposite face, usually at a level where a traditional horizontal d.p.c. would be. The holes are then caulked with electrically conductive mortar. The exposed copper strip between the holes can be bedded in a raked out joint and pointed in, or left on the surface and covered with a mortar fillet, or cased in a p.v.c. channel fixed to the wall; all it needs is protection. In fact the better its contact with the wall the more efficient will be its general action, the whole forming a horizontal plane of contact through the wall similar, shall we say, to a membrane.

L*

At predetermined points along its length, connections are made, via normal electrical outside type junction boxes to 7.044 untinned copper wire cables insulated with p.v.c. sheathing. Untinned wire is necessary to eliminate the possibility of electrolytic action between the two metals. These cables connect to earthing rods made of copper coated steel of about three-quarters of an inch diameter, driven into the soil to depths of 12 ft. to 20 ft. at points between 30 ft. and 40 ft. apart along the wall, but at quite close distance therefrom.

The installation provides an electrical circuit of exceptionally low resistance, which is necessary where very low potentials are being utilised. Electro-osmosis does not dry out a wall—it simply stops recharging of the capillaries with water once they have dried out by preventing creep through them. Thus a treated wall may take a considerable time to dry out after such an installation has been completed, weeks, perhaps months, but its effect at the surfaces will be seen quite quickly.

Efflorescence will occur if it would normally do so upon drying out and any delequescent condition will remain, but so long as dryness is maintained these states can be dealt with at the surfaces by neutralisation and should not cause continued difficulty. There is no strengthening action imparted to the structure by electro-osmosis as is sometimes afforded by some of the other treatments previously noted, but deterioration is arrested although some shrinkage may and probably will occur.

Electro-osmotic treatment has been applied to basement walls, using a grid of holes and connected copper strips, but it cannot deal with conditions arising from static water pressure where pressure is forcing water through the pores either horizontally or vertically.

It is interesting to note that detergents act in a similar way by disturbing surface tensions and also that electro-osmosis has been used by engineers for a considerable time as a means of de-watering soils during excavations (drier soil being generally less liable to slip than wet) and also, for securing damper soil conditions, by a reversal of the process, for electrical earthing.

Several interesting developments using this phenomenon are being tested, for example in water saturated soil, it may be possible to secure the deposit at the outer side of basement walls of gel or pore blocking materials, by using the wall as one electrode and the earth as the other and applying current to cause a flow of proofing materials injected into the soil to the wall. Once a sufficient amount has been deposited, then the current is stopped and is no longer necessary.

Where pores are blocked in this way to quite a shallow depth through the thickness of the structure, any static water pressure will, if it affects the blocking material at all, push it further in, not push it out, as it would if the blockage were nearer the inner surface.

You will see that floors too could be treated, in fact "tanking" becomes a possibility.

There are obviously limits to the application of all treatments. Electro-osmosis requires effective earthing facilities and a possible limit may be imposed by space or distance not being available. The patentees can, however, advise upon this matter. They are the only people who so far have had sufficient experience of its possibilities in the practical field.

Rentokil Ltd., now give a twenty year guarantee in respect of premises where they install electro-osmotic treatment, which together with the acceptance by some twenty five or more local authorities, of these installations as a qualification for improvement grants, is evidence of its effectiveness.

Walls up to 9 in. thick can now be treated without drilling provided copper strips can be secured electrically to both surfaces. This enables application to be made to complicated constructions such as flints externally with bricks internally.

Index

Abortive use of plinths, 84
Absorbent material, 42
Absorption, 43
   of electrical energy, 9
Access to subsoil drains, 65
Actane process, 123, 134
Adhesives, 101, 106, 107
   failure of, to plinths, 55, 84
Adhesion, of membranes, 69, 70, 71, 140, 141
   testing of, 71
Adjoining owners, notifications to, 95
   agreement with, 96
   buildings, examination of, 95
   effect of dampness upon, 57
Air, as insulation, 109
   bricks, insect proofing, 108
Alum, powdered, 117
Aluminium foil, 48
Angle of contact, 20, 39
Anode, 17
Animal fibres, 113
Application of surface tensions, 102
Asbestos fibres, caulking with, 150
Asphalt, mastic, 100, 140
   tanking, 138
Assistance to evaporation, 78, 81
Atmospheric moisture, 78
   pressure, 70
   siphons, 78, 80, 81, 88
Atoms, space occupied by, 3
Automatic pumping, 153

Basement, adhesion testing for linings, 71
   asbestos fibres for caulking, 151
   asphalt lining, 138
      mastic lining for, 140
   bonding pockets for lining, 144
   chases for linings, 144
   caulking cracks in structure, 151
   cracks, caulking with metallic lead rope 151
      grouting, 151
      plugging, 151
   fixings to tanked surfaces, 73
   forces involved in tanking, 69
   lining, 130
      preparation for, 73
   tanking, simple, 73
      by infusion, 133
      traditional methods, 135
      supports to, 77
      shallow, heights for, 77
   unfit, latex siliconate treatment of, 133

Basement, ventilation of, 81
   walls, sealing services passing through, 152
   wetting cracks with detergents, 151
Batten protection, 107
Bitumastic impregnated papers, 101
   emulsions, 141
   solutions, 74
Bitumen, hot, 141
Bonding agents, for membranes, 70, 74, 110
   hot bitumen, 141
   bitumen emulsion, 141
Breakdown of surface treatments, 104
Breathing of walls, 34
Brickwork, crumbling of, 58
   efflorescence on, 36, 56, 164
   pulverisation of, 59
Bridging, of d.p.c., 52, 55, 83, 84, 86
   remedy for, 85
Building examination of, 95
   adjoining, 95
   paper, 74, 75, 108

Canvas, linings internally, 106
Capillary, 14, 21, 26, 33, 38, 112, 159
Capillarity, 25, 158
Cedar boarding, internally, 107
Ceramic tiles, internally, 107
Charges, electrical in materials, 7
Chemical, combination, 112, 155
   adhesive plasters, 54
   deposition, 32
   expansion in pores, 36
   indicators, 54
Choice of materials for horizontal d.p.c., 89
Chromium plating, 32
Clay soil shrinkage, 147
Colloids, 116
Colloidal solutions, 116, 145
Concrete, waterproofing solid, 117
   weight of, 142
Condensation, on surfaces, 43,
   on soft setting coats, 110
   damage to linings by, 105
   prevention of, 104, 106, 107, 126
   on walls, 58, 79, 81, 107, 158
   on hard surfaces, 59, 81
   on solid floors, 78
   on masked areas, 104
   within pores, 35, 41
Conditional moisture retention, 56
Conclusions, drawn from dadoes when surveying, 104

168 DAMPNESS IN BUILDINGS

Conclusions drawn from settlement cracks, 96
Conduction, of heat, 46
Conductor, water as electrical, 157
Considerations of structural settlements, 96
Contact, angle of, 20, 39
Cooling effect of dampness, 58
Cracks, in basement structure, 150, 151
    caulking of, 150
    grouting of, 150
    plugging of, 151
    wetting of, 151
Crazing of renderings, 116
Creep, 23, 38, 39, 164
Creepers, 149
Crystals in pores, 36
Current, electrical flow, 156, 157, 164

Dadoes, batten protection for, 107
    considerations when surveying, 104
    evaporation provision from behind, 107, 108
    linoleum, 107
    protective nature of, 106
    spaced off, 105
    use of, 104
Dampness, as a nuisance, 57
    as a cause of expansion, 56
    softening, 56
    swelling, 56, 112
    cooling effect of, 58
    effect upon adjoining property, 57
    eradication of cause, 56
    lowering level of, 61
    resulting in loss of strength, 56
    resulting in reduction of rigidity, 56
Damage to interior linings, 105
Damp proof course, bridging of, 52, 55, 83, 84
    remedy for, 85
    choice of material for, 89
    cutting in, 91
    effect of pinning up over, 93, 94, 98
    down, 94
    examination of buildings before insertion, 95
    adjoining property before insertion, 96
    horizontal, 77
    insertion of above floor levels, 100
    insertion of slate or sheet, 93
    junction with vertical, 100
    method of insertion, 94
Debris, in drillings, 127
    in sawcuts, 98
    in fractures, 98
Deep latex siliconate treatment, 130
Deliquescence, 50, 164
Depth of insulation, 117, 138
Detection of old remedies, 97

Detergents, 164
Dew conditions, 35
Direction of wall loadings, 93
Disposal of subsoil water, 61
Diversion of subsoil water, 60, 61
Dr. Hurst, 133
Drained cavities, inside, 153
    outside, 51
Drains, soakaway, 58
    subsoil, 53, 56, 58, 60, 61
    access to, 65
    investigations for, 61
    siting of, 65
    size of, 63
    testing for usefulness, 61
    trapping from foul, 67
    trial holes for, 61
Drips, 78
Driven water, 12
Dry areas, 50
Drying out, by evaporation, 83
    effects of, 56, 164
    of walls by warm air fanning, 104

Effect of dampness on adjoining premises, 57
    of drying out, 56, 164
    of heat, 4
    of insertion of d.p.c., 114
    of swelling, 14
    of presence of gels in materials, 114
    of settlement on services, 92
    structure, 92
    of stresses caused by pinning up, 98
    of weather on waterproof solutions, 36
Effectiveness of waterproofing agents, 110
Efflorescence, 36, 56, 164
Electric accumulators, 157
    cells, 156, 158, 162
    charges in materials, 7
    conductor, water as, 157
    current, flow of, 156, 157, 164
    earthing of, 163, 164
    potential, 156, 157, 158
Electron, 6
Electro-osmosis, 68, 91, 154, 155, 157, 164
Electrostatic attraction, 7
Emulsion, 40
    hot bitumen, 141
    rubber, 74
Enamelled boards, 107
Energy, free surface, 158, 159
    gravitational, 12
    molecular, 154
Electrolyte, 157, 162
Electrolytic action, 164
Electro-chemical deposition, 32
    plated materials, 32
Erosion of soil by pumping, 139

Evaporation, assistance to, 78, 81
  at surfaces, 35, 38, 59, 77, 78, 81, 88, 158
  from behind dadoes, 107
  provision for, 108
  prevention of, 101
  result of restricting, 101
Evidence of defects whilst surveying, 106
Examination of buildings for old remedies, 97
  before insertion of d.p.c., 95
  adjoining buildings before insertion of d.p.c., 96
Expanded polystyrene, 42, 104
Expansion of cement during grouting, 94
  and shrinkage of cement renderings, 75
  chemical in pores, 36
Extent of internal surface treatments, 104

Failure of treatments to patches, 132
False floors, 152
  walls, 152
Feeding in thin membranes, 99
Felts, hair, 108
  roofing, treatment with latex siliconate, 134
Fibreboards, 107
Fibres, asbestos for caulking, 151
Fixings to tanked surfaces, 73
Floors, levels for insertion of d.p.c., 100
  membranes in, 74, 79, 103, 142, 144
  plain loading to, 142
  reinforced loading to, 143
  slate, 135
  solid, latex siliconate treatment to, 132
  sumps, 138
    sealing off, 142
Flow of electric current, 156, 157, 164
  water over weirs, 64
Fluid, latex siliconate, 134
  silicone, 10, 116, 134
  purchase of, 126
Foil, aluminium, 48
  reflective, 59
Forces of gravity, 68
  gravitational, 25, 68
  inter-atomic, 7, 9, 11, 12, 14, 158
    strength of, 10, 13
  internal atomic, 9, 11, 12, 14, 158
  involved in tanking, 69
  unbalanced surface, 158
Formation of materials, porous, 32
  non porous, 32
Fortifying against dampness, 117
Foul drains, trapping entry o subsoil to, 65
Free surface energy, 158, 159

Galvanizing, 32
Gaseous matter, 6, 13, 14
Gelatines, 113
Gels, 114
  anchorage of in pores, 122, 165
  effect of presence of in materials, 114
  introduction into pores, 120
  mixing with cement, 120
  pore blocking, 115
  waterproofing with, 114, 145
    renderings, 114, 117, 145
    solid concrete, 117
Glues, 113
Gravitational energy, 12
  forces, 25, 68
Gravity, 19, 22
Grouting, 129, 150
  expansion of cement when, 94
  sawn in membranes, 94

Hair felts, 108
Hardboards, 107
Hard surfaces, condensation on, 59, 81
Heat, effect of, 4
  transmittance through materials, 46, 48
  treatment to latex siliconate infusions, 127
Hedges, 147
Height of tanking, 77
Horizontal d.p.c., 77
  choice of materials for, 89
  clearing debris from sawcuts for, 99
  cutting in, 91
  debris in sawcuts for, 98
  effect on stresses caused by pinning up over, 98
  insertion of above floors, 100
  saws for, 91
  slate or sheet, 90
  junction with vertical, 100
  levels for insertion, 89
  pinning up over, 93, 94
    down, 93, 94
  pinning up over, method, 94
  sawn in membranes, 88
Hot bitumen, primer, 141
  pitch, 135
  tallow, 135
  tar, 135
Humidity, relative, 30, 35
Hydrated lime in cement, 117
Hydroscopic, 50

Indicators, chemical, 54
Infusion, 68, 89, 120, 124, 125, 126, 127
  methods of, 125, 126
  tanking by, 133
Injection, 120, 124, 125
  methods of, 125, 126, 130, 132
Injected membranes, 128

Insertion of sawn in d.p.c., 93
Inside drained cavities, 153
Insulating quality, loss of, 59
Insulation, 36, 38, 46–48
 air as, 109
 by, ventilated cavity, 59
 expanded polystyrene, 42, 104
 in depth, 117, 138
 loss of value by saturation, 41, 108
 restoring to basements, 152
 with building paper, 108
 with hair felts, 108
 with reflective foils, 59
Insurance requirements, 95
Interaction between materials, 9, 16
Inter-atomic forces, 7, 9, 11, 12, 14, 158
 strength of, 10, 13
Interior linings, adhesives for, 101, 106, 117
Internal atomic forces, 7, 9, 11, 14, 158
 strength of, 10, 13
 bitumastic impregnated paper, 101
 canvas, 106
 damage to, 105
 evidence of defects, 106
 life of, 101
 Lincrusta, 106
  stripping of, 106
 matchlining, 106
 metal foils, 101
 metallic based paints, 101
 pitch papers, 101
 timber, 103
 treatments, 103
 varnished papers, 106
 wall paper and decorations, 42
 whole walls, 105
Inspector, public health, 57
Introduction of gels into pores, 120
Investigations for subsoil drains, 61
Inward pull at surfaces, 160, 164
Ions, 158, 162
Irregular walls, treatment of, 130
Ivy, 144

Junction of vertical to horizontal D.P.C., 100

Knapen atmospheric siphons, 78, 80, 81, 88

Latex siliconate, 68, 120, 122
 deep treatment, 130
 fluids, 134
 of unfit basements, 133
 of vaults, 133
 resistance to static water, 135
 roofing felts, 134
 treatment of patches, 132
  or irregular walls, 130
  by heat, 127
Leaflets, Ministry of Works, 151

Levels for insertion of horizontal d.p.c., 90, 100
Life of bitumastic impregnated papers, 101
 interior linings, 101
 latex emulsions, 101
 masking treatments, 103
 metal foils, 101
 metallic based paints, 101
 pitch papers, 101
 wax solutions, 101
Lift shafts, latex siliconate treatment, 133
Lincrusta, 106
 stripping of, 106
Linings, adhesives for, 101, 103, 106
 canvas, 106
 dadoe, ventilation of, 108
 damage to, 105
 evidence of defects, 106
 matchlining, 106
 pores with repellents, 115
 timber, 106
 whole walls, 106
Linoleum, 107
Liquid, properties of, 13, 17, 21
 state of materials, 6, 13, 14
Loading to basement floors, plain concrete, 142
 reinforced concrete, 143
Loss of insulating quality due to dampness, 59
 strength due to dampness, 56
 value, due to dampness, 41, 108
Lowering level of dampness, 61
 water table, 61, 69

Masked areas, condensation upon, 104
Masking dampness, 101, 103
Mastic asphalt linings, 100
 linings, 140
Mastics, sealing services entering basements, 152
Materials, choice of for d.p.c., 89
 effect of gels in, 114
 interaction between, 9, 16
 nature of, 3
 non porous, formation of, 32
 porous, formation of, 32
 shrinkage of, 112
 strength of, 4
 surfaces of, 13
 swelling of, 112
Matter, atoms of, 3
 gaseous state of, 6, 13, 14
 liquid state of, 6, 13, 14
 solid state of, 6, 13, 14
 space occupied by, 3
 vapours of, 34, 41
Metal foils, 101
Metallic based paints, 101

Metallic lead rope for caulking, 150
Membranes, adhesion of, 69, 70, 71, 140, 141
 testing of, 71
 grouting sawn in, 94
 linings, bonding pockets and chases for, 144
 waterproof for floors, 74, 79, 142, 163
 walls, 69
Meniscus, 24, 101, 159
Methods of infusion, 125, 126
 injection, 125, 126, 130, 132
 insertion of d.p.c., 94
Ministry of Works leaflets, 151
Mixing waterproofers with cement, 120
 water, 122
Moisture, atmospheric, 78
 re-absorption, 57
 retention, 56
Molecular energy, 154
Molecules, 3
 in drops, 158
Movements of underground water, 159, 164

Nature of materials, 3
Negative electric charge, 7
Non porous materials, 32
Non wettable surfaces, 34, 35, 159
Notification of intention to adjoining owners, 95
Nucleus, 6

Osmotic electro, 68, 91
Osmosis, electro-, 154, 155, 157, 164
Outside drained cavities, 51

Papers, pitch, 101
 varnished, 106
Paraffin wax, 39
Parovents, 44, 144
P.C.M. solution, 126
Permeable, 33
Pinning down, 94
 up, 93, 94
Pitch treated paper, 42, 77
Plaster, crumbling of, 59
 pulverization of, 58
Plastic tiles, 107
 coated boards, 107
Plated, electro-, 32
Plinths, 55
 abortive use of, 84
 adhesion failure of, 55, 84
Plywoods, 107
Polystyrene, expanded, 42–43 104
Polythene sheets, 74
Pores, 32, 33
 blocking of, 115
 chemical expansion in, 36
 condensation within, 35, 41

Pores (*contd.*), free material, 115
 introduction of gels into, 120
 repellent linings to, 115
 treatments, 37, 112, 165
 vapours in, 41
Porous materials, 32
Position of horizontal d.p.c., 49
Potential, electric, 156, 157, 158
 surface, 159
Preparation for tanking, 73
 of surfaces, 102, 141
Pressure, atmospheric, 70
 grouting, 151
 water, 12, 68, 71
Proofed cement and sand, 24
Property, effect of dampness on adjoining, 57
Prevention of evaporation, 101
Protection of membranes, 68, 74, 79
Protection of battens, 107
Protective nature of dadoes, 106
Protimeter, 54, 85, 96, 162
Provision for evaporation, 108
Public health inspector, 57
Pumping, automatic, 153
 of subsoil water, 139
 water, rate of, 147
Purchase of silicone fluids, 126

Radiation, 46
Rate of pumping, 147
Re-absorption of moisture, 56
Reflection, 46
Reflective foils, 49
Rigidity, reduction of by dampness, 56
Reinforced loadings to basement floors, 143
 proofed cement membranes, 75, 137
Relative humidity, 30, 35
Release of stresses by pinning up, 98
Remedy for bridging of d.p.c., 85
Remedies in old buildings, 95
Renderings, waterproof, 110, 111, 117
Repellants, lining to pores, 115
 mixing with water, 122
 paraffin wax, 39
Requirements, insurance, 95
 surface, 102
Resin bonded hardboards, 107
 plywoods, 107
Resistance to static water, latex siliconate, 133
Restoring insulating value, 152
Restriction of evaporation, results of, 101
Retention of moisture, 56
Roofing felts, 134
Rubber based solutions, 74
 emulsions, 74
Running water, 12

Sandwich treatment to walls, 110
Sap, shrinkage in wood, 114
　swelling of, in wood, 113
Saturated soil, 60
Saturation, 29
　of insulation, 46–47
Sawn in membranes, 88
　clearing debris from sawcuts for, 98, 99
　grouting up over, 94
Saws for horizontal cuts, 91
Sealing off sumps, 142
　services through basement walls, 152
Services, sealing of to basement walls, 152
Setting coat, soft, 110
Settlements, 91, 92
　consideration of, 96, 97, 98
　effect of on structures, 92
Sheet membranes, insertion of, 90
　method of, 94
　pinning up over, 93, 94
Shrinkage, effect of, 114
　of materials, 112, 113
Silicate, sodium, 60
Siliconate, latex, 68, 120, 122, 127, 130, 133, 134
　static water, resistance to, 133
Silicones, 116
　effect of weather on, 36
　fluids, 10, 134
　purchase of, 126
Simple tanking, 73
Siphons, atmospheric, 78, 80, 81, 88
Slate d.p.c., 135
　insertion of, 90
　method of insertion, 94
　pinning up over, 93, 94
Slate floors, 135
Soakage, 11
Soakaway drains, 58
Soap, soft, 117
Sodium silicate, use of, 116
Soft, setting coats, 110
　soap, 117
Softening of materials, 56
Soil, saturated, 60
Solid concrete, waterproofing, 117
　state of materials, 6, 13, 14
Solution, colloidal, 116, 145
　P.C.M., 126
　waterproof, 33, 78
　　effect of weather on, 36
　wax, 101, 162
Sorption, 112
Spaced off dadoes, 105
Spalling of surfaces, 36
Spraying zinc, 32
Subsoil, disposal of water, 61
　diversion of water, 60, 61
　drains, 53, 56, 58, 60, 61

Subsoil, drains (*contd.*), access to, 65
　disposal of water from, 61
　diversion of water by, 60, 61
　investigations for, 61
　pumping out of, 139
　siting of, 65
　size of, 63
　trial holes for, 61
Static water, pressure of, 159, 164
　resistance to by siliconate latex, 133
Strength of materials, 4
　loss of, 56
Structural cracks, caulking of, 150
　grouting of, 150
　pressure of, 151
　plugging of, 151
　settlements resulting from, 91
Sumps, floor, 138
　sealing off, 142
Surface, fixing to tanked, 73
　inward pull at, 160, 161
　non wettable, 34, 35, 159
　of materials, 13
　potentials, 16, 159
　preparation of, 102, 141
　requirements, 102
　spalling of, 36
　tensions, 13, 14, 17, 18, 22, 30, 39, 154, 158
　treatments, 32
　　application of, 102
　　breakdown of, 104
　　extent of, 104
　wettable, 19, 22, 159
Surfaces, condensation on, 43
　hard, 59, 81
　solid floors, 78
　energy, free, 158, 159
　evaporation at, 35, 38, 59, 77, 78, 81, 88, 158
Supports to tanking, 146
Surveying, 104, 106
Suspensions, 39
Swelling, dampness as a cause of, 56, 112
　effects of, 114
　of animal fibres, 113
　　gelatines, 113
　　glues, 113
　materials, 112
　　saps, 113
　vegetable fibres, 113
　wools, 113
Synthaprufe, 86

Table, water, 61, 69
　lowering of, by trees, 148
　with drains, 56
Tailing down, 142
Tallow, hot, 135
Tanking, 67
　asphalt linings, 138

DAMPNESS IN BUILDINGS 173

Tanking (*contd.*), basements, 130
  bonding for, 144
  by infusion, 133
  fixings to linings, 132
  forces involved in, 69
  mastic asphalt, 138
  preparation for, 73
  shallow, height of, 77
  simple, 73
  supports to, 146
Tar, 135
"Tell-tales", 96
Tensions, surface, 13, 14, 17, 18, 22, 30, 39, 154, 158
Testing adhesion of membranes, 71
  for usefulness of subsoil drains, 61
Theory, capillary, 25
Thomson weir, 64
Throatings, 78
Tiles, ceramic, 107
Timber internal linings, 106
Transmittance of heat, 46, 48
Trapped water, 35
Trapping subsoil from foul drains, 65, 67
Treated papers, pitch, 42, 77
Treatments, heat of infusions, 127
  linings, interior, 103
  masking, 103
  of floors, solid, 113
    lift shafts, 134
    patch failures, 132
    roofing felts, 134
    unfit rooms, 133
    vaults, 134
  pore, 37, 112, 165
  sandwich to walls, 110
  surface, 32
Trees, 147
  effect upon water table, 148
Trial holes for subsoil drains, 61

Unbalanced surface forces, 158
Underground water movement, 159, 164
Unfit basements, latex siliconate treatment, 133

Vapours, material state, 34, 41
  within pores, 41, 115
Varnished papers, 106
Ventilation, 80
  of basements, 81
  of dadoe linings, 108

Walls, breathing, 34
  drying of by fanning, 104
  false, 152
  linings, 105
  membranes, waterproof to, 69
  paper, 42
  sandwich treatments, 110
Water, as an electric conductor, 157
  driven, 12
  erosion with, 139
  movements, 159, 164
  pressure, 12, 68, 71
  pumping, 139
  rate of pumping, 147
  running, 12
  soakage, 11
  subsoil, 60, 61
  table, lowering of, 61, 69
    by trees, 148
    in walls, 104
  trapped, 35
  vapour, in pores, 115
  weight of, 142
Waterglass, 116, 162
Waterlogged soil, 60
Waterproof, adhesion of membranes, 69, 70, 71, 140, 141
  membranes, to floors, 74, 79, 142, 144, 163
  protection of, 68, 74, 79
Waterproofing, agents, 110
  effectiveness of, 110
  renderings, 110, 111
    crazing of, 116
  solid concrete, 117
  solutions, 33
    for outside walls, 78
    introduction into pores, 120
  with gels, 114, 145
Wax, paraffin, 39
  solutions, 101, 162
Weight of concrete, 142
  water, 142
Weirs Thomson, 64
Well points, 64, 139
Wettable surfaces, 19, 22, 159
  non, 34, 35, 159
Wetting with detergents, 51
Wools, swelling and shrinkage of, 113
Wykamit d.p.c., 126

Zinc spraying, 32

DAMPNESS IN BUILDINGS

VOLUME 2:
Condensation and penetration above ground

R. T. GRATWICK
B.E.M., A.I.O.B., F.R.S.H.

CROSBY LOCKWOOD & SON LTD
26 OLD BROMPTON ROAD, LONDON, SW7

© *Copyright R. T. Gratwick, 1967*

First published 1967

*Filmset by Keyspools Ltd., Golborne, Lancs., and
Printed in Great Britain by
Billing & Sons Ltd., Guildford, Surrey*

Contents

21	The processes of evaporation	179
22	Surfaces—Temperature and humidity	188
23	Diffusion of moisture vapour and heat through building constructions	195
24	Finding heat losses, surface and interstitial temperatures	202
25	Penetrating or condensational dampness	212
26	Occupational habits and dirty surfaces as a clue to condensational dampness	224
27	Use and placing of added vapour barriers and insulating layers	233
28	Ventilation—Convectional and fan-assisted; dehumidification	242
29	Condensation in domestic flues	253
30	Remedies for results of condensation in stacks and flues	264
31	Penetrating dampness in walls	279
32	Remedial measures for run-off penetration	290
33	Penetrative run-in not directly associated with weathered features	303
34	Jamb, sill, and isolated patches	317
35	External claddings and surface coatings	334
Appendix 1 Thomson weir		338
Appendix 2 Wet and dry bulb thermometers. Hygrometers.		340
Appendix 3 The Kata thermometer		345
Index		349

21: The processes of evaporation

Condensation

CONDENSATION occurs when air containing water vapour is cooled to a temperature at which that air can no longer hold invisibly the amount of vapour it held at the higher temperature. Usually the air which we are considering has carried its water vapour from some relatively distant source of evaporation—a free surface of liquid water, even one overlying ice although most people will visualize evaporation as arising only from the surface of heated water. Evaporation of water to invisible vapour can and does take place at all temperatures, given suitable conditions at and immediately above the free water surface: the difference being simply the speed or amount of liquid evaporated in a given time.

If rising or ground dampness in buildings is probably the most frequent cause for enquiry for remedial measures, then condensation most certainly ranks second. Furthermore, as we have noted in Vol. 1, incorrect remedial measures applied to overcome the effects of rising dampness often result in condensation conditions being produced.

An example to show that condensation does not occur from the cooling of dry air is provided by manufacturers of sealed double glazing units who make sure that the air enclosed between the two glass skins is absolutely dry by assembling the units to airtight condition in dry air conditions. Many "do-it-yourself" double glaziers who adapt existing windows *in situ* discover, at the first sign of cold weather, the result of not taking the precautions to ensure that the air enclosed is completely dry.

We must consider how air becomes damp or *humid*—which is the correct term. If we understand how to prevent undue humidity in air we may avoid the need to remedy condensation. In the final chapter of Vol. 1 the reader's attention was directed to the inward pull theory related to capillarity and away from the surface skin theory.

Whilst the surface skin theory is a better way of understanding capillary penetration of water through porous materials than the inward pull theory, it does not help us when we consider evaporation taking place from the free surface of a liquid in contact with a gas—water and air. In Vol. 1, p. 19 fig. 7c, it was suggested that at the intersurface of a liquid—water in this case—atomic or molecular forces or energy not fully engaged with those of other atoms or molecules of their mass, devoted their surplus energy to forming stronger links with their lateral neighbours. If this is not so, as the inward pull theory suggests, then there is free unengaged energy at that surface. If we accept this we shall be more able to understand how and why evaporation takes place, and how air sustains molecules of water within its mass at one state of heat energy and yet is unable to do so at a lower state.

If we reconsider fig. 3, Vol. 1, p. 6 which is repeated below where we symbolically drew representations of the three states of a substance as circles of influence with dotted demarcation lines between the states, we can see that at critical temperatures molecules might quite readily transfer their station from one side of one of these lines to the other. A closer study of the diagram shows some circles straddling the lines so that they are partly in one sphere and partly in another. We are left to guess whether they are on their way up or down: it could be either. These thoughts give us the first glimpse of molecular activity within a mass of a substance, especially within liquids and gases where it is not difficult to imagine such a state of affairs. It is less easy to envisage such a condition within the surfaces of a solid; but the responses it gives to added heat or the extraction of heat, expansion and contraction, prove that activity exists. The only difference between activity within solids and that within

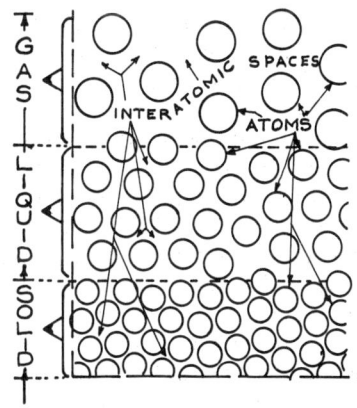

FIG. 3. (Vol. 1) *Symbolic representation of the three states of a substance. Increase in inter-atomic space occurs with increase in temperature and results in a change of state at certain levels. Heat absorption is energy intake.*

liquids and gases is that with solids the relative positions of molecules do not alter with the activity, whereas within liquids and gases they can and usually do so. There is, in fact, within gases very great activity with molecules constantly "colliding" one with another and bumping into the sides of the containers which bound them. It is the intensity of these bumps, in both gaseous and liquid masses, which we recognize and measure as their pressure upon the bounding surface. The more densely the gaseous particles are packed the more numerous will be the bumps against the surface of the containing vessel and, therefore, the greater the measurable pressure. Actual collisions do not occur; the impact and bounce-off is between the "fields" or spheres of influence (see Vol. 1, p. 4).

Whilst this internal activity will be less marked within a liquid at normal temperatures it still exerts bumping pressure upon its containing surfaces, and the appearance of a perfectly still condition upon the free to air surface of static water should not deceive us into believing that no activity exists there. If you leave a tumbler of water in a room at a quite reasonable temperature, the water level will fall appreciably in a few days. Similarly, a rain puddle left upon an impervious surface will "dry up" even in quite cool weather. Both of these happenings show that molecules of the liquid "take off" or are bumped out from the surface in contact with the containing air. We cannot see them go, but we have no doubt that they do. The acceptance of the free surface energy theory renders the possibility of evaporation, that is the passing of molecules of a liquid from its surface into a gas in contact with it, also acceptable. The rate at which the liquid molecules leave the liquid surface will vary with the internal activity state of the liquid mass. It will also be relative to its temperature and the ability of the containing gas to accept the molecules; this, in turn, will be relative to its pressure. If we think a little further about liquids and gases whose molecules are able to move about within the mass—remembering that very minute changes of heat energy content will induce any molecule to seek a change in position within the mass, and that it is extremely difficult if not impossible to have uniform temperature throughout a mass—then it is not difficult to imagine a constant jostling of molecules within the containing surfaces of the mass. Each of these molecules endeavouring, without success, to find within the mass the position ideally suited to its immediate activity state. Furthermore, if we accept the free surface energy theory then those at the surface will probably be even more active in this jostling action. This can result in some leaping or being jostled right out of the liquid and into the gas adjoining its surface, whilst gaseous ones from that mass could be jostled into or bump their way into the liquid mass thereby causing both types to become at least temporarily mixed. This being so we get water molecules in air which can condense, and air in water which will be released when heated. Some of these temporarily displaced molecules are thrown or propelled back into their own mass quite quickly (fig. 46) but some, especially where one mass is moving relatively to the other such as air moving over water, are carried along with the foreign mass. In the case of water in air, these molecules find themselves in an air mass bounded by solid surfaces and are unable to

DAMPNESS IN BUILDINGS 183

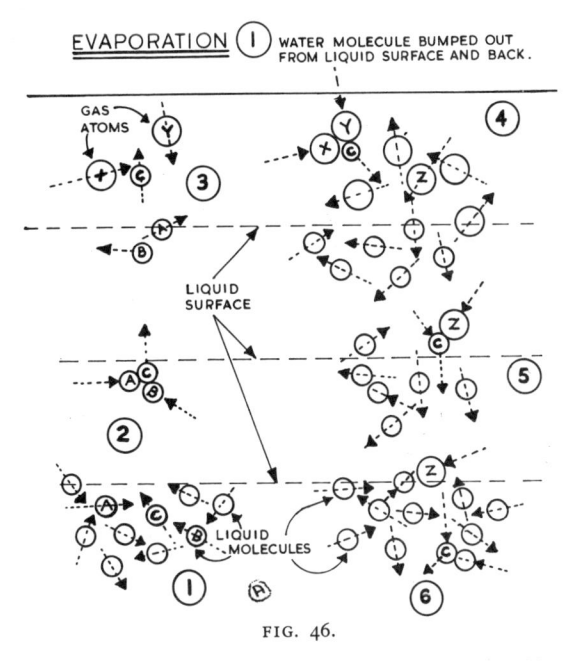

FIG. 46.

regain their original liquid mass at all. Similarly, if gaseous molecules are trapped and carried into vessels, for instance pipes, full of liquid they are confronted with a similar difficulty. Their release and regrouping into an air mass in an upward loop of a pipe, whether cold or warm, or heating radiator, becomes an air lock in a water-filled system; in steam heating and gas service pipes, condensing water gathers to form water or liquor locks in downward loops.

If one imagines these jostling and bumping actions one is reminded of excited human crowd behaviour. Visualize a crowd of people intent upon getting to the centre of an attraction and almost fighting one another in the process: for example at the gate to a football ground when there is to be an important match, or on a rush hour platform at the doors of a London Underground train. There is the dense crowd all pushing inwards, but at its periphery you will see that every now and then some unfortunate individual is

184 DAMPNESS IN BUILDINGS

suddenly ejected. Either he could not stand the squeezing pressure exerted by his fellows on either side, or someone nearer the centre has pushed him violently backwards in a successful attempt to ease his own pressure situation. Physically speaking, the ejected individual has vapourized. He has not, however, been ejected into clear space. There are lots of other people hurrying towards the dense crowd, and often dodging about in all directions in an attempt to gain a vantage point at which to hurl themselves into the inward push. On the other hand, people may be rushing past the particular dense crowd to get somewhere else and are thus acting like the air movement over a water surface. This less densely crowded situation could represent the gas surrounding a liquid drop or adjacent to a liquid surface— the liquid drop or surface comparable with the dense crowd. In some situations it would be noted that people in the less dense crowd were moving about much more rapidly; so rapidly, in fact, that frequent collisions would often occur

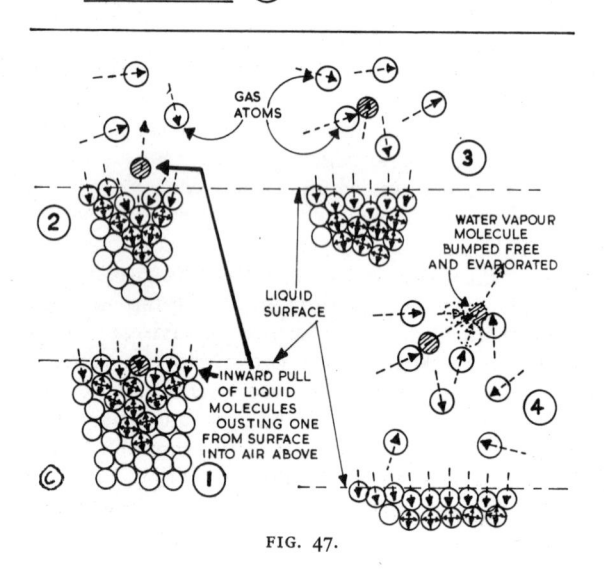

FIG. 47.

DAMPNESS IN BUILDINGS 185

between individuals. Quite often one collision can result in a further series of collisions. It is into this already chaotic situation that the ejected person is violently propelled. He is either violently thrown back or becomes part of the chaos from which later he may be bumped back into the dense crowd, even if he had made up his mind not to attempt a further entry. Similarly, a person hurrying past one crowd might very easily be bumped by a collision into a crowd that he had had no intention of joining. This is what is really happening at a liquid/gaseous intersurface and immediately on either side thereof; molecules are represented by the people in this illustration.

If the struggle continues, one of two things can happen. The dense crowd will increase its general size, if this is possible in the circumstances: this is the process of continued condensation. Alternatively, the passing less dense movement will carry away with it those ejected from the perimeter, and when the cause of the excitement ceases the whole crowd often joins the less dense movement. This represents evaporation proceeding to drying out.

The length of time the dense crowd persists depends upon the continuance of the attraction within it. If the cause is of passing interest then people will continue to join it, pushing to the centre to see as much as interests them and leaving. Usually if you watch a market crowd around a salesman, particularly a "quack" medicine man, many people push back and evaporate out of the crowd directly he suggests that they buy a bottle of "cure". The salesman is not, however, left without a crowd as other curious passers-by push in to replace those leaving. When this happens, there is a layer of people just outside the dense crowd with some pushing in and others pushing out; whilst they are not so tightly packed as the main crowd, these people are jostling in a much more dense mass than those in the outer chaos or stream. If the dense crowd remains of fairly constant size it is because as many people are pushing in as are coming out. When a similar situation occurs at a liquid/gas surface it prevents too rapid, if not all, actual evaporation from the liquid surface.

Evaporation

At given temperatures, liquid/gaseous intersurfaces develop optimum "vapour densities" in the gas immediately adjacent to the liquid surface when equal numbers of liquid molecules are bumping back into and being ejected from the liquid. At this state, reduction in the liquid mass will not continue by evaporation. When you seal a water container which is only partly filled with water, wetted pores in a wall for instance, this state occurs at the water surface when the trapped air can no longer carry off the evaporated water molecules. Temperatures and materials being equal, the less the degree of sealing the more rapid will be the rate of evaporation. It will have been noted that in contact with warm, less dense, moving air, moisture evaporates more rapidly than when warm still air conditions exist and also that with cooler conditions generally, evaporation rates drop. This is because in both of the latter states the air immediately adjacent to the liquid surface more easily becomes saturated with moisture. At saturation level the maximum vapour density relative to the conditions exists in the gas. In the former case, even if such a condition does arise the air movement sweeps away this layer or at least part of its outer layers and permits—we might say even, forces—their replacement. Evaporation then continues but at a rate controlled by that at which the sweeping away occurs. Diffusion of water vapour in air through air-filled pores of a solid porous material is really evaporation taking place in the absence of surface resistance. Ventilation is a sweeping action, disturbing the resistant surface molecule layer. It is interesting to note that one square inch of open ventilation permits as much ventilation air movement through a structural barrier as does 18,000 square feet of diffusion movement through a reasonably porous 9-in. brick wall.

Without evaporation condensation cannot occur; but knowing from whence the moisture vapour might come enables us to take steps to prevent either its evaporation or, if that is not practicable, its condensation. We could, for instance, apply a waterproof seal to a damp basement floor to prevent the air in the rooms becoming sufficiently moist to permit condensation on to cool dry walls. Alternatively, in the underfloor space of a suspended wood domestic floor where it is not practicable to seal the oversite concrete we can provide facilities for regular removal of the moistened air. To achieve this, air bricks are built in to the external walls and sleeper or plate walls are honeycombed. When we adopt the latter procedure we are probably encouraging evaporation, but in doing so maintain low enough relative humidity levels in the air passing through to prevent condense upon surfaces.

22: Surfaces—Temperature and humidity

DURING these considerations of evaporation and condensation we continually refer to "surfaces"; that is those between liquids and gases, or gases and solids. Similarly, reference is often made to "temperature" which is a record of the heat level or quality state of heat energy of a mass of material, and not the quantity level or content.

Alteration of the temperature of liquids and gases in contact affects, respectively, their ability to permit evaporation and to hold the evaporated liquids. In the same way, alteration of temperature at a solid surface will affect its ability to encourage condensation.

Temperature change can only occur if heat energy is added to, or extracted from, a mass of material and this can only take place through its surfaces. Surfaces are thus of vital importance to the consideration of condensation, especially those between warm moist air and cooler water, solids or air.

As mentioned earlier, surfaces are not clear cut lines on section and where mobility of molecules is possible definite activity takes place across the intersurface. Also, molecules of any two masses in contact, if very close to the intersurface, do affect each other even where mobility by actual separation from their own particular mass is not possible. Moisture films adhere to solid surfaces in defiance of gravity: gases, too, can adhere to solid surfaces. Because of this possibility heat energy carried in air could have difficulty in passing to a solid surface adjacent to its mass if some of the air molecules or atoms adhered to the solid surface and formed a much less active boundary layer a molecule or two thick. This could prevent others coming into contact with the solid to which they could pass the heat energy they were still holding. Similarly, if surface molecules or atoms of a solid or liquid have free energy and therefore do not want to accept additional energy from others outside their surface, they too will offer resistance to its transfer. Polishing a metal surface results in disturbance of the electrical balance of its atoms and affects its ability to radiate or accept radiant heat energy. Heating engineers accept these phenomena by allowing for "surface resistances" to heat transmittance when calculating heat losses from buildings.

Heat and surfaces

When in considering heat and surfaces we refer to "surface resistance", it should be appreciated that the actual plane (which after all is a purely geometrical term, there being no third dimension, thickness, to it) is simply that imaginary line shown in our molecular material state diagram (see p. 184) across which molecules may be passing as they change their state or are elbowed out or injected into the different state section.

Air and moisture vapour

With condensation we must first consider air and the moisture vapour that it can carry—that is, carry without its presence being visible. Because if you can see "mist", droplets of water suspended in the air, condensation has already occurred. When air is invisibly holding the maximum amount of water vapour possible, it is then said to be at "dew point temperature" or saturated. The amounts are as follows:

Temperature °F	°C	Weight of moisture vapour which can be invisibly held Grains per ft^3
30	−1	1·97
32	0	2·13
34	1·1	2·30
36	2·2	2·48

| Temperature | | Weight of moisture vapour which can be invisibly held |
°F	°C	Grains per ft³
38	3·3	2·66
40	4·4	2·86
42	5·6	3·08
44	6·7	3·32
46	7·8	3·56
48	8·9	3·82
50	10·0	4·10
52	11·1	4·39
54	12·2	4·71
56	13·3	5·04
58	14·4	5·39
60	15·6	5·77
62	16·7	6·17
64	17·8	6·59
66	18·9	7·04
68	20·0	7·51
70	21·1	8·01
72	22·2	8·54
74	23·3	9·10
76	24·4	9·69
78	25·6	10·31
80	26·7	10·98
82	27·8	11·67
84	28·9	12·40
86	30·0	13·17
88	31·1	13·98
90	32·2	14·85

Note: 7000 grains weight to 1 lb.

This table covers the air temperature range normally found in buildings. If we now select a cubic foot of air at a temperature of, say, 60°F (15·6°C) and note the amount of moisture vapour that it can invisibly hold when saturated— 5·77 grains—then we can understand that if we cool that air to say 50°F (10°C) it must give up 5·77 minus 4·10 which means 1·67 grains weight of moisture in that air will be visible as mist. If the cooling is a result of heat being extracted from the air by a wall or ceiling surface, then the discrete droplets will if they form close enough to the surface be attracted* to and adhere to the cooling surface as condensed water or *condensate* as it is termed. Alternatively, if we raise the temperature of this same air holding 5·77 grains of moisture at 60°F (15·6°C) to about 82°F (27·8°C) it could invisibly hold double that amount. At this higher temperature the air will, therefore, be only fifty per cent saturated and capable of invisibly taking up a further 5·77 grains of evaporated moisture when and if it comes into contact with a water surface or meets a cloud of suspended, condensed, water droplets. By mixing with other air of equal temperature and higher relative humidity, although still below dewpoint, it can also accept some of the moisture vapour in that air and thereby reach an even humidity throughout the whole mass. The term "relative humidity" when applied to air means the percentage, relative to saturation amount, of invisible moisture vapour which could be held at the temperature referred to; that is to say, 66 per cent saturated at 68°F (20°C) if one cubic foot of air at that temperature actually holds 4·96 grains.

Relative humidity can be calculated from temperature readings taken from "wet and dry" thermometers** suspended in air and using dew point tables similar to that from which the extract on page 189 was taken. Use can also be made of a special "Kata" thermometer** exposed dry and wet to air, and making a calculation using a "factor" engraved on each instrument related to the cooling time required for the fluid in the instrument to drop from 100°F to 95°F (37·8–35·0°C)—a range which includes normal human body temperature. The relative humidity of air within buildings is of great importance to the comfort of occupants as well as to considerations of dampness in buildings. Indeed, the relative humidity in these cases often has a considerable effect upon the dampness and *vice versa*.

* "attracted" in this context means the process referred to on page 226 of this volume.

** See Appendices 1 and 2 for details of the use of wet and dry and Kata thermometers.

Every human being evaporates about two-and-a-half pints of water vapour each twenty-four hours; partly carried from the body in exhaled breath and partly as perspiration from the pores of the skin. If this cannot occur at satisfactory rates relative to the degree of activity of the person concerned, then discomfort and even distress will be experienced. The relationship between the moisture content of exhaled breath and building surfaces will readily be seen by breathing on a cold window glass area or even a mirror; condense will then very visibly appear as misting. It will occur as readily but not so visibly upon less polished but similarly cool surfaces of other building materials, clothing, soft furnishings, etc.

Deliquescent materials and moisture vapour

Deliquescent materials and gels, referred to in Vol. 1, will absorb moisture vapour from air. Silica gel is used commercially to dry air where other methods, such as ventilation or warming, cannot be used to produce the desired degree of humidity reduction required; for example, in packing cases containing delicate machinery or instruments, or showcases containing exhibits which could be damaged by too much warmth and where actual ventilation might introduce airborne fungi spores. Where solid gel cannot be used, deliquescent liquids can sometimes be substituted, for example oil of vitriol which is concentrated sulphuric acid. When humid air is in contact with deliquescent materials, animal fibres in clothing, and soft furnishing, condensation is induced at temperatures slightly higher than dew point.

Air containing moisture vapour will at some temperatures reach saturation level and if it is then further cooled, for instance by coming into contact with cooler air, condensation may occur. Cooling of the warmer air takes place because the cooler air is absorbing heat from the warmer in order to try and establish even temperature throughout the whole mass. In this case, this even temperature will be such that if the cooling air is itself saturated the whole mass cannot sustain the amount of moisture which the new lower temperature of the whole permits invisibly. The excess moisture will first appear in the form of suspended mist droplets which will, as they coalesce to form larger drops, sink out of the air to alight upon surfaces. The mist and drops carry heat with them. They are only just below readily evaporative heat level and, unless the surface upon which they are about to alight is at least as cool as they are, re-evaporation will occur into the layer of air immediately above the surface which it has warmed. If, however, the surface is cooler than the droplets then they will lie upon it if it is impervious; if it is absorbent, they will soak into it.

Quite often the complaint of condensation nuisance is indirect. Its effect upon contents is noticed rather than that upon the actual building surfaces; for example: moulds upon dry foodstuffs and leather clothing, dampness in bedding and woollen clothing hanging in the room, "bloom", the misting of polished wood surfaces.

This moulding of dry foodstuffs and clothing occurs more readily in an unventilated cupboard or wardrobe than it does in one such as a ventilated larder where air movement is possible from outside the building. In this country, inside air is almost always at a higher vapour pressure density than that outside. This is the reason why, in spite of the provision of refrigerators, the Housing Acts insist upon ventilated larder facilities being provided where comprehensive improvement grants are sought and in considerations of fitness of dwellings for human habitation.

Where condensation occurs

Condensation in buildings occurs in the air but, as the cooling of the air is usually brought about by its proximity to a surface, the problem of moisture upon the surface normally has to be faced when seeking a remedy for condensation. A complaint of mist in a building is rarely heard although it does occur; most often in bathrooms and kitchens in houses, and in laundries, bakeries and similar industrial premises. If mist conditions are experienced to any marked degree when running a bath, they can be prevented by running in half-an-inch or so of cold water before turning on the hot tap. The housewife deals with her kitchen misting by opening a window, or switching on an extractor fan to increase ventilation—that is, air movement. In this case, increased quantities of non-saturated air are induced to re-evaporate the mist globules and so permit their constituent molecules to diffuse into this air or, by "draught" movement carry the suspended globules out of the room. If this is not done, convectional air movements within the room will carry the globules close enough to a cooling wall, ceiling, fitment, or floor surface for them to be bumped on to the surface and attach themselves to it in the first instance as discrete droplets; if supplemented by further deposits these droplets coalesce to form a film which, in turn, may be drawn into drops and drips from ceilings and ledges or form rivulets and run down vertical surfaces. The first evidence that condensation has occurred is often the observation of droplets upon a cold water pipe, a glass surface such as a window or a mirror, glazed tiles, hard gloss painted surfaces, etc. Matt surfaces such as eggshell finished paintwork, cut expanded polystyrene tiling, unglazed wallpapers, cork flooring, soft clothing, curtains, etc., are the last to show any such evidence. Thus, surfaces are of the utmost importance to our considerations of condensation problems. The fact that a surface cannot exist without substance behind it, however thin, compels us to consider the opposite surface and material in contact with that. In buildings the surface is either part of a finish or of a construction. The possibility of condensation and, consequently, of re-evaporation is affected by the surface's ability to accept or repel heat, to conduct it through its own substance or to retain some of it, and finally to pass it through its other surfaces to another media. Therefore, the subject of heat losses and surface and intersurface temperatures are of vital interest to anyone trying to deal with this form of damp nuisance. So, too, is the study of water vapour diffusion into porous materials, because condensation within pores has a pronounced effect upon the ability of the material to conduct heat. Saturated insulators become efficient conductors. Heat receptive surfaces or efficient conductors are potential aids to condensation.

23: Diffusion of moisture vapour and heat through building constructions

OCCUPIED buildings accumulate heat in their air content from the bodies of the occupants without any additions by way of the burning of fuels or electric power. During very warm weather, occupational heat added to natural warmth derived from the sun and air produces conditions which are too hot for comfort; this problem is even greater where the climate is generally more humid. These conditions are usually associated with over-moist air.

Nevertheless, in this country the air outside an occupied house seldom contains as much moisture per cubic foot as does inside air even if it is relatively more saturated. If we consider inside air at 60°F (15·6°C) which is 70% saturated, it will be seen from the table on page 190 that each cubic foot is holding 4·04 grains of vapour (70% of 5·77 grains) whereas outside air at 40°F (4·4°C) at 80% saturation can only contain 2·28 grains (80% of 2·86 grains). Even if it were 100% saturated it would still hold less vapour per cubic foot than the inside air. This is true even at 50% saturation; only 40% saturation at 60°F (15·6°C) would enable the inside air to hold slightly more vapour than outside air 80% saturated at 40°F (44°C).

Thus the air inside an occupied building, as well as in unoccupied buildings where stored goods sweat or processes produce water vapour, has a higher moisture vapour density than air outside. Where there are two masses of gas—in this case air plus water vapour—having different vapour density and separated by a division which is not gastight, it will be noted that watertightness does not necessarily assure gastightness. There will be a movement of vapour from the denser to the less dense mass, by diffusion through the pores of the division. Diffusion being a form of evaporation, it is useful to observe that light gases pass more readily through porous materials than do heavy. As the water vapour content in air rises, so the resulting gas mixture diminishes in density: the two gas volumes are attempting to equalize their densities and temperature. Osmosis, also, is a process somewhat similar to evaporation. Even if it cannot get right through, diffusion will take place into pores if the air/vapour density therein is lower than the air outside them.

In most ordinary buildings only small areas of construction are gastight; but we are steadily increasing these areas as we supersede traditional construction and finishes with thinner, less porous, denser materials. Expanded polystyrene is not dense; it weighs only 1 lb. per cubic foot but, because of its closed cell formation and the dense nature of the very thin cell walls, it has a very low water vapour transmission ratio. Its ability to absorb liquid water, too, is low; only the cut cells in preformed rigid sheets being able to do so. The first surfaces liable to show internal condensation resist the diffusion of vapour into their pores, but readily accept heat. Where such surfaces are placed on the outside of a building, this quality may not prevent the inner thickness of their supporting structure becoming damp or even saturated from diffused condensed moisture gaining access through their inner surface. If air can get in or pass through, so can moisture vapour. Air does not condense; but if it contains water vapour and is unduly cooled within the pores, the vapour will do so. Once condensed within pores, re-evaporation is an extremely slow process and often only occurs if the actual wall material is warmed. When insulating a wall as a remedy for condensation, advantage should be taken of the fact that a wall with a lower heat loss value is less likely to attract condense than is an uninsulated one, and it must be ensured that a material is used which will not itself become damp to such a depth that re-evaporation becomes difficult. This dampness is the result of moisture, occurring by diffusion or soakage from any surface, being condensed within the pores.

Every material has power to absorb heat energy from a source at higher temperature, providing that the energy can overcome any surface resistance offered by the actual material surface or by this and any boundary layer effect resulting from an adjacent material mass. No material is completely heat-resistant: insulators simply offer either very great resistance to the passage of heat into the surface of their material thickness, or the thickness itself is obstructive to its passage. Surface resistances and the methods of heat transmission through solids and gases were considered to some degree in Chapter 6 of Vol. 1. A rather more detailed study is needed now, however, as we are concerned with the following aspects of buildings: surfaces; enclosing walls; floors, ceilings and other divisional construction features; as well as air content and heat losses from buildings.

"U" Values

Heating and ventilation are inseparable except in the presence of purely fanned air movement. Many textbooks on these subjects contain lists of "U" values. These figures show comparative heat transmittance powers of varying thicknesses and combinations of materials, including cavities in hollow walls. These are all rated in British thermal units per hour per square foot of the construction for each °F difference between the air temperatures on either side of the feature being considered. The most reliable and widely used figures are those published in The British Standard Code of Practice, CP 341.300.307: 1956. Allowance should be made for abnormal weather exposure, but with normal conditions we find that solid brickwork which is $4\frac{1}{2}$ in. thick and unplastered is rated at 0·64; 9 in. work at 0·47 and 14 in. at 0·37. Plastering one side reduces these figures to 0·57, 0·43, and 0·35 respectively. The addition of an unventilated cavity to the construction shows a further reduction to 0·30 in the 9 in. brickwork thickness used as an 11 in. cavity wall, or 0·26 with a 9 in. outer skin and $4\frac{1}{2}$ in. inner. Glass in windows or divisions rates at 1·00 for single glazing and 0·50 for double. For normal glazing, glass thickness is ignored: the very thin material thickness is relatively unimportant compared with surface resistances which we shall consider later. Almost every known building material, and many combinations in a variety of thicknesses, are quoted; walls, roofs, floors and windows are also listed with the variations necessary to allow for varying weather and orientation exposure.

With the aid of this data and information relating to the temperatures which it is required to maintain, together with the rates of air change and degree of ventilation required, the heating engineer can assess the boiler or other heat source capacity which it is necessary to install to counteract the heat lost through the whole or any part of the enclosing structure of the building. If we can assess the heat loss value or coefficient (the "U" value) of a construction upon the surface of which condensation is occurring or might be likely so to do and providing we have information about adjoining air conditions, a remedy can often be specified to combat the trouble or preferably to forestall its occurrence. (See also Vol. 1, Chapter 6).

Resistance and conductivity

The total resistance of a construction depends upon the conductivity of the materials through their thickness and the surface resistances involved. "U" values are reciprocal to this, the total resistance being used as a divisor to unity or one. Therefore, if we have a total resistance of, say, 3·31 then "U" equals $\frac{1}{3·31}$ or 0·30—the figure quoted earlier as the "U" value of an 11 in. cavity brick wall with a sealed unventilated cavity and plastered on one side.

Thickness of material makes a difference to total resistance and, therefore, to "U" value. A 9 in. brick wall has exactly the same surfaces and resistances as has a 14 in. one: thickness is the only varying factor. Thus we find that the thicker the construction the less the heat loss in any given material. In old buildings with thick walls of any material, relative coolness is experienced in summer and warmth in

DAMPNESS IN BUILDINGS 199

winter when heated and draughts are excluded.

Condensation upon wall or ceiling surfaces is rarely a problem in a Devonshire cob cottage with a thatched roof and walls two feet thick, providing both are in good repair, despite the fact that the county is one with a relatively humid atmosphere. When occupied, however, windows will frost up and quite readily show condense if the outside air temperature drops. Each wall has two surfaces and considerable thickness of a relatively poor conductive material; whereas a window, whilst also having two surfaces, has only a very thin thickness of rather highly conductive material.

TEMPERATURE DROP THROUGH WINDOW GLAZING.

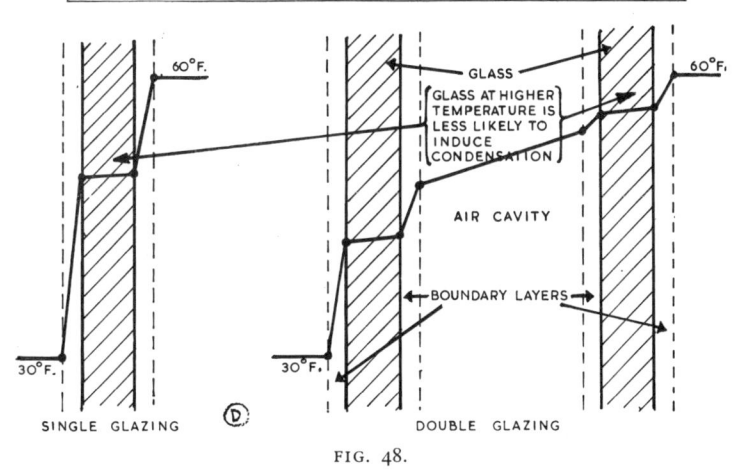

FIG. 48.

Surface resistances are given as constants, the figures used being:

Roofs	External surface corrugated	0·20 resistance
	External surface plane	0·25 resistance
	Internal surface corrugated	0·48 resistance
	Internal surface plane	0·60 resistance
Walls	External surface corrugated	0·24 resistance
	External surface plane	0·30 resistance

	Internal surface corrugated	0·56 resistance
	Internal surface plane	0·70 resistance
*Floors	Considered as barring upward passage	0·60 resistance
or		
*Ceilings	Considered as barring downward passage	0·85 resistance

NOTE: All the above figures are per square foot, per °F difference in temperature.

The reason that figures quoted for corrugated surfaces (meaning definitely undulating, not just roughened, like a rustic faced fletton brick or roughcast plaster) are lower than for plane (flat) is that where reciprocal division is involved the lower the divisor the higher the dividend—in the case we are considering, the heat loss coefficient. This must be correct, because one square foot of elevation of the corrugated surface will have a greater actual area as developed and will, therefore, be able to make greater heat loss or gain contact with air than will a plane square foot of surface. When making heat loss calculations for straight walls or roof slopes, heating engineers do not wish to have to make further calculations in respect of developed or gross areas of building surfaces.

In this list it will be seen that no variation is made for the material of which the surface is a part. We must remember, also, that they relate to contact with air. It is therefore reasonable to suppose that the "resistance" is that resulting from boundary layer air molecules (see pp. 188–189) which cover the surface of the solid.

A short extract from the tables in respect of conductivity of materials gives figures as follows:

Timber generally	1·00
Cork slabs	0·29 to 0·43
Wood wool slab	0·53
Expanded polystyrene	0·22
Foamed urea formaldehyde	0·23
Hardboard	0·71
Plasterboard	1·10

* Considered as plane surfaces: 20% less if corrugated.

Asbestos cement sheet	1·90
Glass wool quilt	0·28
Loose sawdust	0·41
Wet plastering	4·00
Ordinary brickwork	8·00
Ballast concrete	7·00
Lightweight concrete	1·90
Glass	7·00

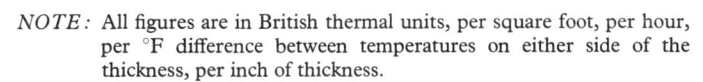

NOTE: All figures are in British thermal units, per square foot, per hour, per °F difference between temperatures on either side of the thickness, per inch of thickness.

Air filled sealed cavities having a minimum width of three-quarters of an inch, but generally not exceeding two inches, are given a resistance constant of 1·00 irrespective of actual width. In these sealed, restricted cavity widths the air is considered as a material, not as free air, and therefore no additional surface resistances are added when they adjoin enclosing materials. Alternatively, if you add external surface resistance plane to internal surface resistance plane (see p. 199) it gives 0·30 + 0·70 which equals 1·0 which is the factor or constant quoted. This rule cannot apply to ventilated cavities which, although often offering some protection to heat passage, by restricting free outside air movement over the inner skin outer surface permit through convectional current air movement directly from and to the outer air. Much depends upon the degree of ventilation which, if considerable, would reduce the effective wall thickness. In an 11 in. wall this would be equivalent to a 4½ in. wall.

Although we can often find from prepared tables the "U" value we require for our construction, the newer techniques employed in construction and material thicknesses used often present problems which we must solve for ourselves. In view of condensation possibilities, it is essential to know how these "U" value figures are obtained—even where the complete figure is available—so that we can discover "surface" and "intersurface" temperatures.

24: Finding heat losses, surface and interstitial temperatures

THE reader who may dislike mathematics or who is wary of formulae is asked to accept the next few paragraphs as a practical exercise based upon facts which are logical and related to real conditions of normal building.

The formula for calculating thermal resistance as a total is:

$$R = Rsi + \frac{L_1}{K_1} + \frac{L_2}{K_2} + \frac{L_3}{K_3} + Ra + Rso$$

This is merely an equation with a series of additions on one side having three of the amounts arrived at by means of simple division. In the above formula:

R is the total resistance of a construction (air to air).

Rsi is the internal surface resistance.

L_1, L_2 and L_3—and as many further numbers following L as are necessary to allow one for each separate material of the construction—represent the thickness of the material, expressed in inches.

K_1, K_2 and K_3 are the respective conductivity ratings of those materials, per inch of thickness.

Ra is the resistance of a sealed cavity.

Rso is the external surface resistance.

Except for the material thicknesses, all the other figures required to take the place of the letters quoted above can be found in the lists appearing on the previous few pages. For an example, we will now consider an 11 in. sealed cavity wall in brickwork and plastered internally; quite a complicated construction for illustration purposes, but a very practical one.

DAMPNESS IN BUILDINGS 203

When tackling such a problem, a section through the construction should first be sketched and the considerations numbered off.

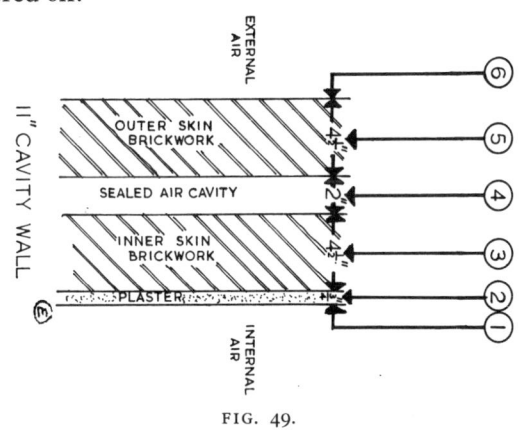

FIG. 49.

Here we have Rsi numbered 1; $L1$ numbered 2; $L2$, 3; Ra, 4; and so on. The solution can be set out as follows:

Number in sketch	Feature being considered	Material thickness (in inches)	Conductivity	Equals	Resistance
1	Internal surface plane (Rsi)	none	none		0·70
2	¾ in. plaster	0·75 $(L1)$	4·0 $(K1)$	$\frac{0·75 \text{ in.} \ (L1)}{4·00 \ \ (K1)}$	0·19
3	4½ in. brick inner skin	4·50 $(L2)$	8·0 $(K2)$	$\frac{4·5 \text{ in.} \ (L2)}{8·0 \ \ (K2)}$	0·56
4	2 in. sealed cavity (Ra)	none	none		1·00
5	4½ in. brick outer skin	4·50 $(L3)$	8·0 $(K3)$	$\frac{4·5 \text{ in.} \ (L3)}{8·0 \ \ (K3)}$	0·56
6	External surface plane (Rso)	none	none		0·30
				Total resistance	3·31

The importance will be seen of dividing the thickness by the conductivity coefficient. The thicker the material the higher will be the resistance: 9 in. brickwork would give $\frac{9 \text{ in.}}{8\cdot 0}$ which equals 1·125 resistance. This is logical and would be expected.

If "U" equals $\frac{1 \text{ (unity)}}{\text{resistance total}}$, then for our 11 in. cavity wall we have $\frac{1}{3\cdot 31}$ which is 0·30. If you substitute a 9 in. brick inner skin, the total resistance rises to 3·875 and the "U" value drops to 0·259. It is, therefore, not difficult to find the "U" value for any combination of materials provided their conductivity coefficients are known.

Once the principle of these calculations has been understood one can judge the relative resistance of constructional features and even applied insulating layers. Reasoned judgements of this nature, particularly when the addition of insulation to a cold or cool wall or roof is contemplated, can help to provide an immediate remedy to condensation conditions. These judgements can be substantiated by calculation, and constructions designed to obviate the occurrence of condensation if air humidity and temperature conditions are known in advance.

"U" values of heat losses through walls and other constructional barriers indicate that heat is lost from the air on one side, normally from the inside of the barrier, to that on the other. As shown earlier, there must be a temperature difference between two bodies for heat to pass at all—the direction of flow being always from the warmer to the cooler body. In the British Isles, heat losses are normally outward at external walls as is the case with vapour diffusion. These losses are upward through roofs and downward through the lowest floors, and either way through party and partition walls and intermediate floors. For external construction under continued strong solar heat conditions, or in tropical humidities, the reverse might well be the case.

Direction of heat flow

If heat losses are to occur or transmission take place there must be a cooler body to which the heat can pass. This means that at all points in the direction of heat flow each particle of material in each layer, whether solids or air, must be cooler than that from which the heat is passed. Similarly, a surface into which heat is to gain admission must be cooler than the surface of the material with which it is in contact or than the source of radiant heat on the other side of intervening space. It is possible to check that this is so by consideration of the thickness of walls and other constructions where temperatures can be taken at internal points. It is also possible to check that the internal air temperature adjacent to a wall surface is higher than the actual surface; externally, the reverse. Ability to discover these temperatures is more important to the study of condensation than actual heat losses but, unless it is understood how the latter are computed, appreciation of the importance of the former and their calculation would be confusing.

Heat loss gradients can be shown graphically

When we discover surface and internal construction temperatures and plot them on a sketch with lines drawn connecting each known temperature, these lines form a gradient like the line upon a graph. If we draw a section of a construction to scale and set up the temperature levels, also to scale, it is possible to use it as a graph and to interpolate quite accurately the temperatures to be expected between given points.

If we now further consider fig. 50 and notes thereto but substitute urea formaldehyde foam filling 2 in. thick in place of the sealed cavity, which can be done to existing cavities by pumping in a foam of shaving-cream consistency, this gives $\frac{L}{K}$, $\frac{2 \text{ in.}}{0.23}$, 8·7 resistance instead of 1·0 with a resistance total of 10.91. Using this total and the same formula as noted to fig. 50, we should obtain an internal plaster

206 DAMPNESS IN BUILDINGS

HEAT LOSS TEMPERATURE GRADIENT GRAPH TO SCALE

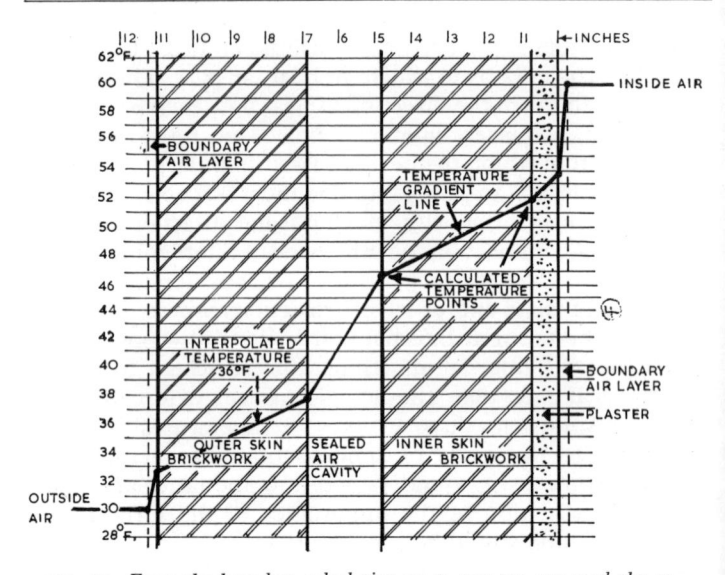

FIG. 50. *From the heat loss calculation on p. 203 we can read the resistances: internal surface 0·70, which is the boundary air layer or surface resistance; plaster 0·19; inner brick skin 0·56; sealed cavity 1·00; outer brick skin 0·56; external surface, boundary layer air resistance, 0·30. Using these and the known air temperatures on either side of the construction, inside 60°F (15·6°C), outside 30°F (−1°C), and the formula given and explained on p. 208–9, we can obtain the following calculated point temperatures. At inner plaster surface, 53·66°F (12·1°C); inner surface of inner brick skin, 51·93°F (11°C); cavity inner side, 46·83°F (8·2°C); outer side, 37·8°F (3·2°C); outer surface of outer brick skin, 32·72°F (0·5°C). It will be noted that the air temperatures adjacent to the construction are set outside the boundary layers of air. It is necessary to show this because the surface resistance temperature drop occurs through this layer. It could not occur in the hypothetical "surface", which has no third or thickness dimension.*

surface temperature of 58·1°F (14·4°C). Thus, if the internal air conditions were such as would produce condense at temperatures above 53·66°F (12·1°C) (even up to 56°F (13·3°C) or slightly above), then the foam filling would prevent its occurrence.

A solid brick wall plastered inside gives a total resistance of 2·31 which, with temperatures of 60 F (15·6 C) and 30°F (−1°C), provides an internal surface temperature of 50.91°F (10·5°C). If we add a $\frac{1}{10}$ in. thickness of expanded polystyrene, hung like wallpaper inside, the total resistance and inside surface temperatures become 2·764 and 52·41°F (11·4°C). The addition of $\frac{1}{2}$ in., as sheet or tiles, gives 4·582 and 55·41°F (13°C); if we added 5 in. of expanded polystyrene, we should have 25·03 and 59·16°F (15·1°C), which means that condense is not likely to occur with air almost saturated at 60°F (15·6°C).

If we know the dew point temperature of air passing up to a surface or diffusing through porous construction, and also the surface and internal temperatures of the construction we can forecast the point—either at the surface or through the thickness—at which condensation will occur. Where in practice we see a wall or roof constructed of thin material of high heat conductivity which has surfaces with high heat absorption and emissivity ratios, we know that if the internal air becomes only moderately humid condensation will occur in cold weather. Corrugated steel or asbestos cement sheets positively invite condensation, particularly if painted with dark hard paints. Thin dense concrete precast wall panels and single glass glazed in steel sashes must also give trouble, so it is necessary to find out a little more about temperature gradients as an aid to forestalling and remedying condensation upon surfaces and within thicker or more complicated constructions.

Surface temperatures and condense

It has already been seen that many complaints of condensation are related to surfaces and, in particular, internal surfaces. Also, that it is the cooling effect of the surface upon the adjacent air which causes the condense. We will now find an internal surface temperature at a ceiling. Fig. 51 shows a section through a concrete flat roof 5 in. thick with no internal plaster or additional finish—an insulating underlay to mastic asphalt outer covering. Re-

208 DAMPNESS IN BUILDINGS

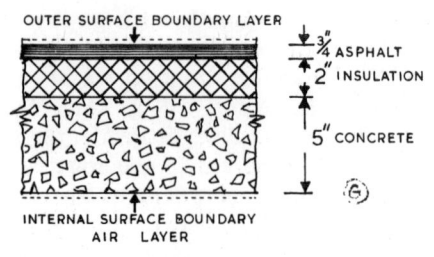

FIG. 51.

sistances are needed, but not the "U" values. In this case it will be assumed that the resistances are:

1. External surface   0·25
2. Asphalt   0·10
3. Insulation   3·30
4. 5 in. concrete   0·50
5. Internal surface   0·60

   Total resistance   4·75

NOTE: Individually and as a total, these figures represent the number of hours that one British thermal unit of heat takes to pass through one square foot of the individual material thickness, the whole construction or the surface, when 1°F temperature difference exists between the air or material on either side.

Another formula must now be used:

$$Tsi = Ti - \frac{Rsi}{R} \times (Ti - To)$$

in which:

Tsi represents internal surface temperature

Ti represents internal air temperature

Rsi represents internal surface resistance

R represents the total overall resistance of the construction

To represents external air temperature.

Assuming temperatures of 65°F inside air and 30°F outside, figures can be written in substitution of the symbols:

$$Tsi = 65° - \frac{0.60}{4.75} \times (65° - 30°)$$

giving an internal surface temperature *(Tsi)* of:

60·58°F.

Finding interstitial temperatures

Suppose the temperature at the topside of the concrete beneath the insulating layer is required. The formula is simply adapted to allow for the added resistance involved, that is the concrete, in addition to the internal surface and therefore:

Temperature at topside of concrete

$$= Ti - \frac{Rsi + \text{Resistance of concrete}}{R} \times (Ti - To)$$

$$= 65° - \frac{0·60 + 0·50}{4·75} \times (65° - 30°)$$

Therefore, temperature
at the point within
the construction
required $= 56.9°F$

Resistances can continue to be added to the top line of the centre part of the calculation: 3·30 for the insulation, a further 0·10 for the asphalt and 0·25 for the external surface. If all the figures are included, the outside air temperature is obtained. If the asphalt surface temperature is required, only the external surface resistance is omitted and we have

$65° - \frac{4·50}{4·75} \times 35°$ giving 30·35°F which is slightly above

outside air temperature; this is the necessary condition if the asphalt is to give off heat to the air above.

Effect of insulation on temperatures

Whilst considering resistances to heat losses, useful study can be made of some of the effects of including insulating material layers into constructions. If rather cold conditions are chosen the value of doing this will be more readily appreciated.

Let us assume temperatures of 45°F (7·2°C) internally and 20°F (−6·7°C) externally with the roof construction previously considered. With the insulating layer, temperature at the underside of the slab at ceiling level will be:

$$45°F - \frac{0·60}{4·75} \times (45° - 20°) = 41·84°F \, (5·5°C)$$

If the insulation layer is omitted, thereby removing 3·30 of the total resistance, then:

$$45°F - \frac{0·60}{1·45} \times (45° - 20°) = 34·75°F \, (1·5°C)$$

A much lower temperature is noted at this surface, in fact quite close to that which would cause condensation if the internal air at 45°F (7·2°C) and in contact with it were normally humid. If its relative humidity were high then condensation would most certainly occur.

Assume that this air at 45°F (7·2°C) is at 66·66% saturation, which means that whereas it could hold 3·44 grains of moisture vapour without this being visible, it actually only holds 2·3 grains. If this air is cooled to 42°F (5·6°C), by bringing it into contact with the cooler soffit, whilst it retains the same amount of vapour it will become 74·67% saturated. At 42°F (5·6°C) it could hold invisibly only 3·08 grains. Condensation is unlikely to occur since it is still at a temperature and condition well above saturation or dew point. If, however, it is cooled further to 35°F (1·7°C) it will become 96·2% saturated. Condensation is still unlikely to occur unless the surface concerned is coated with a deliquescent layer resulting from previous re-evaporation of condensed absorbed moisture, or some decorative or surface treatment material; any of these conditions could induce condense at dew points less than saturation or if the air is permitted to take up more moisture vapour.

Rather cold conditions help us to appreciate the value of insulation. It is not unusual for outside air temperatures immediately above asphalt roofs to drop to 20°F (−6·7°C) in this country when the general air temperature out of doors is at freezing point or even slightly above. We could, with all the conditions we have considered in the case we have been discussing, expect condensation to occur. (See also Vol. 1, p. 41). Under clear night sky conditions the external surface resistance of asphalt roofs is reduced by "exposure condition" to nil. Thus the divisor for the uninsulated roof will become 1·20 only, when the external surface resistance factor is deducted from the total resistance. This produces:

$$45°F - \frac{0·60}{1·20} \times (45° - 20°) = 32·5°F \; (0·3°C)$$

at which temperature this air will become 105·89% saturated and this must produce condense to the extent of 0·128 grains of water per cubic foot of air cooled. Air at 32·5°F (0·3°C) becomes saturated when one cubic foot holds 2·172 grains of water vapour. The air which we have considered held 2·30 grains, but could no longer do so under the further conditions produced.

When we know the conditions likely to arise, we can therefore forecast the occurrence of condensation and the amount of condense likely. If we know the absorptive power of porous materials it is also possible to predict, these conditions prevailing, the number of hours it will take for the known bulk of the material to become saturated. Thus, reversely, it will be seen that if it is proposed to use an absorbant material behind the surface concerned, it could be said that given thickness A in. the condense will all be absorbed whilst condense conditions prevail; whereas if A in. minus 50% thickness were used, condense will commence to show as unabsorbed moisture—as a film gathering to drops on the ceiling surface—after X hours. This information is particularly useful for the night condition considered here, since its duration also can be forecast. The provision of insulation to offset condensation need not, therefore, be guesswork.

25 : Penetrating or condensational dampness

APPRECIATION that condense can occur within porous material thickness, or if it occurs upon an absorbent surface that it can penetrate possibly to saturation point, enables us to consider prevention and cure. The appearance of moisture upon internal surfaces of a building is frequently mistaken for effects of water penetration from the outside. In such a case remedial action considered and perhaps used may take the form of:

(a) Waterproof hard rendering outside; coating the external surface of the construction with water repellent solutions; or, doing either of these operations internally, which action would be an even worse attempt at solution of the problem.

(b) In waterside areas, tarring the outside and painting with cement paints often incorporating some waterproofing additive.

(c) In rural areas, washing with lime and hot tallow and applying to the inside waterproof materials, proofing solution, oil, chlorinated rubber paint, or impregnated papers.

None of these treatments is really a permanent remedy for condensation. Some slight improvement can result, mainly where the cause of the condensation is partly due to the cooling of the wall thickness as the result of a degree of penetrative dampness. If, however, the wall or other construction is saturated as a result of long absorption from any cause, pore blocking—waterproofing the outside—will prevent external re-evaporation of this absorbed water whether it arises from penetration or condensation. Proofings which can "breathe" (see Vol. 1, p. 33) will permit external re-evaporation providing that the structural thickness as a whole can be warmed. Since application of these proofings alone in no way improves the thermal resistance of the thickness, this reaction is unlikely. Internal applications too, unless they have some insulative quality, give no benefit in this direction. They simply stop absorption which often results in an immediate increase in intensity of the amount of condense to be seen upon the surface. When confronted with a wall area, such as a whole width to dadoe height or a panel, upon which condense appears occasionally it is always advisable to investigate the surface immediately beneath the decoration. A glazed plaster surface may quite often be found and this is evidence of the use of a waterproofing fluid. A layer of waterproof paper or foil, or a hard rendering could be alternative causes. In a case of this kind it must be established, before attempting to remedy condensation, that the dampness is resultant from that cause; similarly, it must be ascertained that penetration dampness is in fact occurring. To combat condensation we need to add insulative quality to the construction; the greater the intensity of the condense, the greater is the need for more insulation. Air sealed in tiny sacs, or pores, entangled within fibrous matting or confined in sealed cavities of reasonable width is the cheapest, and one of the best, structural insulators.

External cladding

Where there is some doubt as to the whole cause of dampness in a wall and "rising" dampness can be eliminated as a possible cause, penetrative dampness can be remedied and anti-condensational conditions improved if not wholly remedied by the addition of external spaced off tile/slate hanging or weatherboarding. Such claddings shed water and add some material thickness and insulation to the wall. In the latter case, the real value is the air space provided between the cladding material and the outer surface of the existing wall; this is achieved by battening off. Battens 1 in. thick are sufficient. Timber cladding of the shiplap joint type on vertical battens offers the best insulation. Cross or horizontal battens at close vertical intervals cause short circuiting of upward convectional air currents in the cavity, and this assists heat loss across its width. Such air currents would assist outward evaporation of moisture, however, where condensation is the major cause of the dampness.

The recent re-introduction of tile bricks hung to brickwork or studding, a feature of many old buildings at Lewes in Sussex which produces an appearance of actual open jointed or if pointed, realistic brick facing, offers another attractive alternative cladding.

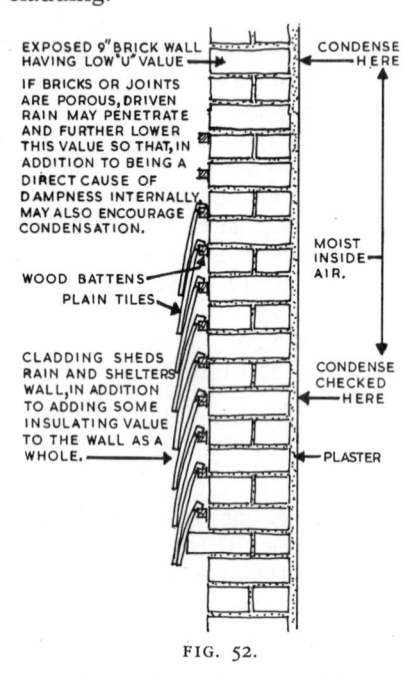

FIG. 52.

Counter battening, where horizontal battens are needed to hang the cladding, add insulative value. Close-jointed boarding is preferable to tiles or slates in cases where insulation is of most importance. The provision of underfelting, often specified for such cladding, needs careful consideration. If prevention of penetration of water or vapour alone from the outside is all that is necessary, underfelting should be included; but it must be borne in mind that it will inhibit evaporation of moisture and the passage to the outer air of vapour arising from inside the wall or building. It will, however, add insulative value to the complete construction and so mitigate internally against condensation. External claddings, in the form of windshields and anti-frost shields, also add protection to their backing walls. In terms of "U" values, they convert severe exposure to normal or normal to sheltered. Vertical spacings of horizontal battens for vertical cladding can be increased over those used to roof slopes; laps of slates reduced to $1\frac{1}{2}$ in. and plain tiles set to $4\frac{1}{2}$ in. gauge are quite sufficient.

Prior to Town Planning restrictions and legislation controlling advertisement hoardings, many houses with exposed flank and even front walls were clad free of charge to the owners providing approval of the fire safety precautions was first obtained from the local authorities concerned. In fact, the owners received an income from the cladders who used the cladding as advertisement hoardings. Timber battenings, or more substantial framings, plugged to the wall supported coverings of matchlined timber or sheet (galvanized steel) metal. These shed rain water, and the spacing off sheltered and insulated the walls. Building owners who "let" their walls for the application of advertisements which were actually painted on the structure, often regretted this later. Pores filled with paint prevented moisture diffusion from inside the building and did not help materially to raise the insulative value of the wall, except perhaps to prevent any increase in dampness. If such surfaces were in prominent positions and appeared to be worth long term use, they were rendered before being used as paint surfaces; however, unless the paint was maintained regularly, crazing and cracking brought the troubles shown in fig. 53.

A wall which is subject to penetrative dampness can still occasionally be treated free of charge and also produce an income in the manner described; instances are very rare, however, as the necessary planning permission is seldom granted now. Permission to clad a wall with more acceptable surfacing materials for purely remedial, non-commercial, purposes is probably more readily obtained but the cost will have to be borne by the owner and there is, of course, no prospect of future income. Any of the materials suggested earlier would be suitable, as well as vertical, tongued, grooved and vee-jointed cedar boarding left in its natural colour. If essential, the boarding may be coated to preserve its colour; but this will reduce possibilities of vapour movement, resulting from internal diffusion or evaporation, through its thickness. In order to reduce gloss effect the use of polyurethane varnish, preferably thinned, is advised in preference to linseed oil which will oxidize in patches to give a very mottled effect and will also darken the colour. When adding tightly-jointed cladding to increase insulative values, all edges of the cavity should be sealed; otherwise, "shelter" only is being added. It is preferable that outside rendering, when used, should be as soft as is practical whilst maintaining sufficient surface resistance to weather. Hard, dense, trowelled cement adds little insulative value and invariably develops fine hair or capillary cracks very soon after application unless it is very skilfully applied, tooled and wet cured. When this happens, driven rain running over the hard dense surface cannot soak in and reaches these hairlike cracks in sufficient quantity to feed capillary soakage through them into the porous substructure from which re-evaporation is difficult. Continued absorptions of this kind eventually produce saturation effects through the wall thickness, thus completely defeating the object of the rendering. If the substructure to which such rendering is applied contains soluble chemicals,* reactions encouraged by—in fact made possible by—the absorbed water may result in rendering spalling off. Some lime is usually contained in the mix for softer renderings, if only in the finishing coat in two-coat work, and this permits a degree of absorption into the coat which prevents run down in quantity to points of possible access to the interior except

* This matter is dealt with later.

DAMPNESS IN BUILDINGS 217

DRIVEN RAIN DOES NOT SOAK INTO HARD DENSE RENDERINGS. IT RUNS DOWN AND FEEDS CAPILLARY PENETRATION INTO HAIRLINE CRACKS AND, BECAUSE IT CANNOT RE-EVAPORATE OUTWARDS, SOAKS INWARDS.

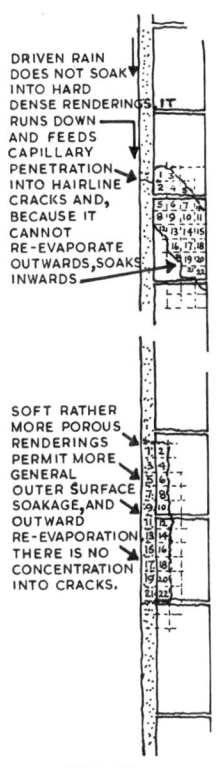

SOFT RATHER MORE POROUS RENDERINGS PERMIT MORE GENERAL OUTER SURFACE SOAKAGE, AND OUTWARD RE-EVAPORATION. THERE IS NO CONCENTRATION INTO CRACKS.

FIG. 53.

after prolonged exposure to driving rain. Lime incorporated into the mix can, by its gel properties, also assist in preventing too much penetration whilst still permitting re-evaporation. (See Vol. I, p. 117).

National Building Studies, Bulletin No. 10, published by Her Majesty's Stationery Office, entitled: *External Rendered Finishes for Walls,* gives a considerable amount of information about applied renderings, their suitability and durability.

Whilst the addition externally of water shedding cladding or of suitable renderings adds some insulative value to the wall and by combating rain penetration from the outside may also remedy internal condensation conditions, it may not completely solve the problem; its use may in fact be prohibited by practical difficulties or for aesthetic reasons, for example Town Planning consents. Such treatments may be stated to "alter the character of the property" to a sufficient extent for approval to be withheld by the administrative authority.

Simpler remedial measures

Cost, too, often compels owners to seek simpler remedies for condensation; such remedies usually take the form of internal applications of insulative sheet materials. Reference could profitably be made at this point to Vol. 1, pp. 104 to 109. As stated therein, insulated dadoes are often erected to mask rising dampness; similar treatments can, however, assist in "insulating" cool walls—and wet walls are cool walls—from humid room air and so prevent condense thereon.

As stated previously, when treating surfaces for condensation where rising damp conditions exist or might be induced, care must be taken not to apply a remedy which robs the surface of its evaporative powers. Whilst the use of vapour proof air sac insulators for anti-condense linings is usually considered preferable to non-vapour proof air pored insulating materials they would not be suitable in such cases. Very thin expanded polystyrene sheeting and anti-condense paints are other possibilities and will be dealt with later; they can, however, only deal with intermittent or slight condense conditions interspersed by drying periods.

Insulative linings

Linings capable of overcoming long or more severe condense periods or conditions must add sufficient insulative value to the construction in order to raise the new internal surface temperature to above dew point of the air which it will contact, (see p. 207). Modern gas sac or air pore insulators offer high insulative value with reasonable thickness. Expanded polystyrenes; polyurethane; mineral wools; fibreglass mats or quilts in half, three-quarters, or one inch thickness give values equal to several inches of wood or cork and to even thicker lightweight concrete, brickwork, etc. The use of such linings will now be studied.

List of Relative Thermal Conductivities

Material	"K" value per 1 in. thickness per degree Fahrenheit temperature difference per square foot per hour—in British thermal units.
Freon blown polyurethane	0·16
Expanded ebonite	0·20
Expanded polystyrene	0·22
Kapok quilting	0·22
Foamed urea formaldehyde	0·23
Expanded poly vinyl chloride	0·23
Mineral wool blanket	0·25
Glass fibre blanket	0·25
Water blown polyurethane	0·30
Cork board	0·30
Loose granulated cork	0·33
Fibre boards	0·39
Loose exfoilated vermiculite	0·45
Compressed straw board	0·60
Wood wool—cement slab	0·60
Foamed concrete	0·60

The fact that amounts of condense can be forecast and thicknesses of absorbent materials adjusted to accommodate these amounts must, however, be related to the problem of re-evaporation. Unless there are means for re-evaporation at the further side of the porous material, any moisture absorbed can only re-evaporate from the pores at the surface through which it was originally absorbed. As has been shown in Vol. 1, chapter 4, whilst moisture can penetrate into capillaries quite readily, evaporation of that moisture from other than very slight depth below a surface is much more difficult. It would be a mistake, therefore, to assume that if we used A-in. thickness of absorbent material below the surface the appearance of condense would never occur thereon. We should have to evaluate the re-evaporative possibilities. These would be influenced by relative humidity of the adjacent air when condense conditions cease, and the temperature condition which the absorbent material will attain during non-condense periods. Furthermore we must not forget that a saturated porous material loses much of its resistance to heat passage, which will result in further cooling of the surface. The longer the duration of the condense or external driven rain soakage conditions, the less the value of porous absorbent backings to a condense surface or outside rendering. Only where slight quantities of moisture are likely to condense internally over longish periods, or more massive amounts over quite short periods, can absorptive internal backings to porous surfaces be considered as a remedy. Even then it must be ensured that (a) there is a satisfactory movement of relatively dry air over the surface between condense periods or (b) the absorbent material will be warmed during those times to above condense dew point temperature. It is preferable that both these conditions should prevail and, further, (c) that the moisture-saturated absorbent will not suffer deterioration as the result of saturation; encourage the growth of fungi; or alter, irretrievably, either physically or chemically.

Build-up of heat in enclosing walls, etc.

Before considering the problem of heat absorption into walls and other building surfaces, which is a necessary pre-occurrence to condense upon the surface, further thought should be given to heat losses from buildings. It is often asked how a room, or a whole building, and its enclosing walls, roof, etc., can become warm when the heating input provided and the calculated heat losses under the air temperature conditions stated—say 60°F (15·6°C) inside and 30°F (−1°C) outside—are those which will balance. It is this statement of "balanced" heat losses which is misleading.

The loss calculation calls for an input equal to temperature difference multiplied by the "U" value of the enclosing structure plus the loss by ventilating air. In the case being discussed the losses will be: 30° × (say) 0·3 Btu per square foot per hour plus a substantial addition for the heat carried out by ventilating air. Dry air requires approximately 0·2 Btu of heat energy per cubic foot to raise its temperature one degree Fahrenheit, so that for a 30°F difference one cubic foot will require 6 Btu. Thus at ascending differences greater amounts of heat up to this figure will be carried out of the ventilated room with each cubic foot of extracted air. Moist, more humid air can carry even more heat.

This maximum calculated rate of loss will only occur when the inside temperature reaches 60°F (15·6°C). Until then it will be less, commencing at possibly 2° × 0·3 plus, and rises gradually as the air temperature becomes 3°, then 4° and so on. Since the heat input apparatus will be designed to counterbalance calculated maximum losses, at this stage it will be providing heat at a greater rate than the losses: the degree will depend upon the type of generation or the source. An electric fire or fan heater, and most heaters sited in an actual room, except solid fuel fires, immediately or very quickly give full potential heat output: the calculated amount. Underfloor electric and hot water radiator types warm up more slowly but, nevertheless, they must be at higher than room air temperatures or no heat output will occur at all. Thus this heat input, which is surplus to actual losses, can be and is absorbed from the inside air by the wall and builds up the heat gradient until at the 60°—30°F (15·6°—1°C) air temperature levels the input is balanced to the loss. We can appreciate this process better if we consider that the reverse is the case when heat input ceases. We do not get an immediate and sudden air temperature drop. The greater the amount of heat the walls etc. can hold, the more gradual will be the warming and cooling processes; but, also, if walls etc. have little heat holding capacity then the more efficient the heat imput apparatus is in providing quickly the calculated warmth required, the more rapid will be the inside air temperature drop when it is turned off.

Wall areas which may attract condensation

Since many types of room space heaters emit heat by radiant rays, wall and other internal surfaces exposed to these rays will gather heat more rapidly than those not so exposed. Thus we find that in one room, one wall only or even part thereof may "attract" condense on heating; others not being affected. This occurrence often leads to the mistaken conclusion that the portion upon which the surface dampness appears has penetration ability from an outside defect: to many people there appears to be no other reason. This effect can occur upon any surface screened from radiant rays, or where air able to warm a surface or to evaporate moisture therefrom cannot freely pass over it. Constant or occasional patches of condensational staining of wallpaper, and possibly black or brown spot fungi growths, often occur behind solid pieces of furniture or goods stacked very close to walls; if the backs of the furniture or the goods have slightly deliquescent surfaces they, too, may become damp and possibly show moulds. These areas of dampness arise firstly from the lack of absorbed radiant heat; this will prevent the surfaces warming the adjoining air. Secondly, this air which is restricted within the narrow gap will not have the additional moisture evaporative powers gained by room air adjacent to warmed wall areas. Therefore a convectional air movement will be created through the confined air space and this will bring the warmer and probably more moist air closely past the surfaces where condense inducing conditions exist.

If this condense occurs and continues, perhaps with only short drying out periods, the wall may develop a slight or even severe deliquescent condition at its surface, condensed moisture having been absorbed and then, during drying periods, leaching deliquescent salts to the constructional surface where they are left at evaporation. If this is absorbed into the decorative paper cover or porous paint then here, and upon backs of adjacent furniture upholstered in natural fibres, condense will be induced, at temperatures even slightly above normal, to become almost continuous.

Screening may well be the cause of the trouble: this diagnosis can be confirmed by the temporary removal of the screening article; or the re-siting and re-aiming of the source of radiant heat, or its temporary reflection during critical periods on to the affected surface. The condition may well be remedied by the application of a micro-thickness of vapour proof cellular insulator beneath the wallpaper.

Whilst considering deliquescent wall surfaces, it should be remembered that sands and aggregates derived from sea beaches and dredging can, if unwashed with fresh water before use in mortars and plasterings, contain substances which will leach to evaporate at surfaces with absorbed moisture. Cases have been known to the author where animal fouling of heaps of builders' sand has almost certainly resulted in similar trouble. Also, where stable blocks or adjacent premises—salting rooms for bacon curing, etc.—have been converted to living or other accommodation, walls against which manure or salt heaps have rested for long periods or where stable or bench washdown water has splashed have shown similar conditions even through new plastering. In one case where a manure heap was the cause, the trouble only showed behind a large upholstered settee.

Where deliquescent conditions exist in depth below a surface, or can be traced to penetration from an outside source, a cure can only be effected by cutting out the existing plaster; treating the structural backing with at least two coats of a chlorinated rubber paint; or fixing a keyed bitumen impregnated sheeting to extend at least nine inches further than does the condense or efflorescence in all directions; and then re-plastering. Lead or aluminium foils used alone on the structural backing would not provide sufficient key for re-plastering.

26: Occupational habits and dirty surfaces as a clue to condensational dampness

WHERE dense concretes—particularly those used for precast panels formed under pressure, or upon vibrating tables, in smooth metal formwork such as are normally used where the panels are structural—constitute the finished internal surfaces of rooms, considerable amounts of heat are necessary to build up sufficient warmth to secure an internal surface temperature close to room air temperature and so prevent condensation.

The author has recently concluded an experiment using the typical dense concrete panel construction now adopted for industrialized flatted dwelling construction. A 5 in. internal structural self-finished slab, a 1 in. expanded polystyrene insulating, and a waterproofing barrier with a 2 in. concrete weather cladding outside were all cast as a unit. Using an internal air temperature of 70°F (21·1°C), maintained from built-in underfloor electric heating at 15 watts loading per foot super of floor area and allowing reasonable ventilation, nearly eight weeks continuous heating was needed before any internal air temperature rise above 70°F (21·1°C) indicated that the wall slab was at that temperature. In this country the early autumn months usually produce quite humid weather, so it is not surprising to hear complaints of condensation upon such wall surfaces particularly as they are almost waterproof to the condense.

Aggravation of these conditions occurs when whole families are away from home during the daytime and they consider it uneconomic to continue general heating throughout the day. Occupiers switch off floor and, less often, storage heaters. They find that air space warms up more rapidly from a portable fan or convector electric heater than from the built-in facilities, and use only these for an hour or two in the morning and when they return in the evening. Without continuous general heating the structural slab will seldom really warm sufficiently to ensure freedom from condensation, especially in kitchens, bathrooms and bedrooms.

Modern causes of condensation

Study of reasons given by occupiers of council and private flatted housing who had ceased to use the installed "off peak" electric heating systems, shows that with the occupational habits previously described they complain that the ebb flow of heat from the cabinets and floor slab storage—that is the falling heat flow which occurs for a time immediately before and after charging re-commences—coincides with their homecoming and extends into the evening, whilst the best output occurs around mid-day when the house is unoccupied. The situation is aggravated by taking off outdoor clothing which has conserved body heat and itself become warmed during wear; the rapid cooking of the evening meal also releases clouds of steam into relatively cool air which condenses upon cool surfaces.

Unfortunately much of the criticism occurs during the first autumn and winter of occupation, soon after completion and before the structural materials have had adequate time to build up residual heat stores to compensate these ebbs. Floor storage systems are likely to be criticized more at early stages of new occupation than cabinet systems. This is because structural concrete temperatures cannot be raised during charging periods to levels which can be permitted in cabinets. Our temperatures would therefore fluctuate more rapidly were it known to occupants that these fluctuations would smooth out, as they do if continuous heating is maintained and as the heating season proceeds to give only a few degrees rise and fall over a twenty-four hour period, then many complaints would not be pressed for action. This is also the period when many re-housed families are spending additional money on increased rent, new furniture etc., as a result of moving; they may, therefore, wish to economize in heating costs. The portable paraffin oil heater which is cheap to buy and which, because the fuel is purchased in very small quantities, appears very economical to operate, offers an attractive substitute heating method. In burning, however, these heaters produce one gallon of water vapour from each gallon of oil burned and discharge this saturated warm air into the rooms. Similar discharges are also produced by many washing machines and most heated spin driers which evaporate large quantities of water. Where drying rooms or grounds are not easily accessible, hanging of "drip dry" clothing and small washed items on internal lines adds to the problem. Rather than endure consequent humid condense conditions, many people who may in fact own washing machines often prefer to make use of launderettes.

Local authorities might avoid a lot of unwelcome public criticism of new buildings if they preheated all dwellings sufficiently before occupation; alternatively, they might supply heating-up current free or very cheaply for the first couple of winter or autumn months.

These problems are real, even although temporary, and architects, councils and others who design or commission these works are having to modify their thoughts on heating and structural insulation in view of new occupational routines and reactions.

People who are rehoused from sub-standard houses, condemned as unfit for human habitation partly on grounds of dampness whether rising or otherwise, resent paying the inevitably higher rents—however superior in equipment, appliances and environment the new housing may be—where dampness is experienced even if it is "only" condensation and of limited duration. Once decorations are stained or new curtains or bedding become damp or spoilt, intense criticism is created which is not satisfied with any explanation of the cause and temporary nature of the conditions. Complaints of spoilt decorations may in fact precede those of damp conditions.

Dirty surfaces may be condense areas

Dirt-soiling of building surfaces, where not directly attributable to rubbing contact with some soiled article, is usually caused by the deposition of airborne dirt particles thereon. The cooler the surface in relation to the adjoining air, then the dirtier it is likely to become. It has been shown that surface resistance, or boundary layer, conditions and the heat conductive ability of the material behind it control the amount of heat energy which can pass from air adjacent to a wall into and through that wall or other constructional surface.

On p. 184 it was observed that molecules, particularly in gases, are very active and actually have frequent collisions; also, that extraneous particles in air—water vapour first of all, and now for this consideration minute dirt or solid particles—are bumped about by these movements. An aeroplane is only kept aloft by similar collisions; many more on the underside of its surface, the aerofoils or wings, than on the upper. It will have been noticed that a paper dart which is skilfully folded, "floats" or glides in windless air longer than does a similar unfolded piece of paper.

The less dense the air, then the warmer it is and the more active the molecules therein; warm air has, therefore, more bumping energy than cooler air. Glider pilots seek warm upward air currents to give their craft added lift in order to gain height for prolonged engineless flight.

The air in all buildings which are not air-conditioned carries suspended dirt particles. Air cooled by loss of heat energy to a cooling surface loses some of its ability to bump dirt particles. Air further from the cooling influence retains its higher ability in this connection, and will thus bump more particles into the cooler air than can be bumped back to it; "condensation" of dirt particles into the cooler air mass is therefore seen. The cooler air is really only the boundary layer or slightly more and, since it soon becomes relatively saturated with dirt, it bumps more dirt particles on to the adjacent cooling surface than would be bumped on to a warmer surface. Thus dirt is pushed on to cool sur-

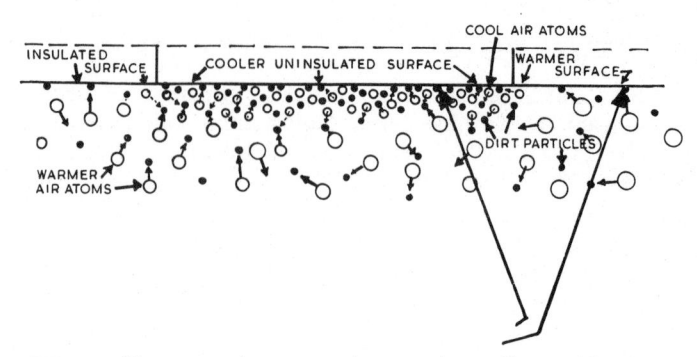

FIG. 54. *More energetic warmer air atoms bump dirt particles more strongly towards the cooler surface, than the cooler and therefore less energetic ones, nearer that surface, can bump them away. Thus a concentration is built up, close to the surface, and more will be bumped on to the cooler surface, than can be bumped on to the warmer. Water molecules and condense droplets are similarly 'bumped' on to cool surfaces.*

faces. This will happen from very dry air without condensation of moisture vapour occurring at all, and is more noticeable than with moist air conditions; principally because drier air is more likely to be dirty than moist. Dirt particles tend to form a centre to which water molecules coalesce at temperatures above normal dew points, thus producing water droplet-coated dirt particles which are too heavy to remain bump suspended; they therefore settle out. This is true also where the water vapour concentration of the dirt saturated air is increased by the cooling surface to very near dew point; the condensed water droplets themselves having dirt nucleii being bumped on to the surface. Alternatively a cool surface, already moist from condensed moisture, will provide a more readily acceptable anchorage for bumped dirt particles than would a non-ionized dry surface.

Radiator smears and pattern staining

The intense dirt-soiled smears which occur over heating radiators are so because air is streaming close to the surfaces by convectional movement and, because that air is very much hotter than the wall surface, a greater gradient exists between them. This produces severe "pushing" action towards the wall. The fitting of a radiator shelf deflects the very hot air away from the wall and causes it to mix with much cooler air before regaining contact with the cooler boundary layer; this much reduces the push bumping action as well as broadening the area over which it is taking place. The soiling therefore becomes generalized and is only noticed eventually by comparison with cleaner surfaces.

Metal bridges spanning insulators, such as cavity ties in both traditional cavity walls and industrialized sandwich

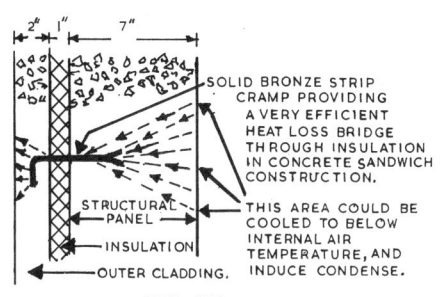

FIG. 55a.

construction, will show pattern stains as roughly circular patches of dirt on otherwise clean walls. If the "bridge" in a cavity wall is also supporting a dropped blob of bricklayer mortar—also bridging the cavity—penetrating dampness from the outer skin may saturate this mortar bridge and further raise heat transmission rates over this area, thus causing condensation and greater soiling. The fact that

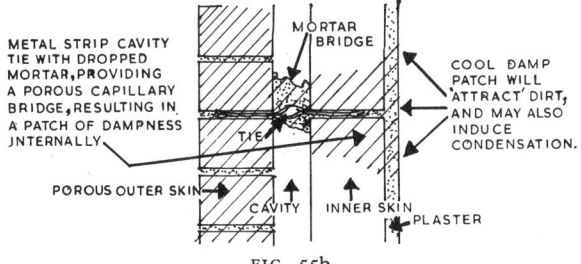

FIG. 55b.

dirt-soiling does not occur immediately in the corners of right-angle wall and ceiling junctions, although it is quite intense close thereto and thus gives an almost striped effect, is due in the case of the wall junction to the cooler surfaces nearby, because there is a greater mass of material behind the surface, to which accepted heat can be passed, relative to their areas in contact with the room air than is present in other wall areas. This is counteracted, right in the angle, by the meniscus-like curve of the boundary layer air which provides a deeper barrier layer of cooled air through which the more active molecules in the warmer air further out are unable to bump dirt particles far enough inwards to effect contact with the surface. The more closely packed layer acts as a cushion over the deep meniscus air. Furthermore, convectional currents passing close to a right-angle junction are swept out by the meniscus before reaching the actual junction and so less dirt is carried close enough to be bumped inwards.

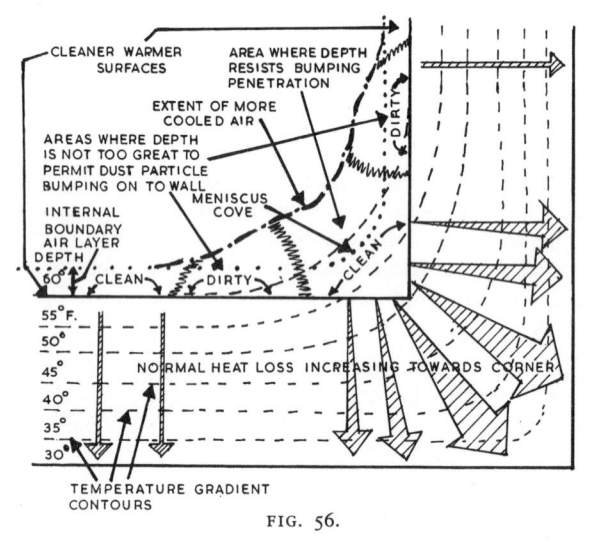

FIG. 56.

A coved corner presents an even thickness of boundary layer air together with greater material or insulating thickness of material which brings the heat resistance nearer to that of the adjoining plane surfaces. Thus coved internal angles can be regarded as an economical addition where periodic redecoration or washing down is related to appearance condition.

Fungi spots

We are not concerned with the cleaning or decorative aspects, but soiled areas can often give us a clue to actual or possible condensation areas. A further indication is given by the fungi growths in the form of minute brown or black spots which often occur upon a surface in these areas. These grow from spores, which are usually airborne, bumped on to the surface in exactly the same way as is dirt and fed by the condensed moisture. Spores are probably also attached to other wall areas of the same room, but these do not grow because no condense occurs thereon. Surfaces upon which fungi spores form moulds should be washed down with spirit or aqueous fungicidal solutions. A 2% solution of shirlan in methylated spirit, or a 6 oz. in 2 gal. water zinc silico-fluorite solution is recommended: there are also many proprietary solutions.

When hanging vinyl coated wallpapers it is necessary to use fungicidal paste. If this is not done then the mixing water would assist the growth of any spores trapped beneath the paper itself; the surface preventing normal drying out evaporation through the paper. If moisture can evaporate rearwards through the wall then other vapour could later diffuse back and condense behind the vinyl vapour barrier, particularly when it is on the wall of a cold, unoccupied room adjoining a warm moist bathroom which may even be in an adjacent house. This condense moisture would then cause the trapped spores to grow.

Diffusion through a membrane or wall, porous to molecule size particles only, is osmotic movement. It can occur through thin rubber sheets when they are stretched. It only takes place, however, when the molecule activity levels are unequal within the masses of gas or liquid on either side.

The movement is from the more active to the less active mass. A child's rubber balloon deflates by this action even when there is no air leak through the filling nozzle. Bumping action is similar to osmotic movement, but without the membrane.

27: Use and placing of added vapour barriers and insulating layers

INSULATING layers in concrete sandwich construction are placed nearer to the outside of the wall slabs and to the upper surface of floor or roof slabs in order that better structural joints can be made. They are also part of the design to provide the greatest possible thickness of heat-holding material behind the inner surfaces to the rooms. Once heated, they provide a compensating heat emitting surface, near to room air temperature, during ebb input heat flow periods. This would be a good defence against condensation if occupational habits did not upset the design consideration. Generally, it can be said that given dew point air conditions at a surface, the length of time which condense to the surface will continue is in inverse ratio to the thickness of the conductive substance behind that surface; also, the greater the heat absorbing capacity of the material, the longer the condense. Lightweight materials of low heat conductive capacity reduce condense time, in fact if their conductivity is low enough they prevent it altogether.

Insulating layers to floors are also placed nearer to the upper surface to permit placing *in situ* beneath screeds needed for covering support and reduce noise transmission to the room below. Those to roofs are similarly placed to permit site screeding for coverings.

The solution to the problem would appear to be that the attachment of the insulating layers to the underside of horizontal slabs—which normally span room widths—should take place at the manufacturing works; in fact, this defeats the object of industrialized construction production.

This is the provision of constructional elements in finished sections capable of being made, handled, transported, and erected speedily without damage. If the insulating layer were exposed, damage would be inevitable. Wall slab internal insulating layers would, if exposed, not only be vulnerable to these damages, but also to occupational damage when fixed. Experimental work is in process using internal linings covered with plastic laminate; but, in addition to adding to the overall cost of the finished slab, a problem of jointing is posed because laminates, being flexible, usually curve outwards at their edges unless fixed to rigid backings.

Draught proofing may encourage condensation

The problem of condensation in new housing is not confined to industrialized flatted construction; it is occurring in new houses of relatively traditional design and construction. The causes are similar in many instances to those noted earlier coupled often with draught-proofing of doors and windows by which action natural ventilation is reduced. This economic measure does not take into consideration, however, the consequent rise in relative humidity which is produced by occupation without any corresponding increase in the insulating standards of the roof and other constructional enclosures.

A general reduction in the cost of electricity for space heating, to below even "off peak" levels, or the introduction of cheap district heating would solve more condensation problems of this type than would all the remedial measures which could be prescribed.

Cold roof spaces, condensation on ceilings

Low rise housing with pitched roofs covered with single lap tiling, slates, and sheet materials which do not require continuous support, comply with the building regulations relative to the restriction of heat losses through complete enclosing constructions, provided they are constructed with underlying sarking felts of thin bitumastic hessian—

or even heavy building papers—covering roof spaces over plasterboarded ceilings with aluminium foil reflective insulating backing. The thin outer coverings do not, however, always prevent quite cool air conditions developing in the air spaces above the ceilings. The principal heat loss restricting feature of the construction is the aluminium foil which, being a reflective insulator, is only resistant to radiation losses. It has little, if any, effect upon convective loss and practically none upon conductive loss. About 50% of the heat lost through ceiling to roof spaces is by radiation; the remainder is by convection. The reduction of loss by radiation when foil is employed is not more than 90% which means that 45% of the possible radiant heat loss is intercepted; none of the convective-conductive loss is restricted. Although air cannot move through the aluminium membrane, the foil acts as an exchange surface to convection currents lifting heat to contact its underside, by conducting the heat and passing it from its upper surface to those above. The plaster thickness is useful in respect of convective-conductive losses. The roof spaces are seldom windtight and, whilst this may help to "dry out" moisture from woodwork and air within the loft space, it also cools that space particularly when outside air conditions are cold. As in a similar situation with ventilated cavity walls (see p. 201), inside protection is greatly reduced; in the case of this type of roof, heat loss resistance is reduced almost to that offered by the tiles and felt.

Unfortunately, the plaster thickness is not impermeable to either water or its vapour. Thus air laden with water vapour, rising as it will to the ceiling, then diffuses up through the plaster and comes into contact with the foil which, if cooled by cool loft conditions, will provide condense conditions for the vapour. If this situation continues, the plaster will become saturated and thereby lose its insulative qualities. The appearance of condense upon the ceiling surface will commence at this stage, and droplets will collect into drips (see Vol. 1, p. 21, fig. 9). Only a prolonged drying out condition will prevent the frequent re-appearance of droplets once this plaster condition has arisen. In a bedroom it will do so each night if occupied; exhaled moisture vapour raising the relative humidity of the air to near dew point at ceiling contact levels. When the room is vacated each morning the condense will re-evaporate and leave the ceiling surface, together with perhaps one-sixteenth of an inch depth of plaster, with a dry appearance for a few hours late in the day as the relative humidity of the air is lowered by ventilation. If the ventilation is insufficient then the gain in internal air temperature caused by raised daytime outside air temperatures, or warmer drier air circulating from other parts of the house, will assist in the drying-out process.

Aluminium foil offers no appreciable resistance at all to heat passed to it by contact, so moist warm air from the room below permeates the plaster and is virtually in contact with the cold loft air; condense must, therefore, occur as the heat lost thereto reduces the lower air to dew point temperature. Also, re-evaporation of the moisture from the plasterboard can only take place back and downwards into the room air; unfortunately, since moisture laden air is less dense than drier air at similar temperatures, the least favourable conditions for re-evaporation will exist adjacent to the ceiling plaster.

If we omit the foil vapour barrier and use only a porous insulator—plain plasterboard—even one covered with, say, fibreglass matting, or loose vermiculite filling between joists, then the moisture laden warm air will rise through it into the loft space and condense will occur upon the underside of the outer coverings; possibly on the felt underlay or on the rafters and other cooled surfaces. If it can reach the topside of the underlay, through laps in the felt where this is bitumastic or otherwise impermeable in the sheet, then the condense might drip from the battens or run between the tiles to the outside of the roof. Where, however, it drips from the underside of outer surfaces on to the upperside of the ceiling, most occupiers (and also many not too well-experienced technicians, interested laymen, newspapermen and other newsseekers) assume that the roof is leaking and complaints of "raining in" are made. If a comparatively new roof is involved, much unwelcome public criticism may well ensue.

Remedial measures

Condensation upon top floor ceilings of this type can be prevented by maintaining suitable space heating within the rooms over a sufficient period, combined with a reasonable degree of ventilation preferably with the incoming air brought from the outside of the building. But, of course, this practice increases the cost of heating as these rooms may well be normally unheated at all during daytime. Where a non-heating solution is sought, then sufficient ventilation alone may suffice. If the ceiling as a whole is permeable, then ventilation of the loft space as often advised would indeed provide a solution. It is wondered, however, whether contained within this remedy there is perhaps a breach of the building regulations in respect of restrictive demands imposed therein against heat losses. If the loft is ventilated from and to an external air mass, the above ceiling space should be regarded as having an "external surface" to the loft; and the only resistances to heat loss upwards which can be recognized for the calculation of the heat loss coefficient—the "U" value—will be those of the ceiling alone. In this case, the outer coverings only "shelter" the ceiling. An upward correction in heat loss from "normal" to "sheltered" alone is unlikely to bring the "U" value into line with the regulation requirements. Some additional insulation would have to be added to the ceiling; when assisted by some space heating and normal ventilation, this usually provides a satisfactory solution to the problem. Where there is already a vapour barrier below it with an absorbent depth of material, for example foil backed plasterboard, then once that absorbent depth is dry—and this is important—a further vapour barrier fixed with airtight joints below the absorbent layer will prevent diffusion of vapour-laden air upwards into the absorbent layer and its contact with the cooled upper vapour barrier. Providing that it is airtight it will also prevent the depth of absorbent insulator becoming saturated with condense, even if some still occurs upon the new surface, and so the absorbent insulator will maintain its heat loss resisting quality.

Care in use of vapour barriers

Where some condense still continues intermittently, a depth of absorbent material below the added vapour barrier will take this up invisibly and allow its re-evaporation when drier air conditions recur. Even a layer of absorbent ceiling decorative paper may do this, particularly the unglazed relief patterns, pebble dashes etc. It is unwise to paint such ceilings with impermeable paint as non-absorption of slight condense could result in drips; water-thinned paints and some emulsions are useful. The application of a further layer of foil backed plasterboard, foil side upwards, would serve the purpose of added vapour barrier and additional absorbent underlining. Airtight foil joints must be secured by the use of impervious applied adhesives or tape. Expanded polystyrene underlinings to ceilings are very popular and, since this material has a very low moisture and vapour absorptive value, it acts as a combined insulator and vapour barrier. Proprietary two-millimetre thick roll materials, which are sold to underline wallpapers, present a problem because the thickness is insufficient to add enough heat loss resistance to the ceiling considered as a unit. Where tiles of thicker substance are used, then trouble could arise in the joints if they provide permeable channels for rising vapour-laden air through to the upper barrier.

Insulating ceilings

When replacing a ceiling where condensation has frequently occurred or installing a new ceiling where its occurrence might be suspected, then a suitable thickness—three-quarters to one inch—of air pocketed or gas expanded insulation material of a non-porous nature should be used. If porous, then a material sealed on both sides within an impervious vapour barrier is indicated. There are several proprietary forms, including cellulose fibres and paper based types. All are lightweight and easily fixed, usually with adhesives, to existing soffits or joists.

The only alternative treatment (but this should not be

applied in roof spaces into which moist air can gain access and condense) is to cover the topside of the existing ceiling with a similar thickness of air pocket insulating material, either over the joists or closely fitted between them. The loose exfoilated vermiculite types are most easily filled in but glass fibre mats, slightly over in-between joist spacings in width, tucked in can also prove useful. Incidentally, the mats can be removed completely and easily without loss or damage if so desired at a later date; the loose fills cannot. In all cases of laying over joists or between joists in pitched roofs, especially those of low pitch, difficulty arises near the eaves where working space becomes very restricted in height. It is important, however, that all areas of the affected ceiling should be covered if patches or strips of condense are not to be left. The eaves often prove to be the worst areas where this placing difficulty occurs: stiff insulation boards or mats can, however, usually be pushed into these tight places.

If the roof space is unventilated and there is an effective vapour barrier in the ceiling, lining the underside of the rafters with almost any type of insulator can prove satisfactory if it gives the roof construction a better "U" value as a whole and a suitable added resistance to heat loss below the outer covering.

The spread of flame values must be considered when considering the provision of new or overhead insulation to the underside of a ceiling or soffit in any building subject to control under building regulations. Plasterboards are satisfactory; but expanded polystyrene would most certainly have to be of the self-extinguishing grade and many of the cheap tiles are not.

Expanded polystyrene

Expanded polystyrene is a fragile material if exposed to abrasion or impact. Its use without a protective covering is not recommended in positions such as dadoes or walls, or even at higher levels if liable to surface damage. Neither should it be fixed where adjacent temperatures are liable to remain at 175°F (79·4°C) for other than very short periods, for example around hot water and heating pipes and tanks; also, it should not be used within close range of a hot air fan or immediately above or within range of radiant heaters. Convectional hot air currents rising from conventional radiating surfaces or hot air warming system outlets can also create too high a temperature to make its use satisfactory. An important point to remember in this connection is that so long as heat is applied, it is gradually built up, or stored, in all kinds of air and gas pocketed insulating materials with reflective surfaced pockets (see Vol. 1, p. 47, fig. 18).

Expanded polystyrene melts at about 212°F (100°C), the boiling point of water, and even if it is of self-extinguishing grade it will burn all the time it is in contact with an independent flame. Fortunately there is so little actual solid material in the expanded sheet, not more than five per cent, that when it does burn it adds little to the fire as a whole. The author has seen several instances where, as the result of a pan of cooking fat catching fire in a domestic kitchen, tiled expanded polystyrene ceiling coverings vanished in almost a matter of seconds. The use of this material also restricts decoration: oil paints soften the material and papers can only be stripped from it with suitable adhesive solvents. Knife stripping cannot be contemplated. Where papers are pasted over this material they, too, become very vulnerable to damage by abrasion. Where airborne dirt alone is the soiling agent, it remains cleaner as an exposed covering than would an uninsulated surface because it presents a warmer surface to the room air; and also dirt particles are not so readily pushed thereon (see p. 226). Warm, moist air rises in rooms by convectional movement; in kitchens, particularly, this air often carries grease or fat molecules evaporated from the liquid during cooking. The rising action of the warmer contaminated air creates pressure beneath the ceiling which is just as efficient a "bumping" force as would be that resulting from more static mass density pressure. Care should therefore be exercised in the use of this and similar materials, particularly when exposed on soffits or near sources of heat.

Tiles of this and other insulating material having a vinyl

or other moisture proof plastic surface, from which deposited condensed grease and adhering dirt can be wiped, are more suitable for kitchens or even bathrooms. The surface barrier, here, is not required as a vapour barrier but as a suitable protective surface presenting a smooth washable face rather than the pitted one of the cut pores or cavities of the expanded insulator. There are some tiles and sheets on the market which have a glazed finish, secured by extrusion process manufacture, moulding or heat treatment instead of the more usual cutting from blocks. With these the surface will be without cut pores and therefore responds to wiping with a cloth. They present a rather artificial sugar-like glazed surface, appearing constantly wet in comparison with the matt, brilliant white of the cut type. Furthermore, the moulded type are usually slightly ribbed to a pattern or have a textured raised lined surface; thus they are likely to be difficult to wipe over without leaving dirt or grease smears along the raised features.

28: Ventilation—Conventional and fan-assisted; dehumidification

THERE is no doubt that sufficient ventilation to and from the external air is the best remedy to offset condensation in a kitchen, bathroom, or any other room where steam is generated. The most effective room ventilation is obtained from natural convection induced air movement by having low level inlets and high level outlets in the same wall; the reverse when a fan is used. A fan will be most effective if it propels air inwards, provided that openings other than the ventilation outlets from the room are kept closed. This effects a far better general air change than can an expulsion fan which tends to stream air to comparatively restricted paths from inlet to outlet without causing turbulence and general movement. Where it is impossible to keep outlets such as doors closed, this being the case in many domestic kitchens, the high level expulsion fan is the only reasonable and practical mechanical aid. The kitchen cooker is, however, the principal source of steam since the output is maintained possibly over several hours. Sinks and even wash tubs have less lengthy usage; in fact nowadays some modern washing machines pump their hot waste water direct to the waste pipe from sealed tubs so that very little steam, if any, is released into the room. Cooker steam and vapourized fats can be dealt with by fitting hoods over the cooker area. With the addition of a fan exhaust direct to the outside air, these also considerably reduce condensation problems in kitchens; they are essential where "open planning" of a house results in the kitchen portion on the ground floor being open above working top level, perhaps through open divider units, to the lounge or living-room/dining-room section and especially so if this section is itself open to the stairs to an upper floor. Where extractor aids are not provided there are always moist air movements from the ground to upper floors and, if the walls, ceilings and windows of the upper rooms are not well insulated against heat losses, then condense will almost certainly occur not only on walls and ceilings but also on bedding, clothing, etc. Extractor hoods are particularly valuable here because they not only reduce condensation but also prevent grease vapour and cooking odours travelling upstairs.

Condensation on to cold surfaces

It is true that central heating from a source on a lower floor heats the rooms upstairs in "open planning", but it must be remembered that warm air can carry invisibly more moisture vapour than can cooler air. Therefore, with only slight heat losses in the upper floors, dew point can easily be reached. Even if walls and ceilings do not present cooling surfaces, the following surfaces do so: windows, cold ceramic vitreous enamelled cast iron bathroomware and particularly plastic water closet flushing cisterns which are, of course, constantly filled with cold water. Incidentally, plastic laminated furniture, fitments, doors, etc., have hard glazed surfaces and so resist heat gain into supporting structures to which they are bonded that they, too, remain cold and mist over, particularly in kitchens, cool bedrooms, bathrooms, and on landings. If a hood is not used in the kitchen, this misting often includes condensed grease which, unlike condensed moisture, will not re-evaporate. P.V.C. handrails on steel cores also invite condense and become misty and slippery to touch especially where metal brackets, pinned to walls, penetrate into cold conductive materials and act as heat loss bridges. Suspicion of a leaking W.C. cistern can often be attributed to condensation over its surfaces running down to drip from a rib or bracket as the discrete drops gather. This will happen during moist summer or autumn weather even in outside water closets equipped with cast iron cisterns. Water from company's mains or drawn from other than very shallow wells, seldom exceeds 40°F (4·4°C) in temperature; W.C. cisterns fed directly would be unlikely to attain a shell temperature much above this unless they stand unflushed in a warm room for a considerable period. Moist plastic water closet seats are a nuisance.

Estimated speeds, actual direction, and conditions of turbulence of air movement can be traced and observed if a visible vapour which has a specific gravity similar to air and which does not readily diffuse or condense is released into the air: titanium tetra-chloride, a liquid, will give off such a vapour if an uncorked bottle of it is placed in the airstream under investigation.

Cold water storage tanks in roof spaces also provide efficient condense surfaces to moisture carried into the loft through pervious ceilings. In bygone days, drip trays were provided beneath the tanks to catch condense drips; to-day these are never seen, and are unnecessary provided the tank is enclosed by insulation having its own or an added outer vapour barrier. The reason for lagging a cold tank is usually protection from frost but, indirectly, heat gain from surrounding air is also prevented; if unduly moist, this air would condense some of its moisture on to the tank side should its heat level be lowered by loss of heat thereto. Here again "roof leaks", dripping on to ceilings, can result from condense drips from unlagged cold pipes and tanks above; this can be actually seen where such pipes etc. are exposed to view beneath a ceiling.

Anti-condensation paints

Condensation on to cold pipes and tanks can, if the condition is not too severe, be prevented from recurring or the condense temporarily absorbed by coating the surfaces with anti-condensation paints. These paints have powdered cork, asbestos fibres, or some other porous material as a filler carried in a binder that is not anti-capillary in action; they thus provide a very thin absorbent insulation layer between the moist air and the cold metal surface. They prevent the tendency to slight condense or, if some does occur, hold the droplets and prevent drips forming; therefore, providing the condense period is not prolonged it will re-evaporate when drier air conditions return. Thus they are useful where short periods of dew point conditions, interspersed by longer drying times, are likely to occur. One disadvantage in the use of these paints on plain steel pipes and surfaces is that the paint soon becomes rust-coloured if vapour proof priming coats are not used.* Sprayed asbestos is now available and provides a better and more permanent remedy, as also do prepared vapour-proof preformed plastic insulators. For this purpose, expanded polystyrene is suitable for cold water pipes and tank surfaces; but polyurethane would be required for heating service pipes which are liable to cause condense during non-heating seasons. As with tanks and pipes, we are keeping the air heat out!

Cork-filled anti-condensation paints are not suitable for application to walls or ceilings. They soil very rapidly and, as is the case with most soft absorbent surfaces, are difficult to clean; in addition, these paints leave surfaces which have a pimpled finish. Any rubbing action breaks the bond between the soft fillers and the binder and usually leaves bare or smooth patches. It is preferable to carry out renovation by cleaning off completely and re-coating; this is the only method which should be used in kitchens where condensed grease has been absorbed.

Treating walls and ceilings

Surfaces liable to induce condensation in kitchens, where condense, or grease, extractor hoods are not provided, should be lagged with pre-formed units; or sprayed coverings with grease resistant membranes on the outside may be used. The surfaces can then safely be cleaned with soap and water,

* The following publications all give valuable information about other paints in relation to problems of damp conditions:

    Building Research Station Digests (September 1953), No. 58 and Second Series (revised, January 1966), No. 21.

    Ministry of Public Buildings and Works, Advisory Leaflet No. 57 (1964).

detergents, or grease solvents. Suitable lagging materials could be surfaced with various non-ferrous, stainless steel and plastic materials; thin vinyl sheeting, if bonded securely to rigid insulation with vapour-tight joints, can also be useful.

Micro-thicknesses of expanded polystyrene serve the same purpose as anti-condensation paints and, except that they have built-in resistance to vapour diffusion, can be used instead providing the considerations relative to cleaning and protection are first noted and allowances made. They are not, however, suitable for surfaces where consistent surface heating exceeds 160 to 170°F (71·1 to 76·7°C), or where vapourized grease or fat will be carried in the air streams passing over them.

Anti-condensation paints with asbestos fibre fillings are sometimes used as underlinings to a papered finish on wall areas where limited condense conditions exist. This could be a satisfactory remedy providing that re-evaporation can take place through the paper; whereas the use of micro-thicknesses of expanded polystyrene, which will not absorb condense, might result in more than saturation conditions occurring in the paper covering. Everything will depend upon the thickness of the polystyrene, the intensity of the humidity of the air, and the conductivity of the wall. An anti-condensation paint—"Inertol Dinaphon V. 33", which is a material having a dispersion of plastic resin nature with crystalline and granular fillers—has been used successfully on ceilings and upper wall surfaces to a swimming pool and to an abattoir.[*] Any thickness of porous paint and expanded polystyrene also provides a degree of acoustic sound deadening to surfaces so treated.

De-humidification may be essential

De-humidifiers have to be used in cases where it is essential, for reasons of hygiene, to have hard non-absorbent

[*] Manufactured by Intertol Company Ltd. West Carr Lane, Stoneferry, Hull. The material can only be pump-spray applied and the minimum thickness is said to be $\frac{1}{10}$ in.

wall and ceiling surfaces in rooms where high relative humidity will exist and sufficient air change ventilation cannot be provided. Kitchens, tobacco leaf sorting rooms, laundries etc. are not the only rooms which might necessitate the installation of de-humidifiers; cool, or even cold, stores can develop very high relative humidity of air content from moisture evaporation from stored goods and the use of this treatment may be indicated.

De-humidifiers usually mechanically cool incoming air to produce condense within their containers, and then release the drier air at a suitable re-warmed temperature which again reduces relative humidity; de-greasing of air can also be achieved by similar apparatus. Some units will perform both functions and they can be obtained in quite small sizes for use in domestic kitchens as a substitute for extractor ventilated hoods over cookers. Where mechanical cooling cannot be used, deliquescent chemicals are indicated; in such units, however, arrangements have to be made for drying off the absorbent material or for its periodic replacement. Mechanical types usually require means of condense drainage for collected water and, if they also have to deal with grease, the replacement of grease absorbent filters is also necessary. In commercial installations, de-humidifiers and air de-greasing units are often used as heat exchange units to other warming plant through the moisture condense section; the de-greasing section utilizes grease solvents from which the greases and fats can be recovered by distillation or specific gravity separation. A refrigerator is a de-humidifier unit; the condensed moisture vapour freezes to ice upon the cooler coils.

Condense may create structural hazards

Fish and potato chip frying ranges present the combined problems of steam from the fish and potatoes plus the vapourized cooking oils or dripping. The solution nowadays is the use of covered ranges with hoods coupled to trunking through which the vapour laden air is drawn to condensers and separators; the cleaned and dried air is then discharged into the furnace chimney of gas-fired ranges or the extract vents to electric ranges. Where older premises are equipped only with hoods over the ranges the furnace flues, or extract flues to which they are connected, require the following: salt-glazed stoneware, grease and moisture-tight linings, and suitable condense drainage. Buildings have been seen by the author in which the whole of the breast, large areas of adjacent wall brickwork, plasterwork thereon, and wood linings and fittings to cupboards and adjoining the wall, became saturated with condensed grease and drying oils in cases where old domestic flues had been used for frying ranges. This nuisance not only affected the premises concerned, but also rooms in the adjoining property because the wall in which the flues were contained was a party wall. If a fire had occurred, the brickwork itself would have burned like a torch as the oils vapourized; without fire, the nuisance was that of a rank oily odour, severe greasy surface staining which collected dirt and fluff, and grease-soiling of clothes hung in the cupboards. The only real remedy was complete demolition and rebuilding of the chimney breasts with new bricks and properly lined flues; steam and detergent degreasing of the brickwork; stripping of plaster to adjoining areas and replastering, with grease resistant rendering as the first coat; and the removal and renewal of all the saturated woodwork.

A case was referred to in Vol. 1, p. 59, where renewal of brickwork became necessary as the result of frozen condense rupturing the actual bricks. Thus we are reminded that condensation is not just an inconvenience or a nuisance; it is the primary cause of many and various cases of structural weakness and failure.

Dealing with misty glass

Readers will be familiar with the anti-misting devices employed to keep clear windscreens of motor vehicles, aircraft, and railway locomotive cabins. Usually a warmed air stream flows over the inner surface and thus heats the glass sufficiently to prevent condense or, alternatively, to reduce its intensity to an extent that individual molecules do not coalesce to form droplets upon the surface. Such devices can be fed with warmed air from exhaust or cooling engine heat; also, they may be electrically heated from batteries or generators. External icing and freezing of internal condense, if the latter has been allowed to occur, are dealt with at the same time. Anti-misting solutions simply provide a surface upon which water loses its surface tensions and so cannot gather or retract into globules or droplets which, by reflecting light from their surfaces and refracting light internally, produce the misting appearance—the continuous sheet of water produced by the loss of tension gives little reflective or refractive distortion. Shop windows, in fact any window, can be kept free of mist condensation by these methods. An unheated oscillating electric fan will often utilize room air to effect this; alternatively, low-powered tubular electric heaters placed along the bottom of the glass panes provide warmed air convectional upward flow over the inner surface to keep the glass clear, as will domestic radiators placed beneath glazed wall areas. Severe down draughts are also prevented, from otherwise unwarmed glazed surfaces. Even cold wall areas are protected against condense by these methods. The use of a room wall length heating pipe at low level or a skirting radiator to an exposed wall, instead of the conventional radiator at one part of it only, can greatly improve a borderline condense condition on the other areas.

Heat induced convection currents keep walls dry

Buildings which are liable to condense upon walls—even if induced by deliquescent surface conditions—or where slight rising or penetrative dampness occurs, can be protected by these methods providing, of course, that the moisture vapour induced by evaporation can be conveyed away from other condense surfaces either by mixing with large quantities of drier or warmer air or by external evacuation. Placing low-powered, 60 watts per linear foot, electric heating tubes as skirting heaters and creating warmed convection currents over cool, slightly damp wall areas has proved successful in keeping intermittently occupied houses dry during vacated periods. These heaters have also prevented condensation occurring when re-occupation of the premises initially created higher relative humidity. A room in a Dorsetshire cottage where condense occurred on the inner surfaces of external rubble masonry walls two feet thick having no damp-proof course and rendered inside to dadoe level, has been protected for the past three years with two four-foot tubes used only during autumn, winter, and early spring periods of non-occupation. The room measures 22 ft. 0 in. × 12 ft. 0 in. with a ceiling height of 9 ft., and its solid floor is over 12 in. below street level to two walls. The condense had previously occurred regularly during periods of non-occupation and in the absence of normal heating. As is the case in this cottage, the exhaust heat from small domestic refrigerators placed near cold slightly damp walls—such as in a walk-in larder or pantry—will also keep dry the wall areas behind and above them. Protective devices other than the refrigerator can be operated by switches responsive to air humidity, and so prove very economical in the prevention of spoilt decoration and furniture etc. placed near to such walls. Not only is any slight rising and penetrative dampness dealt with, but the air movements and ventilation induced and maintained completely clear mustiness arising when premises have been closed for a time.

Condensation grooves and channels

Where condensation on the inside of glazed windows, or other cold vertical areas, cannot or need not be prevented the provision of externally drained condensation collecting channels at the foot of the areas prevents water damage to decorations etc. below. Inclined and domed roof glazing needs condensation slots over its curbs, or channels to prevent collection and dripping of gathered condense where free under-surface flow is interrupted. Slot gaps should be wide enough not to become dirt-particle filled—either from dust deposited internally with the condense moisture or driven in by outside wind—and so as not to induce capillary access of rain flowing over the outer surface. $\frac{1}{8}$ in. wide drainage slots or $\frac{1}{4}$ in. diameter tubes are normally sufficient. Tubes should be lined with non-ferrous metal or plastic if the material through which they are drilled is not itself resistant to air/moisture corrosion.

Cold bridges

Condensation on to cold bridges spanning metal ties through sandwich construction or traditional cavity construction is, if arising in small patches, quite clearly of very borderline proportions and occurs when dew point conditions are almost present adjacent to the adjoining non-bridged areas. The patches usually appear as slightly dirtier or discoloured areas in decorations; rarely are moist or wet actual surface conditions seen.

Very little added insulative material is needed to combat such patch condensation; paper-thin expanded polystyrene is sufficient. Alternatively, one or perhaps two coats of anti-condensation paint with a smooth surface finish can also be used; this treatment is less likely to suffer abrasive damage than the polystyrene and will not show ridging around the perimeter of the patch. The paint can be thinned-out around the edges; this is not possible with polystyrene.

Solid bridging, caused by cavity closure building, where slates nailed or mortared to the skins, or bricks built tightly

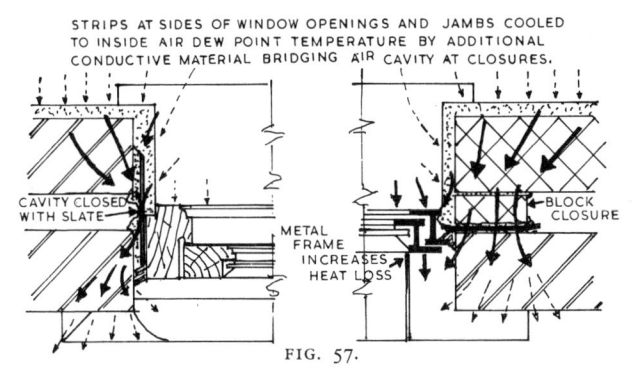

FIG. 57.

out to vertical slate or bitumastic felt damp-proof courses, call for similar treatment; but this has to be in strips, with the insulation carried about three inches wider than the dirty or stained wall band. One must not forget that part of the jamb, or reveal, surface coldness is due to air cooled by the glazing or metal window framing passing close over these surfaces. The added insulation will in this case prevent the surfaces losing heat to that air. Bridging caused by boot lintels arises by contact with the outer skin through the overhead damp-proof course; this will be more pronounced

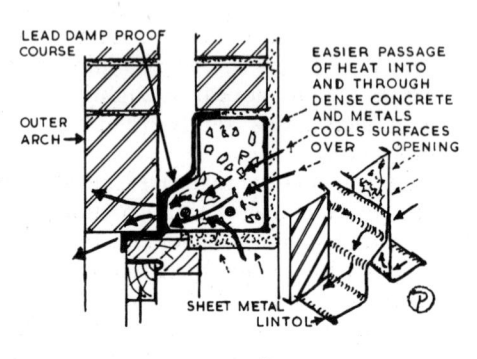

FIG. 58.

if the course is lead than if it is a felt. Pressed steel lintel supports to soldier arches, too, can cause bridging; so can pressed metal door frames used externally. The risk of bridging will be considerably reduced by the use of asbestos filled anti-condensation paint as undercoats internally to the frames, and the application of a liberal thickness of bitumastic or chlorinated rubber paint to the lintels before fixing.

29: Condensation in domestic flues

DOMESTIC flues are not immune from the effects of condensation. In this case the causes may be either the fuel, or a combination of fuel and burned household refuse; usage and exposure must, however, be added to either possibility. A constantly used domestic flue, irrespective of the fuel being burned, will not suffer from condense except for very short periods immediately after the fire is lit. Condensation of normal flue gases is unlikely once the structural enclosure has had time to warm up—i.e. the lining or, if unlined, the brickwork or other enclosing material; flues exposed to severe external cooling conditions are, of course, exceptions.

Before discussing the results of flue condensation, it is necessary to know from whence the moisture which is to condense comes.

Solid, oil, and gaseous fuels all contain hydrogen, and the process of commencement and continuation of combustion is a chemical reaction requiring oxygen. Coals and gas require about fifteen pounds weight of air per pound of fuel to burn efficiently. Oil fuels need twenty to twenty-two pounds. During combustion, hydrogen combines with oxygen in the proportions, one pound of hydrogen to eight pounds of oxygen, to give nine pounds of water (H_2O). The actual combination being two hydrogen atoms, as a molecule, combining with sixteen oxygen atoms. Each lb. of solid fuel consumed in combustion produces 0·4 lb. of water as a vapour; gas produces 1·33 lb., and oil 1·2 lb. Since, however, we usually buy our gas by the therm (100,000 Btu) it is useful to know that each therm produces 10·4 lb. of water vapour when burned; one gallon of paraffin produces 10 lb. This is why flueless oil stoves appear to be so efficient as space heaters; gas fires, too, where they are permitted to be used without flues. Release into the room of the moisture vapour of combustion very greatly increases relative humidity and thus the cooling power of the air is reduced; accordingly, people occupying the room begin to feel too warm because the evaporation of excess body moisture can no longer remove unwanted heat into the air. They will only feel cold when more body heat is lost than that which is necessary to maintain correct body temperature, 98·4°F (37°C). Actual air temperature is relatively unimportant to this body cooling process; one can be cool in dry air at 100°F (37·8°C) but warm in very moist air at 60°F (15·6°C) or even lower. Continuing inability to lose sufficient body heat leads to distress and even collapse.

Heating methods may aggravate dampness

Evaporation of moisture from walls—damp from other causes—into rooms where such heating methods are used is also reduced or even rendered impossible and the moisture will become noticeable where previously the dampness was perhaps not apparent. The affected wall or ceiling, or even floor surfaces, become saturated and will constitute a serious condense surface. The whole condition will revert to drying out when the heating season ends, but in the meantime decorations will suffer perhaps irreparably; also action resulting in deliquescent material formation, may cause recurrence of surface dampness during humid days of the non-heating season. Unless occupiers are aware of all of these facts they will assume that dampness, if this occurs on humid days, is exuding from the interior of construction or, if on an outside wall, from soffit or floor; and, therefore, will think that there is a penetrative leak. Much condensation into deliquescent surface material, or immediately behind porous surfaces, is mistaken for penetrative dampness.

Gel materials—such as paperhangers paste, gelatinous binders in adhesives and decorative materials, distempers etc.—if not thoroughly cleaned from plastered surfaces before redecoration, often take up atmospheric moisture at above dew point air temperature; they show darkened patches upon newer, superimposed porous redecorative covering membranes—distempers, wallpapers, etc.—and are similarly mistaken for penetrative leaks. When supposed or real dampness occurs upon internal surfaces on a dry day, or even immediately before rain commences, the surface material and its immediate backings should be carefully investigated. Where deliquescent conditions are believed to be the cause, the use of a paraffin stove in the room during a cold dry spell will confirm that internal atmospheric moisture is the cause of the trouble; a steaming kettle would also serve this purpose. Such tests are also useful where the possibilities of condensation occuring in a room are being investigated prior to proposed changes in heating or ventilating methods; also where change of user or alterations could result in raised relative humidity levels.

Structural additions may also aggravate dampness

The enclosure by an added extension room covering the windows or air bricks of an existing room with direct external means of ventilation will cause totally different air conditions in the room; this could cause a build-up in relative humidity sufficient to produce condense upon a formerly adequate remaining external wall. It could result in the appearance of rising dampness in that wall surface which was previously controlled by evaporation. Quite small changes in relative humidity and evaporative powers can cause startling results upon critical surfaces. An unexpected result of the addition of such extensions is that in winter the expected draught protection to the enclosed room does not, in fact, occur. When massive condensation upon the extension roof glazing or translucent sheeting occurs, indicating severe cooling of air in contact therewith, severe convection currents are set up in the air enclosed; these will, through ill-fitting partition windows, air bricks, open connecting doors or other aerial means, draw air from and push it into the enclosed room as efficiently as outside air movements and wind did previously. If the cost of complete reglazing is prohibitive, this should be carried out to the roof of the new building as this is the most important cooling surface; these measures will remedy the situation substantially although, of course, not completely as would the full and more costly procedure. An internal sun blind drawn below the roof glazing at night, when heat loss conditions are often most severe, will very considerably reduce the trouble where double glazing is not fitted; heavily folded curtains to windows and wall glazing also assist. Care should be taken, however, to maintain some ventilation to the external air or, with occupation, relative humidity may build up to uncomfortable conditions. Fans causing only turbulence within a confined air mass reduce temperature and humidity and so produce a cooling effect providing the ceilings, walls, windows or floor surfaces, against which they propel the air, are able to cool it. This will be relative to their surface heat condition and the heat conductive capacity of the material behind the surface. Cooling of saturated air, as long as it persists, results in condensation arising on the cooling surface. This will be unnoticed as long as it is absorbed into the surface; but when deposition rate exceeds that of absorption or when condense commences upon an impervious surface, the usual visual signs will be evident. In both cases, if the material behind the surface is not very conductive and able to pass the heat on to some other mass, the continued absorption of heat will result in warming both the surface and its backing with the resulting loss of cooling power to the air in contact.

Production of air with high relative humidity in a room by artificial, normal, or exceptional user means can be a method of identifying cold internal surface areas however small, and may enable the observer to decide their character and the extent of the insulating remedial measures necessary.

* * *

It is hoped that this diversion from condense conditions in chimney flues may have clarified some rather important points: now we return to discussion of combusion products in flues and the resulting damp conditions.

Combustion processes

Combustible substances commence to burn when sufficient oxygen is in contact with them and ignition temperature is reached. Quite often it is not necessary to actually apply a flame or spark to the fuel/oxygen mixture; ignition in this case is said to be spontaneous. Once ignited, combustion continues while ignition temperature is maintained and fuel and oxygen are present in the correct proportions and quantities. Gases, including those given off by solid and liquid boiler-fuels, have higher ignition temperatures than carbon left in the grate of a coal fire. It is therefore necessary to maintain a higher temperature over the fire if these are to burn and not be carried unburned into the flue; air, necessary for combustion, must be well mixed with these gases or vapours.

As solid or oil fuels heat up to ignition point they give up any moisture contained; the hot carbon then takes up oxygen from the air, releasing CO_2—two oxygen atoms combining with one carbon—and heat is released during this action to the extent of about 14,500 Btu per lb. of carbon involved. This added heat enables the CO_2 to combine with a further carbon particle to form $2CO$; in doing so, 9000 of the released Btu are re-absorbed. This cooling causes the combustible gas to combine with further oxygen from the air above the fire to form $2CO_2$—which reaction releases a further 10,000 Btu per lb.; fully burned, the carbon therefore provides 15,500 Btu per lb. Further useful heat comes from hydrogen in the fuel, $2H^2$ plus O which gives $2H_2O$, 52,000 Btu being released per lb. of hydrogen providing the moisture produced stays as vapour. Condensation of this amount of moisture vapour will release a further 9500 Btu, usually by heat losses to the flue casings and structure. Sulphur from solid fuels combines with oxygen to form SO_2 whilst providing 4000 Btu per lb. of sulphur. Oil is almost pure hydro-carbon: gas is a mixture of hydrogen, methane, and carbon monoxide plus a little sulphur.

Solid, and some liquid fuels also contain tarry, spirit and oily materials which evaporate during the heating processes before, during, and after, ignition temperatures. These vapours from volatile substances may burn or oxidize in the furnace or the lower parts of the flue or, without burning, they may be carried to the higher, cooler parts as a vapour. If they condense here, the liquors will soak into bricks, joints and, through porous plasters or renderings, to inside or outside surfaces where they will be visible as brown or black staining. There is often a pungent odour from such internal stains.

Acids produced from combustion may cause dampness

From our point of view, the significance of the reactions in the process of fuel combustion is that carbon dioxide and sulphur dioxide together with water, can produce liquid acids, carbonic and sulphuric. Both of these can be aggressive towards building materials, with results which ultimately cause conditions of dampness, or at least may aggravate the position.

Sulphur dioxide, SO_2, can take up a further oxygen molecule from air to become SO_3, sulphur trioxide. This substance can then combine with water, H_2O, to form sulphuric acid, H_2SO_4. The reaction from SO_2 to SO_3 is necessary because SO_2 is not readily soluble in water. Initially, SO_3 plus H_2 produces sulphurous acid, H_2SO_3; then, more slowly, the additional oxygen atom from the water completes the process to H_2SO_4. The acid is dilute but, unfortunately, dilute acids are often more aggressive to building materials than are concentrated.

Carbon dioxide plus water, CO_2 plus H_2O, gives carbonic acid, H_2CO_3, which in its dilute state readily dissolves calcium carbonate to form calcium bicarbonate solution. The latter, flowing out of limestones, evaporates on the surface to leave fine crystals as efflorescence. Sulphurous acid more readily attacks these crystals than the original material. In fact, upon stonework and other materials with a calcium carbonate content the two processes are seldom separated. Carbon dioxide is released when a sulphurous attack upon calcium carbonate occurs.

The flues of a building under consideration may not themselves be the cause of such attack: industrial and other combustion, road transport, etc., may all add water vapour, carbon/oxygen and sulphurous products to the air. After a period of years, buildings which are constantly exposed may suffer material deterioration. Where combustion within the building itself is the cause, evidence of the action and severe results may appear within months; everything depends upon condense conditions in the flues, the state of the linings thereof, and the thickness of the enclosing brickwork. The effects will be most severe where soft solid fuels and kitchen wastes are burned together or where fires are lit only intermittently during cold weather, especially where the flue is exposed. The severity will be controlled by the degree to which the brickwork can become moisture saturated, either from internal condense or soakage from an external source, together with any drying influences. The thicker the work, the less likely the trouble. Exposed stacks, enclosed with half-brick thick work and only mortar lined or parged, will suffer most; parts which remain wet longest will be more affected than those which either do not get wet or dry off quickly. Thus a domestic flue on an internal wall seldom suffers. The use of "coked", smokeless and sulphur free fuels, reduces the possibilities; these still produce the CO_2 and the water vapour, but the SO_2 is absent.

Smoke abatement and clean air legislation have done much to reduce the quantities of suspended solids in metropolitan air, but analysis of the records from apparatus in London during the six years immediately following the application of the Clean Air Act of 1954, shows the following:

Year	SO_2 in parts per million of air by volume	Solids (smoke) in milligrams per 100 cubic metres
1955	8·0	33
1956	8·3	34
1957	7·8	29

Year	SO_2 in parts per million of air by volume	Solids (smoke) in milligrams per 100 cubic metres
1958	8·1	27
1959	7·4	25
1960	7·4	19

From this table it can be seen that whilst there has been a systematic reduction in the solids, the sulphur dioxide has remained relatively steady.

Crystallization and efflorescence

Ordinary flues, unless constructed or lined with acid resisting materials such as salt glazed stoneware pipes, sulphate resistant cement or high silica (refractory) bricks bedded in fire cement or sulphate resistant cement mortar, contain oxides of calcium, magnesium and sodium. Aluminates are also present where Portland cement is used.

All acids readily combine with metals to form salts. The substances mentioned above are metals and the salts formed when the acid is sulphuric include: calcium sulphate, magnesium sulphate, sodium sulphate, and sulphoaluminate. The combinations also include the production of water. Calcium oxide, CaO, plus sulphuric acid, H_2SO_4, produce calcium sulphate, $CaSO_4$ plus H_2O; magnesium oxide, MgO and the other oxides produce similar products, a sulphate and water. The sulphates are powders, but water enables crystallization to take place. This involves increase in bulk or expansion. Added water, such as additional condensate from a flue or penetrative rain, can take these substances into solution; the calcium dissolving most slowly. Solutions of magnesia and sodium produce the characteristic white powdery deposit, efflorescence, when they are evaporated at a surface from pores. New brickwork often shows this quite quickly: the added water in this case coming from the mortar itself or the bricks where it has been absorbed during erection of the building or during storage in stacks.

The sulphates are often present in bricks in minute quantities as the result of the burning processes of manufacture; efflorescence from this cause will cease after a time. Calcium sulphate is seldom a cause of efflorescence. These surface deposits do no harm, except to aluminium alloy metals; this is why 99·9% pure aluminium is recommended for roof covering and, particularly, weather flashings. Even then fresh cement mortar will attack the aluminium whilst its setting processes continue, ceasing immediately they are completed. It is advisable to paint the turned-in edges of flashings with bitumastic paint to prevent this action where strong cement mortars are used for pointing.

Spalling of surfaces

If, however, the crystallization takes place within pores near the surface the expansion of formation will, in a softish or brittle material, cause portions to burst off; this action is called spalling. The effect of dissolved gases within a structure often shows first where pointing of porous brick or rubble stonework, shallow in depth, is hard or dense. This defect is often erroneously attributed solely to frost.

If spalling occurs beneath an impervious surface, paint for instance, the paint will blister and hard dense renderings will burst off their backings. It will be realized how important were the considerations of hair cracks in such renderings and, further, how applied spaced-off claddings can assist in preventing driven rain penetration from outside whilst moisture produced and absorbed inside is permitted to evaporate. Internal surface plaster eruptions very often result from such penetrations and, when they occur adjacent to flues, are nearly always the result of condense from the flue gases.

In mortars as well as lime and cement plastered coats and renderings, where silica sands form the aggregate, it is the matrix binding these grains together which is attacked and where the crystallization and expansion take place. This results in the loss of material strength within the material and its ability to adhere to its supporting backing. Brickwork or stonework, the joints of which are badly sulphated, become piles of bricks or stones held apart by the mortar instead of being held together by it. Susceptible stones and soft bricks can become shapes of powder mixed with crystals which, if they dehydrate or dry, also become powders. Plasters will soften, swell, then dry and powder off with the slightest abrasion; if held back by paper decorations they become deliquescent "sponges", ready to absorb moisture vapour from the air, at above normal dew point. The sulphates also bleach the papers.

In the northern hemisphere, in cases where distortion occurs in a slender chimney stack or thin parapet wall where the joints are unequally affected due to varying degrees of saturation, this usually takes the form of curving over to the south—because the sun dries off the southern aspects from time to time, whilst the northern remain damp (see fig. 59).

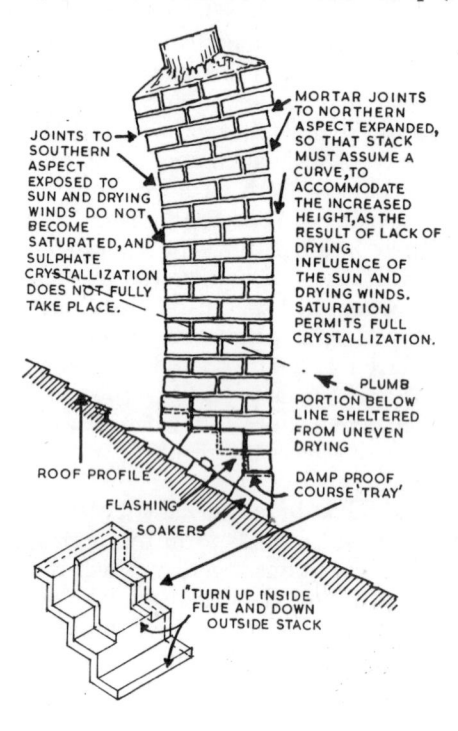

FIG. 59.

Therefore, greater amounts of expansion occur in the latter joints than in the former; the effect of this being a "wedging" up of the northern elevations to form the outer curve. Any portions of the stack sheltered all round from drying conditions, remain straight.

FIG. 59a. *Both chimneys serve domestic boilers. Right hand is solid fuel fired, in constant use and is slightly out of plumb. Left hand was solid fuel fired, intermittently used but went out of plumb badly where maximum sulphating occurred just above roof. Its terminal is a metal liner, put in when the boiler was replaced by a gas fired one, plumbed up, you will notice.*

30: Remedies for results of condensation in stacks and flues

CHIMNEY stacks cannot be repaired once they have become sulphated above roof level. The fact that they are affected is evidence that crystallization has taken place from inside, and is therefore present to the full thickness of the walls and any remaining linings. Repointing or outside rendering, which is often carried out as an attempted remedy, will only remain intact for a few months even if there is no distortion from vertical. Such measures merely add to the difficulty which absorbed condensed moisture encounters in reaching the outer evaporative surface, and the longer a sulphated material

FIG. 59b. *Lower Courses were only repointed—a few months later this had burst off. Upper part was rebuilt with clean bricks and new mortar.*

remains wet the worse are the effects. The pointing or rendering will, if absorbent, rapidly become affected; if dense, it will burst off.

Complete rebuilding of the affected stack is the only satisfactory solution and, ultimately, is the most economical. It is essential to insist that all affected bricks and jointings are pulled down until sound work is exposed, even if this requires going below roof covering level. If the stack had a proper damp-proof course tray at six inches above roof slope or outer surface level, to weather the flashings, then it is unlikely that any work below that level will be affected—except in very exposed conditions, or where the stack continues vertically downwards on one or more elevations as part of the external wall or as a projecting breast. If the defects do extend downwards, demolition should be continued to avoid any risk of having to do this after the upper work is completed—a very expensive job.

Sulphated demolition materials should not be re-used

None of the material arising from the demolition should be re-used in rebuilding—not even "sound" bricks. In their estimates builders, in particular, should ignore architects' or surveyors' instructions in specifications to: "clean and set aside sound bricks for re-use" or, "rebuild the stack with existing sound bricks and make out with new to match existing." Do not even contemplate re-using them for hardcore filling under concrete pavings or floors. They are saturated with sulphates and will rapidly transfer these to new concrete laid over such fillings, especially if the soil below is wet. The only use that should be even considered for bricks from sulphated demolition would be as loose fillings to surface water soakaway pits providing they are sited where soakage therefrom cannot wash sulphates in solution to gain contact with other structural or service work. Sulphated mortars and lime renderings must not be re-ground in mortar mills for re-use. They, too, will cause similar trouble; if anything, the mortars are even more potent than are the bricks. They are, however, valued by horticulturists for use as fertilizers for some shrubs; they should not, however, be used for plants growing against walls of buildings or where soakage could contact underground services or structural work.

Conformation with Building Regulations

If the requirements of the building regulations are complied with, rebuilding of the stack and flues will today, and in future, prevent recurrence of sulphating except that occurring from chemicals from the bricks of the outer construction or the mortar in which they are jointed and arising from external rainwater penetration only—not from internal condense. The current regulations require that all flues must be lined with acid resistant linings jointed so as to prevent condense running or soaking into porous enclosures, and rendering or parging is not permitted as a lining. Additionally, in London the topmost twelve courses of brick construction—and presumably a similar height, 3 ft. 0 in. of stone or other porous constructional materials—must be jointed, not just pointed, in cement mortar.

In a case where exposure conditions are severe and the exposed length of a stack above the roof has been rebuilt with half-brick enclosing work only, coating the outside surfaces with a colourless water-repellent solution after constructional moisture has thoroughly dried out will assist in combating sulphation occurring from the brickwork itself for a few years. This treatment need only be applied to the elevations which will become, and remain, wet; but treating the whole will not cause complications.

The alternative would be to rebuild with 9 in. surrounding brickwork, using bricks of very low sulphate content.

Flexible metal flue liners

Suitable flue linings have been mentioned previously (see p. 260); to these can be added stainless steel which can be obtained as very flexible tubes. These tubes should be used where: the whole flue is not demolished; where a sound but unlined existing flue is to be brought into use for a new fuel which is likely to produce considerable condense, gas or oil for instance; or where a slow combustion or magazine solid fuel boiler is to be used. Only the pot and a course or two of existing brickwork will need to be removed and rebuilt as the tube can be threaded down from the top of the stack. Flue linings do not necessarily prevent condense in the flue; they can, however, assist in this way if they are spaced off the outer structural enclosure, and if the resulting cavity is either filled with lightweight concrete or some other non-combustible and decay resisting insulating material or can be sealed airtight.

In the event of incomplete combustion in a boiler firebox or other appliance which is either gas or oil fired, any unfilled cavity could act as a trap to hold explosive gas mixtures unless the inner lining can be guaranteed to remain gastight. The dangers of this are obvious, but from our consideration of this subject we should insist (a) that linings which convey condensible vapours and gases which can dissolve into their condense do not permit penetration of either gas, condense, or solution into the structural work, plastering or rendering, and (b) that they do not cause cooling of gases or vapours to condense condition. Thus the primary reason for the requirements of the regulations is also our consideration.

Spaced off flexible gastight metal liners with an unfilled cavity left around them from which condensate cannot, and heat cannot readily, pass can be of other cheaper metals when gas or oil fuels are to be used. Outer aluminium with a lead inner lining interleaved with building paper is recommended for gas; for oil, both plys can be of aluminium. Messrs. Unitubes Ltd., of 197 Knightsbridge, London, S.W.7, provide a full descriptive leaflet dealing with installation of such tubular liners. *Building Research Station Digest* (second series) No. 60, dated July 1965, gives valuable information with regard to domestic boiler chimney design.

In cases where flues are subject to intermittent use and cool condense conditions will frequently occur, vitreous stove-enamelled or salt-glazed vessels should be provided—

at the lowest soot door at a point accessible for removal—to catch condense dripping from the base of impervious linings, otherwise saturation of the structural work will occur at this point.

Solid liners

Where flues require lining to facilitate use for alternative fuels or in order to bring them into conformity with the current regulations, the use of dense concrete pipes of acid resistant concrete is permitted providing the joints too are in acid resistant mortar. Two specialist firms, The Economic House Drain and Flue Repair Company, 17 Linhope Street, Dorset Square, London, N.W.1, and Messrs. J. Murphy, Civil Engineering Contractors, of Highbury, London, N.7, both offer *in situ* processes for cement/aggregate flue lining. The former use tubular liners lowered in and end jointed; all crevices and hollows outside its round shape are grouted leaving a gas and condense-tight lining. The latter utilize a pneumatically inflated rubber tube liner with off surface centralizing spacers around it; pressure cement mortar grouting is then pumped around to fill out to the existing flue shape, and when this is set the liner is deflated and withdrawn. Providing that the latter linings are carried out to a thickness sufficient not to be regarded as pargetting only, using acid and heat resistant concrete, and can be guaranteed moisture and vapour tight—which is believed to be the case —then they would comply with the regulations.

It should be remembered, however, that lining flues only adds to the enclosure thickness and prevents future condense, liquors, and gases from entering the structure. It does not help in any way to cure sulphating which has already occurred or to prevent condense on to room surfaces of the breast already in a deliquescent condition; neither does it prevent rain soakage externally into the brickwork, stacks, or exposed breasts.

Where stacks have substantial horizontal or slightly weathered areas of mortar flaunching, or even brick cappings, over which sulphurous gases may be streamed by down

DAMPNESS IN BUILDINGS 269

draughts from dwarf height pots, rain and snow may collect and soak in; covering with sheet lead weatherings, properly dressed to drips all round, will prevent disruption of the topmost courses from sulphation. Two bonded courses of carefully cut, bedded, and weathered clay tiles or slates could also be used.

External soot doors encourage condense

Soot doors placed externally in flues, lined or not, or in cold roof spaces are exposed points of access to the flue vapours and so attract condense. Doors with only a single thickness of thin metal will, when so exposed to hot flue gases, considerably cool them and condense will occur on the inner surface; one often finds staining from condensed flue liquors below such doors. Building regulations require that

FIG. 59C. *Note also the few courses of pointing adjacent to soot door affected by sulphation.*

such doors shall be airtight. Double skin doors improve matters considerably and under extremely exposed conditions packing the cavity between the two metal skins with mineral wool will help, also.

Nevertheless, doors placed at the bottom of flues should be at a level below the smoke pipe entry so that flue gases do not impinge upon them. The well provided should, however, not be too deep. If it is there is danger during times when the fire is burning inefficiently that too much unburned gas will collect there and may be exploded by a spark or even the heat of increased burning from the firebox when the damper is opened or a forced draught fan comes into action. This is not an unusual occurrence with domestic magazine boilers: a useful well depth is 12 to 18 in.

Supplementary air inlets to solid fuelled boilers are sometimes provided near the bases of flues. These permit additional air to enter the flues and mix with gases after they leave the firebox; this air is additional to that normally required for complete combustion of the gases in the appliance (see p. 00). When they are placed low in the flue and are not too extensive—two inches square being sufficient—they assist further combustion reaction of unburned gases by supplying added oxygen. If the air is warm, perhaps being drawn in through inlets from within the boiler room, this will help flue draught and also mitigate against flue condense by keeping up flue temperatures. Some information on this subject simply refers to this air as a diluent to the chimney gases. This is so, so far as its humidity is concerned, if the additional air is drier; it would dilute other gas-air mixtures if too cool to permit the further combustion. Dilution will slow flue draught—combustion increases it. Additional air inlets are not permitted to be fixed if they draw in outside air which, being cold, would encourage condense. All gas boilers are fitted with inlets to their exhaust flues.

Care in the placing of supplementary air inlets

Care must, however, be exercised in the use of low level supplementary air inlets. If they are operating when the fire is obtaining plentiful underdraught but insufficient overdraught, unburned gases and volatile vapours will burn and ignite in the flue which can then become overheated; if this situation is prolonged the brickwork becomes too hot for safety. Where older flues are only parged, too much heat rapidly causes disruption of this rendering and it soon ceases to give the lining protection which it is supposed to afford to the brickwork—in particular, to improperly filled vertical joints in the half-brick thick enclosing walls or dividing widths. The Building Regulations require that flue entries of supplementary air inlets shall only be situated so as to draw air from the room in which the appliance concerned is placed. Furthermore, the inlets must be capable of being closed or the flue must be fitted with a draught stabilizer. This means that air is not permitted to return to the room neither can too much air enter the flue. Gas-fired appliances usually require such supplementary inlets and, where this is so, they are built into the exhaust pipe as part of the appliance.

Solid-fuelled, convector type room heaters whose flue connecting joints are not airtight and which are operated with their overdraught dampers almost closed but underdraught air inlets open, quite often produce structural flue conditions which result in plaster cracking and heat seared markings to decorations along these cracks. Thus, brown seared markings along cracks or over areas of applied paper decorations are not due to condense liquor staining. They are scorch marks and should be regarded as evidence of potentially dangerous conditions.

Chimney stacks are seen with a short length of stoneware pipe let into their sides near the top to give an upshot angle into the flue; such inlets are intended to counteract downdraught. This they may do; but they should not be positioned too far down from the top or the cooling effects of the air they introduce—when acting as supplementary upward air intakes—whilst not counteracting downdraught will, during humid and cool weather, increase the possibilities of condense above this point. Where downdraught occurs, the terminal speed of the flue gases is too slow: the warmer these gases are in relation to external air, the greater will be their terminal velocity. Cooling them is not the best means of overcoming downdraught. Louvred pots or terminals which create updraught, by diverting wind flow across the top of the flue, do so without cooling the gases within the flue and therefore provide a better remedy.

Liquor staining on walls and ceiling

Where the effects of sulphating, often accompanied by liquor stains, appear at the junction of the ceiling and wall of the topmost room and spread or occur to the wall alone near to the ceiling, it is possible that this is due to the absence of a damp-proof course tray linking with the flashings providing

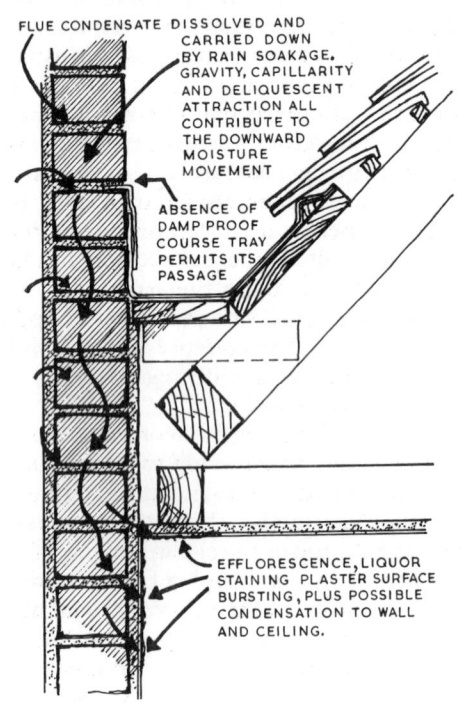

FIG. 60.

weathertightness where the chimney stack passes through the roof coverings. First indications will normally be the darkening of decorations during humid weather conditions, when atmospheric moisture condenses thereon, brought about by the cooling of the brick and plasterwork and the deliquescent salts which penetrating moisture carries with it; liquor staining follows as more severe evidence of actual moisture on the decorated surface. Blistering of paint and bursting off or crumbling of plasterwork will complete the final stages of degradation.

Positions just below top ceiling levels are most usually affected, but these symptoms can and do occur at lower points of a flue as it passes upwards behind the inside wall surfaces in rooms or roof spaces towards its terminal. It is not unusual to find patches a foot or two in area halfway up the height of a chimney breast—even in a lower floor room. As with domestic boiler flues, the location and severity of patches will be related to the outside exposure of the flue, the fuels used and their condition, and the regular or otherwise usage of the heating appliance which it serves. Dry and hard fuels produce less condense than those which are wet or soft; continuous burning appliances maintain generally warmer flue conditions and, therefore, also induce less condense. This type of defect can appear even on breasts or on the wall of rooms behind breasts to interior walls; those in external walls will be discussed first.

Cool flues on outside walls

Flues having only a half-brick thick wall dividing them from outer air will remain cool for considerable periods after the initial lighting of the fire. Where the bricks or joints are porous this thin enclosure will occasionally become damp to varying depths inwards from the outer surface from absorbed rain. It may even, during long rainy spells or short intense storms, become saturated to the extent that moisture oozes out into the flue or, at least, is evaporated into the flue air by air ventilating from or to the rooms. Thus we can get moist air in such flues, even when no fire is burning. The mention of air ventilating into a room via a chimney flue may appear surprising, but this is quite easily possible. Where for instance two rooms have an intercommunicating opening or doorway, or even aerial connection via a passage or lobby, a strong upward chimney draught in one room can cause convectional current air movement into that room from the other one providing air can be drawn into the latter room by some means. In the same way, smoke can be drawn down an adjoining flue. This can also happen with an adjoining house. The evaporating effect will be the more intense, the cooler the drawn in air. A cooled flue, not in use as an exhaust outlet to some form of combustion, can quite readily become the trunk from the outside air by means of which these induced currents within buildings are supplied. This will be the principal reason for the appearance of patches of dampness attracted to deliquescent surfaces on breasts to flues on interior walls in a room with an unlit fire.

If condense occurs in a flue from any cause whatever the inside surfaces will, unless they are impervious, absorb the moisture. Whilst they are moist the acid gases may be dissolved and the solutions will penetrate by capillary, encouraged perhaps by evaporative conditions on the further side.

Porous flue linings absorb condense

Flues which have been used will be coated inside with dust, ash and, perhaps, soot. These materials are all absorptive and will act like blotting paper, holding the condensed moisture in contact with the flue linings. Condensed spirit vapours too may be absorbed and dissolve tar etc. from the other deposits; this is a source of staining liquor. In severe conditions, condense of all kinds may saturate the immediate linings and run down to concentrate or pool into crevices and other depressions. A blob of dropped mortar lodged at a bend or stuck to a flue side, can often be a point of concentration and saturation. If repeated, such concentrations can soak through the internal or external brickwork and present conditions identical to those caused by rain-assisted soakages

FIG. 61.

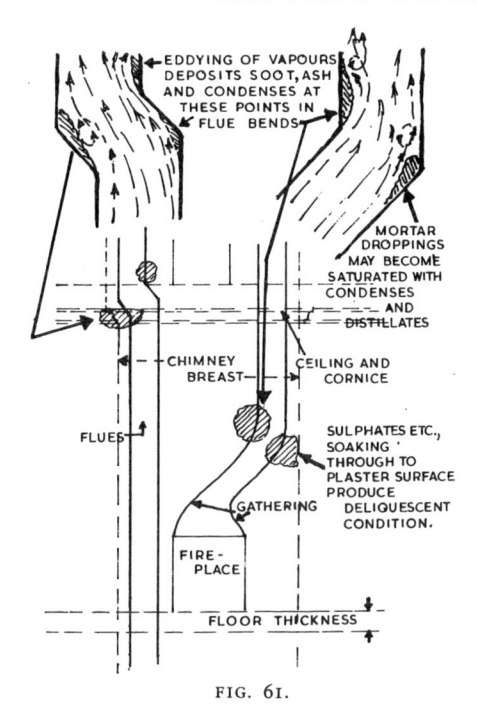

nearer roof levels. Contrary to popular belief, it is seldom these days that rain drops down chimney flues to cause soakage in rooms lower than those on the topmost floor. The more modern chimney with its diameter restricting pot, particularly when sooted, only permits raindrops to enter for quite a short distance and in very restricted quantity; this penetration would only add to sulphating of the topmost few courses. Only in flues down which (or was it up which?) chimney sweeps' apprentices used to climb, could rain or snow cause trouble to floors lower than the topmost.

The fact that the appearance of the condense damp condition on the cooled or deliquescent area immediately precedes rain, but perhaps is not noticed on the surface until it is known to be raining, leads to the assumption that the cause is the penetration of rain by some means. The fact that rain is imminent or is falling means that relative humidity generally is high and condense is therefore then most likely to occur.

Mysterious damp patches on walls

Flues, without solid fuelled or gas appliances at their base, which are cooled by exposure to external or very much cooler adjacent room air and serve as exhaust air ventilation shafts, may be extracting very moist air from the room they so serve. This may condense to produce damp patches where earlier sulphating has led to the formation of deliquescent surface areas. These are the mysterious patches of dampness which people cannot understand. They occur during cold dry weather periods and, furthermore, they may not appear in the room from which the moist air arises but on the wall of a higher room or one in the adjoining house.

For an hour or two after a fire has been lit, severe dampness occasionally occurs a foot or two above fireplace opening level to ground floor chimney breasts or walls backing on to them. This can be caused by heat driving out rising dampness from the fireback and jambs. Steam actually forms in capillaries close to the inner surfaces and pushes moisture to saturation level through outer, room interior, surface pores. This condition, whilst of temporary duration, causes much of the decoration bleaching found at such points.

Remedies for flue condense patches

Where internal surface condense occurs upon walls and the cause can be traced to flue condense, or downward soakage carrying flue condense, no remedy can be regarded as complete if the condense or soakage will continue; only temporary relief may be achieved. If severe efflorescence, evidence of surface crystallization, or liquor staining exist, the only practical remedy is to remove all affected plaster together with a precautionary area about six inches wide into the not yet affected perimeter. If the structural brickwork behind is also sulphate saturated, severe crystallization of mortar joints will indicate this condition, then this should be cut out and rebuilt as has been suggested for flues and stacks. Reinstatement of plastering upon rebuilt brickwork can then proceed with rendering coats in ordinary cement mortar 1 : 3 with sand mixed with a mortar plasticizer or with sulphate resisting cement, one part to three parts of sand. National Building Studies, No. 10, *External Rendered Finishes to Walls*, recommends a mix of one part high alumina cement, one part ground chalk or limestone (not ordinary building lime) and six parts of sand over brickwork which may remain damp and where sulphates could continue to be present. There would appear to be no reason why such a mix should not be used internally as an undercoat, providing the surface which supports it does not also become hot in addition to remaining damp. This is unlikely, however, in the situation we are considering; the basic cause here was cooling of the brickwork and, with flue linings added, even cooler surface conditions would be present. A lime or gypsum plaster setting coat can complete the reinstatement.

Less severe cases can be masked for redecoration, by replastering only or treating the remaining brick surface with bitumastic paints or 'Synthaprufe' and then applying normal —preferably high insulative value—plaster. Aluminium foils sandwiched between two coats of such "paints", used as adhesives, add to the sulphate resistant barrier; where painted applications are not convenient an aluminium backed plasterboard with the foil side to the brickwork, and fixed with a bitumastic adhesive (or painted with it), could be attached to the wall to receive the plaster-gypsum-setting coat. In all cases where brickwork is not removed, as much drying out time as is possible should be allowed to the exposed brickwork before covering in; brushing down should also be done before covering, to remove efflorescence from the surface. Where condensational flue dampness will not continue, because the flue has been lined or rebuilt, repeated wetting of the exposed brickwork followed by drying out periods—hot air or radiant heat assisted if desired—and repeated brushings will serve to remove a considerable amount of sulphated material thereon as efflorescence.

Surface masking

More temporary, but very effective, masking can often be achieved by removing existing decorations but leaving the plaster and brushing down well after drying-off the surface naturally or artificially; aluminium or lead foil should then be applied with red lead paint made up with goldsize as a suitable adhesive. Finally, this should be covered with an anti-condensation paint or a micro-film of expanded polystyrene to reinstate the surface heat absorbent condition of the patch to nearer that of the surrounding untreated plaster. Where the defects are not too advanced and remedial measures to prevent further bad condense or soakage to the surface from the flues have been taken, one of the following measures can suffice after brushing treatment: two coats of aluminium paint, application of a pitched or resinated waterproofed paper secured with a fungicidal paste, or even a vinyl coated paper similarly fixed.

Ceiling reinstatement, if the plaster needs removal, is preferably carried out with foil backed plasterboard with the foil linked to the wall foil by bitumastic lap bonding. Surface treatments can be those applied, where suitable, to the walls.

31: Penetrating dampness in walls

WHEN dampness appears on internal surfaces and its cause is neither capillary rise or condensation, penetration from rain is suspected. Above ground level, rain itself, wind-driven spray droplets whipped up from surface water, or driven rain and atmospheric water vapour, penetrates by finding a passage through materials or openings or joints between their units. Penetrative possibilities are affected by: the duration, frequency and intensity of the rain or "mist" condition, the strength of driving wind, drying influences such as the sun and certain winds, likelihood of run-off, and evaporation as the result of material warmth. Situations where water upon a surface cannot run off readily materially assist penetration

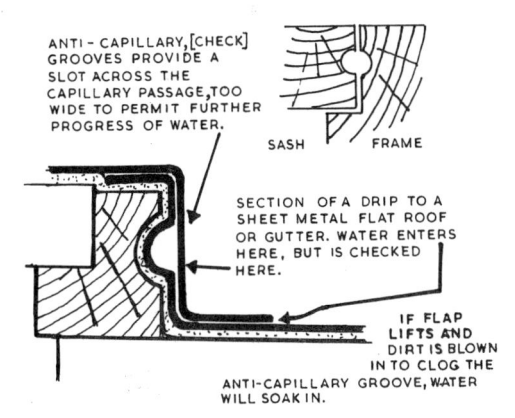

FIG. 62.

into porous materials. Care should be taken to avoid hasty conclusions, however; the fact that a surface is porous or even has open holes, need not mean that penetration will occur. We have seen earlier that somewhat porous renderings can prove more weathertight, in certain circumstances, than cracked hard ones. On the other hand, we deliberately enlarge cracks, by providing storm and capillary grooves, to counteract driving forces attempting to push water through them.

Water may enter by being deposited or held on to horizontal or sloping surfaces, and then being driven into holes adjacent thereto. It may run in by gravity, or be drawn in by capillary action: movement by gravity will naturally be downwards, but not necessarily vertically; whereas capillary and driven movement may be in any direction. Evaporation and subsequent condense within pores may assist progress, whilst vapour entry and its subsequent condense interstitially might precede any further progress.

Surface holes of just less than 0·2 in. and upwards diameter will admit driven rain freely; whilst prolonged strong winds will force fine rain or run-off water into holes a few thousandths of an inch in diameter. Fine driven snow will pass through quite tiny holes, particularly in thin sheet material. Run-in by gravity alone, where the surfaces of the material surrounding the pores is impervious or have angles of contact of 90° or over, requires holes at least 0·02 in. diameter; capillary penetration to any great depth is relatively ineffective through holes of that size.

Method of penetration may change

The bore of holes and the width of slots and cracks in building materials generally tend to become reduced, after initial widening by drying shrinkage, with the ageing of the material; the reduction arising both from natural causes and as the result of many maintenance and renovation processes. Thus, driven-entry often reduces with age and gravity procedure slows down, but capillary progress or possibilities thereof become more widespread. An alternative description which is often used for capillary movement is soakage.

Reduction in the size of passages is often the result of the moisture itself causing swelling of gel materials, such as with wood across its grain, or those airborne as particles into other pores and by its effect upon deliquescent material in pores. Even inert dust and minute debris which become attached to pore walls, either whilst they are wet or as an effect of ionization, will affect penetration: more often to encourage it than to discourage. Spaces between slates and sheet metal flashings or two sheets of material, one weathering the other, often become capillary paths when wind or waterborne dirt lodges therein in sufficient quantity; without this assistance, no water would penetrate. Continued build-up of gel material within pores will, however, eventually block them to liquid run-in moisture. One other means of pore blocking results from the growth within pore ends of minute plants, mosses, and lichens—or habitation by colonies of protozoa, minute animal cell structures which feed like plants. The spores, seeds, or cells are borne on dust or separately in air when dry, and proceed to grow when vapour or liquid moisture is provided. Quite often these growths prevent run-in or, by absorbing liquid which has penetrated by capillary movement, prevent penetration to opposite surfaces of the material (see fig. 65 and p. 288). Newly burned roofing tiles are sometimes quite porous, but after the first rainstorm develop practical watertightness to penetration by one of these means.

High winds assist penetration

Strong winds produce horizontal, and in the case of upper parts of some exposed buildings even upward, thrust pressures which can drive water collected or lodged in horizontal joints, cracks, or on designed ledges, upwards through shiplap joints or to a sufficient degree between weatherings to permit further travel upwards by capillary means. When horizontal pressure is maintained against water trapped in a horizontal slot from which there is an upward passage—of greater width than will permit capillary movement—surrounded by impervious material, the side wind pressure can

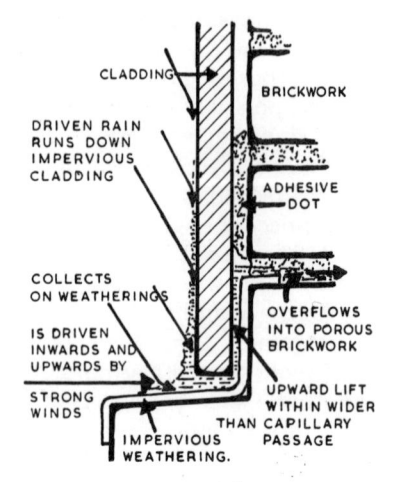

FIG. 63.

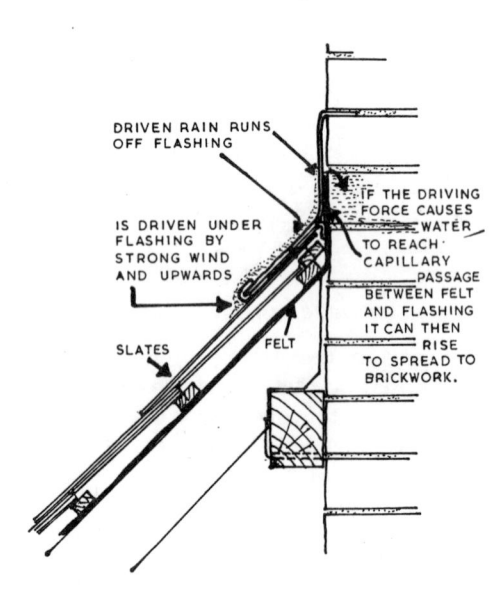

FIG. 64.

be regarded as a substitute for depth of water or static head pressure providing the base of the upward passage is covered with water. This pressure will, if there is free air at the top, lift the trapped water up the passage to a height similar to that which static head pressure would be expected to raise it. This height may not permit passage to an overflow point or to contact with an absorbent material; if this is the case then it will drain out when the wind pressure subsides. If, however, it can overspill (fig. 63) or, by absorption or capillary action, become trapped, it can then possibly penetrate further into and through the construction to show dampness upon an interior surface. Where it does not penetrate further, it may become the means for fostering decay or other deterioration of materials. Its presence in a porous insulating mat will lower the value of the mat as an insulator; if it does this sufficiently, the cooling effect could produce condense conditions to internal surfaces or within the construction.

Wind speeds will produce horizontal pressures as follows:

Wind speed in miles per hour	Horizontal pressure exerted in pounds per square inch	Equivalent to inches static water head
10	0·0020	0·058
20	0·0083	0·220
30	0·0190	0·520
40	0·033	0·920
50	0·051	1·420
60	0·075	2·090
70	0·100	2·800
80	0·130	3·620

Ledge and joint drainage

Where large vertical impervious areas, such as those provided by glass and metal curtain walling, drain on to weathered ledges flashed in a way similar to that shown in fig. 63, the ledge should be constructed as a gutter with

FIG. 65. *Horizontal run-off gutters every 4th floor.*

outlets drained to downpipes so that run-off water does not accumulate in sufficient depth to cover the base of the slot behind the cladding.

If this problem is seen to be likely to occur and drained joints are provided, all internal boundaries of the joints should be sealed with impervious materials. If they are not, the widths of the slots necessary to permit drainage allows wind-driven "mist" to penetrate into the interior construction. If prolonged, this can cause a condition as damp as the forms of penetration against which the drainage was designed.

A similar problem occurs where large weathered areas, cornices, wide window sills, balconies, open landings, etc., deliver considerable quantities of run-off water over verges on to vertical fascias; where at the base, runback on the soffit is prevented only by narrow throatings. Strong

DAMPNESS IN BUILDINGS 285

FIG. 65a. *Both horizontal and vertical features to large buildings need special attention to deal with run-off driven rainwater.*

maintained wind blowing directly at right-angles to the building or fascia surface and which is deflected upwards or is even holding air trapped in the angle between the building face and the soffit by its pressure, will cause run-off water to fill the throatings. This provides a bridge enabling further run-off to spread over the soffit beyond the throating, run down walls below, drip from ridges and projections shielded from wind movement, or find its way freely or with wind pressure assistance into porous materials and capillary or larger passages between impervious units which the throating was put there to protect. To prevent this we must design with deeper and wider throating grooves or drip projections and, when painting throated soffits, make quite sure that the dimensions and efficient shape of the groove or drip is not reduced or distorted by the paint or, for that matter, by any other material.

Decay often results from absence of throatings

Much internal dampness and decay is caused by failure to provide throatings or drips to weathered projections, or the loss thereof by degradation or erosion of material—or as the result of incorrect maintenance and alteration. The existence and efficiency of a throating or drip edge to projections should be investigated where damp patches occur beneath window openings and below other projecting external features.

Continued painting of wooden or stone sills often results in the hitherto efficient throating groove becoming deformed, or even filled with paint. This permits water running off the weathering to cling to the soffit and spread back to the wall apron below the feature. Capillary cracks quite often exist here due to differences in the thermal and moisture reaction of the projection material and the wall or apron. Where this is so, penetration is certain. Specifications requiring periodical burning-off of paint to such features are sound, providing that the supervisor ensures that the throatings have in fact been cleared of old paint before repainting is done. Where deformation of the throating alone is the cause, remedial work consists of restoring the throating to its proper shape and dimensions and carefully caulking the crack with an elastic mastic pointing. Drying-out of the dampness can normally take place from the inside, if penetration has reached that far; otherwise, pointing of the crack externally should be delayed until drying is seen to have taken place.

During alteration and extensions to buildings, the preservation of existing efficient weather drips and throatings must be maintained. Fig. 66 shows a badly wet rot decayed internal portion of a wood sill to a window, whilst photograph in fig. 66a shows the external alteration which brought this about. An extension building with a flat asphalt roof and gutter has its skirting flashing turned in under the wood sill of the window. The wood sill had a completely satisfactory and efficient throating groove when it overhung a stone sub-sill the projection of which was cut away. The asphalters filled the throating leaving—when existing paint-

FIG. 66. *Internal sill badly decayed as the result of penetration below wooden sill externally, resulting from loss of throating when tucking in asphalt skirting.*

work degraded and later when swelling and subsequent shrinkage of timber occurred—capillary space between the asphalt and the wood sill. Subsequently run-off from the sashes was able to gain access and decay commenced; sound timber which had withstood fifty years of weather needed complete replacement within five years of the addition being erected; several windows in the building were similarly affected, others, where no alteration was made, remaining sound. The outside photograph also shows, across the asphalt at right-angles to the window, severe cracking at the drip where, because no reinforcement to the asphalt was used, thermal expansion has taken its toll. The dark line is a luxuriant strip of moss growing in the dirt washed into the

288 DAMPNESS IN BUILDINGS

FIG. 66a. (a) *The cause of the inside decay to the sill.* (b) *A surface defect assisting penetration of the addition roof, but partially remedied by moss growth in dirt washed into crack.*

asphalt crack; the lighter strip below it is lime salts leached during saturation from the asphalt aggregate and, possibly, the concrete from the roof substructure but left as a white powder deposit when water holding the solution and behind the moss dam evaporated. It is interesting to note that here, although the asphalt cracks were as much as three-eighths of an inch wide in places, the dirt filling and moss growth had prevented severe run-in leakage into the building below. Only dampness showed upon the inside concrete soffit; no actual drip or run-in was evident. The evidence was that as the asphalt crack widened, it was progressively filled with washed in dirt or growth debris over which grew the moss— a natural reduction to possible ingress of run-off water in quantity. Hard rendered plinths are often seen carried up to the underside of window sills and similar projections which to the plasterer, and probably also the specifier, appear to be a suitable completion point for work as it is an overlapping weathering. However, dampness is certain to penetrate if the throatings are filled and shrinkage away from the sill of the new rendering leaves a capillary crack.

32: Remedial measures for run-off penetration

WHERE throatings have been omitted whether deliberately or in error and the feature concerned projects beyond the wall face, they can be cut; if it does not so project (e.g. a wooden

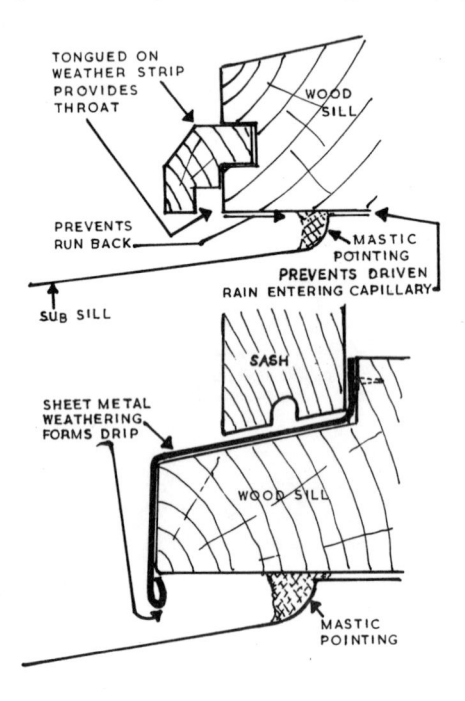

FIG. 67.

sill set over a sub-sill) then it will be necessary to groove the face and tongue on a throated extension weathering glued to the sill with red lead paint if the repaired sill is to be painted, or else with a waterproof resinous glue. The only other alternative is to cover the wood sill with a non-ferrous metal weathering taken in under the sashes and turned down over the fascia to extend a quarter of an inch or so below its bottom edge to form a drip (see fig. 67). No attempt should be made to dress the metal weathering down over the sub-sill, unless that too is without a throating when the metal could weather this also and finish as a drip to both. Complete casing-in of wooden sills is not recommended; this could promote conditions conducive to rot. Temporary prevention of penetration can be gained by "gunning" in joints between wood and sub-sills with building mastics alone (see fig. 67). Providing that these are not exposed to direct sunlight for long periods, protection of up to five or ten years can be gained; this proviso is usually complied with by not putting too much mastics into the space below the wood sill and so keeping the surface in the shade. Bitumastic trowel- and knife-applied sealants have an exposed-to-sunlight life of about five years. Hard-setting cements or mortar pointing should never be used in such positions.

Degradation of stones must be stopped

Where loss of throatings has occurred on stone members by means of chemical degradation or physical erosion, the remedial measures will depend upon the extent to which they have deteriorated. If the chemical action is severe enough to result in loss of the throat, it is very likely that the general surfaces of the stones will also be affected: if this is so, the cause of the chemical degradation must be found. The speed of occurrence may give some indication here. If a period of years is involved, this would indicate atmospheric attack. In many sedimentary stones a close examination will probably reveal that the matrix holding the aggregate together has suffered and the surface left has a pimply effect; in stones with finer aggregate, rubbing with the finger will remove the powdery surface. There may be considerable soot and grime deposits below the feature and also discoloured stone powder run-down stains. Earlier remarks regarding acid attacks on stone are also appropriate here.

Incompatible materials

More rapid development of chemical erosion is usually the result of run-off from incompatible material above. Some limestones and artificial stone reconstructed with crushed limestone aggregates produce run-off from acidic atmospheric attack which can very rapidly attack siliceous sandstones. Calcium and magnesium sulphate solutions destroy the cementing material holding the sand aggregate together. Run-off from brickwork containing sulphates can also have this effect; lime and cement renderings above may also be responsible. Every effort should be made to prevent recurrence after restoration of the affected feature. Where replacement of the eroded stone is necessary due to the severity of the attack, the use of a compatible stone is the best remedy. If this is not possible, or is for some reason undesirable, the repaired work must be shielded from run-off by covering the weathering or upper surface and its fascia with properly dressed non-ferrous sheet weatherings. Either asbestic-bitumen heat manipulated sheet material or mastic asphalt is well worth consideration where the more traditional sheet metals might themselves produce aggressive or staining run-off. Natural slates and clay tiles can also be used if they are bedded and pointed in sulphate resistant mortars, set to good weather, overshoot the projection needing protection by about one-and-a-half inches, and are also bedded and pointed at their top edge into grooves cut into the plane facework above or apron flashed thereto with sheet flashings. These do, however, alter the elevational appearance of the projection. Nevertheless, sub-sills to windows are frequently constructed in this manner and prove satisfactory; replacement repairs of this nature, if extended to all of the sills on an elevation, would cost considerably less than stone replacement. Where a wood upper sill is left, a combination of the metal covering described on page 291 and the tiles or slates mentioned above offer a useful remedy. If plain tiles are used, these can be obtained with continuous nibs so that, bedded head down, a drip is formed; two courses, properly lap bonded, of either slates or tiles should be used. If appearance or change in the colour of the sill or projecting feature is not an objection, similar possibilities are offered by hard engineering type bricks or tiles specially designed with weathered upper surfaces or set weathering and provided with drip or throats. Painting upper surfaces will, at best, provide only short term protection. Coating with proofing solutions seldom prevents all penetration on almost horizontal surfaces.

Clear waterproofing solutions

Clear waterproofing solutions of any kind, even those which can "breathe", applied to vertical surfaces and fascias give somewhat longer protection to re-formed work but, applied to older surfaces, may trap soluble salts beneath the skin surface which they form—this later results in bursting-off or spalling of the surface. There appears to be no reason why silicon esters, siliconate-latex, or gel-forming waterproofers should not materially assist in enabling re-formed artificial stone work to better resist deterioration by water-carried run-off if they can be used in the wet mix at formation, or can be infused deeply into a porous mix when set—even, where the material so permits, by repeated submerged soakage of *in situ* surfaces or precast blocks. Whilst the Building Research Station in its published information on this subject suggests that in the case of silicon ester, soakage or immersion may be helpful, it does not appear generally to consider that there is any conclusive evidence that silicone water repellents or metallic siliconates can be regarded as more than relatively short-lived as surface penetration resistant treatments against rain. Nevertheless, since so many of the water repellent liquids designed for surface application have only short guaranteed lives and have to be renewed every few years, it does not appear that their use could cause irreparable injury even if no lasting good is achieved. Re-use should not, of course, be contemplated if they prove injurious or useless on first application. Any reputable manufacturer who is requested to advise upon the use of a product on a particular surface would, when given all the facts, most certainly not advise its use if he had reaon to believe that any harm at all could result. In cases where rectification work can be readily undertaken should harmful effects become evident, the manufacturers should be asked to advise whether limited experimental usage should be carried out.

Re-cutting may be possible

If stone features are bold in proportion it is often possible, where erosion is the result of long atmospheric exposure or

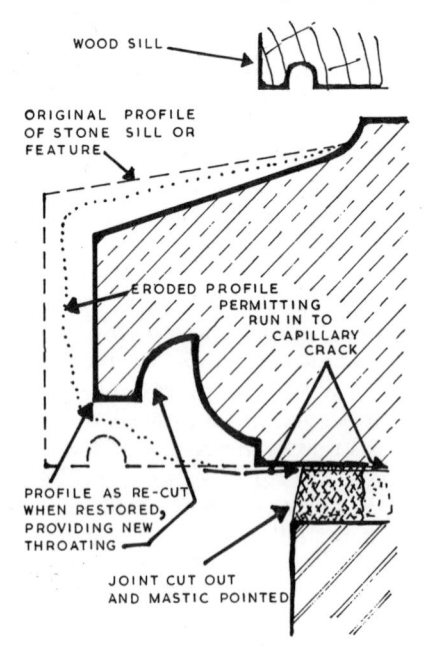

FIG. 67a.

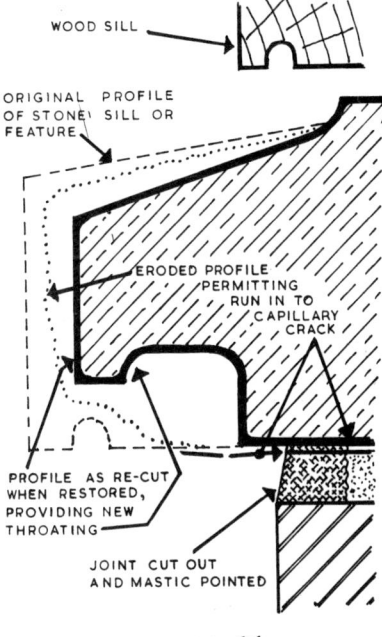

FIG. 67b.

where measures have been taken to prevent a recurrence of run-off, to re-cut *in situ* to new sections incorporating effective throatings or drip edges. Sometimes, however, the expense of re-cutting or the resulting deformity prohibits such action and in these cases plastic repairs can often be carried out using artificial stone with cement, cement/lime, or resinous matrix binders.

The replacement of sections having very small cross sections, such as re-running the fillet between a fascia and a throating, is impracticable; similarly, building-up upon a surface subject to lamination is not advised. Some sandstones show this defect, either as the direct result of actual grain lamination naturally occurring in the stone and which ought to have been detected before it was originally used, or as the result of cementitious material dissolved by penetrative moisture being deposited in pores a little distance below the surface at which re-evaporation takes place. Surfaces subject to repeated wetting and drying—such as sills and thresholds, steps, etc.—most often suffer in this way if the stone is susceptible. If this is so, the natural bed of the stone has very little bearing upon the result; in fact, stones which react like this seldom exhibit a clearly visible grain. Either the stone must be replaced—and there is really no other course possible if natural lamination exists—or it must be cut back considerably to enable quite a bold sectional plastic replacement.

Restoration is a job for skilled craftsmen. Masons who have first mastered the art of stone appreciation and cutting can judge the restorative treatment most likely to produce permanent results and should always be employed on important works. Local masons, well-experienced bricklayers and plasterers can and do, however, often carry out very creditable local repairs.

Plastic repairs to stonework

The principal advantage claimed for plastic restoration is the lower cost compared with replacement with new stone; in many cases there is also less disturbance to other features. Many jobbing builders successfully re-run defective stone sills and external steps, however, by liberally cutting away the old stone and casting extensions in cement and sand, even crushed shingle concrete, suitably anchored by reinforcement to the old stone and facing with white cement, crushed stone mixture. A small amount of waterproofing powder or liquid added to the mix both encourages rapid setting and plasticization for working to a dense finish and prevents moisture deterioration of ferrous reinforcement or anchors. Properly weathered, stooled and throated, which is not difficult *in situ* casting, gives very long lasting repair. Plasterers successfully run the finishing profiles without formwork. The skill of the workman in mixing, and placing the core concrete and finishing the weathered surfaces so that shrinkage crazing does not occur, are the secrets of success.

Moist, but not wet, mixes throughout materially assist. Where re-running without formwork is contemplated, a roughly cut core of brickwork is first set leaving about one inch to finished profile which is then plastered on and tooled to finished profile.

Preparations for plastic repairs

Plastic restoration using cement-lime matrix must be preceded by careful cutting away of all affected stone, including not only that required to level off portions actually eroded but also areas impregnated with salts whether deliquescent or not, so that building out can commence from sound solid clean surfaces. In any event at least three-quarters of an inch depth is necessary; where it is intended to use reinforcement, at least that amount of cover over this is necessary. Too great a cut back is preferable to too little. Perimeter edges should be cut to straight lines so that finishing tooling can be done at right-angles at all points from the plastic to the existing work. Whether the cut sides are vertical or slightly undercut appears to be a matter of personal choice; restorative experts disagree on this point and each method seems to produce as many good results as the other. Remaining surfaces should be keyed and thoroughly cleaned of dust; if reinforcement is necessary, copper or brass anchors (screws can be sufficient) plugged to the existing work provide wired fixings for copper or brass rods. Everything should be wetted with water if cement/lime mixtures alone are to be used; reliable bonding liquids suited to the stone, either watered or incorporated into grouts, can help. Neat cement grout thoroughly brushed in is still a reliable bonding agent. Resinous mixtures will usually require a proprietary bond, and the suppliers' advice should be sought. Cement/lime mixes using suitably coloured sand as aggregate are recommended—crushed igneous rocks being regarded as sand—but care should be exercised when limestones or calcareous sandstone are being repaired to ensure that such sand is compatible. Crushed limestones should be reserved for only thin top coatings *in situ* cast if there is no other way of matching the existing stone so that the reinforcement is protected and as much of the restored depth as practicable is as impervious as is possible. White or cream coloured cement and the lime content of the mortar will usually give to the mix all the lightness of colour required. Mixes in the nature of 1:1:4 or 6, cement, lime, sand, by volume are usually used. Stone dusts are not recommended as aggregate in cement/lime mixtures even in toppings; they tend to produce glazed effects under tooling and this sometimes results in subsequent crazing. Build-up mortars and concretes should not be stronger than the material being repaired—strength lies in the matrix.

Modern stone paint finishes to plastic repairs

The use of reliable stone paints over fully profiled cement and sand *in situ* core castings can often give satisfactory results, especially some of the modern resin bonded products. These products have the advantage that they bridge cracks and crevices so that if extended over existing work more complete cover is provided. Care should be taken that the one selected does not give an artificially glazed finish. This might not matter when used over a whole feature but when used for patches could clash with the existing surface—in fact, it is likely to remain so clean for such a long period that it becomes increasingly evident that it is a patch. Cleaning down the entire surface and completely re-painting might, therefore, be the better proposition.

I have had no actual experience of the use of entirely non-cementitious stone repairing mixtures, those using hydrated and hydraulic limes or "Roman cements", but these materials would obviously be suitable for "stucco" repairs and in addition, it is well known that "mortars and concretes" rich in lime and non-Portland cements suffer less from setting shrinkage than do Portland cements. Resin bonded, fibreglass aggregated mixtures too are offered. Messrs Peter Cox Preservation Company Ltd., of 2 Cross Keys Close, London, W.1. offer a non-cementitious process, P.C.100, which could be in the former category but might be resin bonded. They claim that shrinkage is so slight, if at all, as to be negligible so far as possibility of surface cracking or joint opening is concerned. It does, however, require careful curing and takes a considerable time to set through a built up thickness. This is consistent with the setting of limes. When they have completed to a surface, it is treated with another of their preparations, which protects the repair whilst curing and full setting takes place. To be useful and effective over an ordinary lime mortar this would have to be a silicone based liquid waterproofer which enabled "breathing" through treated surface pores to take place. Lime mortars set by chemical action with atmospheric carbon dioxide gas. Hydraulic limes can, however, set under water. The use of fibreglass would appear to be more suitable for pre-formed replacement items which could be cast into moulds, off the site and then cemented into place, rather than for *in situ* build up. One would suspect that its setting tensions would be too much for most natural stones, and that the material would pull some of the stone surface away.

Resinous mixtures composed of:

Plaster of Paris	100 pts. by weight
Urea Resin	50 pts. by weight
Hardeners	5 pts. by weight
Water	50 pts. by weight

have been used in plastic work and for castings.

Careful curing is vital

Plastic repairs are carried out with no slump mixtures in cement and lime-cement bonded work so that surface grazing and shrinkage generally is reduced to a minimum. This requires that they should be properly cured when complete so that full setting and hydrolization is effected. Covering with polythene sheets or spraying with resinous seals such as is done with structural concrete work is effective providing sufficient water has been incorporated into the mix to effect hydrolization. On smaller works, damp cloths are useful. These can be wetted further to provide additional water for absorption into the work where very dry mixes have been used. Any curing should continue for at least seven days.

Run-in through fractures and open joints

In cases where the material is chemically sound and has not lost its throatings from physical damage, isolated damp patches occurring immediately below sills, cornices, and copings, indicate open joints or fractures. Externally the evidence of this condition is a run-down damp patch, often dirtier than protected areas, with a perimeter of white surface efflorescence showing up during drying periods. If sulphating of the mortar has occurred or frost has had its effect, burst-off pointing will result. Internal dampness from this source is usually at a somewhat lower level, due to gravity pull acting upon the run- or soak-in: sometimes considerably lower—if unfilled internal joints or tracks of porous material give it passage.

Open joints are usually the result of thermal or moisture expansion causing movement from which recovery could not occur: stoolings forced under loaded jambs to sills, returns pushed over free parapet ends to copings, or jointing materials crushed out from between the units of copings, cornices, etc. In such cases, prevention of further run-in requires cleaning out and remaking the open joint. Allowance should be made for future expansion by using mastic material if the joint is filled to a sill; utilizing a metal underflashing to an open drained joint in the case of a coping; or a metal weathering covering to a saddle joint to a cornice or weathering. Before rejointing sills, particularly where there is evidence of sulphating or frost expansion of mortar joints below, levelling the disjointed stones may be necessary. Sulphating or expansion could have caused upward pressure below the site of the leaking joint which has lifted the unrestrained ends. If the leak is through a fracture, in a ground floor situation, this upward pressure could have been the cause. In all cases, if the lift cannot be readily seen it will be necessary to check alignment with a straight edge. The old bedding mortar should then be raked out from below the sill, together

DAMPNESS IN BUILDINGS 301

with that over the stoolings, leaving only a small portion below the sill and just clear of the jambs, so that after some weak and almost dry mortar has been caulked-in the stones can be levelled and aligned before the open joint is made good. A length of metal or bituminous felt underflashing will add an additional barrier to future possible run-in if set into the remade joint below the sill to span the site of the fracture or open joint and made to slope outwards or is lipped up at its inward edge. (See fig. 68.)

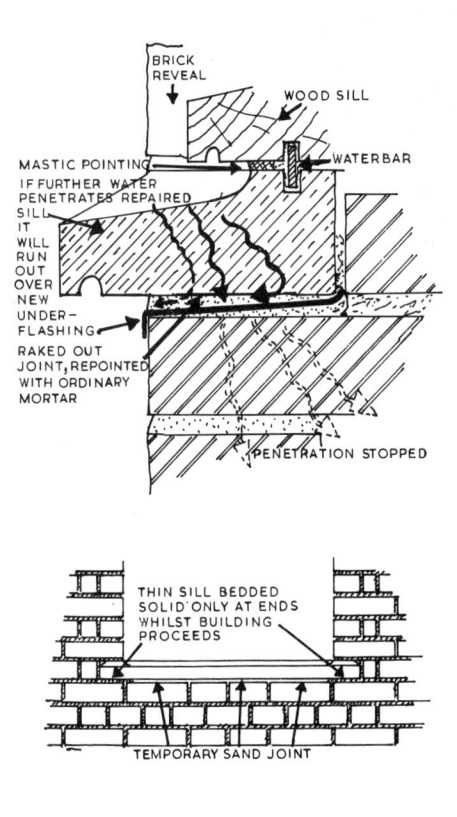

FIG. 68.

Setting and re-setting thin sills

Relatively thin stone sills should be bedded in sand only whilst new building proceeds across their span; they should only be pointed solidly when the whole structural load is on the wall. This prevents early fracturing of sills; brick and weathered roofing tile sills also require this treatment. It is good practice to bed in only the stoolings when the work is rising, and complete the open portions as cleaning down and pointing proceeds. The procedure of including such references in specifications appears to be dying out; it ought to be continued. Providing run-in is stopped and the sulphated joints below are not too badly affected, the allowance of sufficient drying-out time will permit deep raking-out and reinstatement of the pointing below the site of the run-in. Where upward displacement of the facing bricks or stones has occurred, rebuilding of the apron or the other facework disturbed should be undertaken as part of the remedy. Similarly, if the internal plastering has become soft and friable and possibly is saturated with deliquescent salts, this should be treated as suggested for chimney breast damp patches. Adequate time must be allowed for drying-out the stripped brickwork.

33: Penetrative run-in not directly associated with weathered features

ISOLATED patches of internal dampness showing at the ceiling to wall junction to a topmost floor room, where flat roofs or parapet gutters exist, can often be traced to penetrations through copings set only a few courses above. In these cases, the moisture will have found its way downwards within the parapet wall and around the back of the roof skirting or cover flashings to the upstands of roofs or gutter coverings. The action is very similar to that noted on page 273 and illustrated in fig. 60, p. 272. The placing of a continuous horizontal damp-proof course along parapet walls immediately below the weathered coping is a good practice. It provides an additional barrier to downward penetration if coping joints open for any reason. Tiles or slates creased and cement mortar weather filletted undercourses to brick on edge copings, perform a similar purpose providing that the slate or tile courses do not fracture if a brick joint opens. A couple of shillings per linear yard for a damp-proof course of bitumastic felt or polythene plastic is not an expensive addition to this part of a structure. It will well repay its cost where thermal or moisture expansion is likely to cause joints to open. The fact that such damp-proof membranes shed any water they intercept down the wall face, means that even if water does penetrate it has a better chance to re-evaporate when drying conditions return. If the water so shed runs in through the whole thickness of the wall it is possible that it may not have re-evaporated from the centre before the next wetting occurs. Prolonged wetting is a major factor in sulphate expansion. Care should be exercised in the selection of the bricks and mortar when building exposed brickwork parapet walls. The Building Research Station Digest, 65 (second series), December 1965, *The Selection of Clay Building Bricks*, and No. 123 of June, 1959, *Sulphate Attack on Brickwork*, together with second series No. 58 *Mortars for Jointing*, all provide very useful information in this respect.

Where the site of joint opening is limited to one or two isolated joints, the remainder perhaps being cramped together, remedial measures similar to those adopted for sills etc. would provide the answer: the lifting of the stones or bricks on either side of the open joints, and the insertion of a short length of membrane—bitumastic felt, polythene sheeting of the dimpled type which is specially made for damp-proof courses, or non-ferrous metal could be used. These will scarcely be visible in the rebedded work.

Dampness may by-pass flashings

Normal run-off from properly weathered and throated copings does not usually, if there is a reasonable distance of exposed wall above the flashing, result in dampness showing within the building. Where an exposed parapet wall exists and there is a continuous band of dampness along a ceiling to wall junction below, penetration is probably occurring through a route behind the flashing. Copings should be examined to ensure they are weatherproof. Evidence of this is that the wall below, at least for a couple of brick courses or a similar distance on other materials, is cleaner, drier, and not showing efflorescence along its length to both faces. If below that level it is dirtier or shows efflorescence then wind-blown soakage from coping run-off is a contributory cause to its damp condition. Where this is so, one would expect to find porous bricks and/or joints in the parapet wall; with old walls, the open joint pointing may be the principal means of penetration. The fact that dampness has penetrated into the building indicates saturation of brickwork to a considerable degree. Every effort should be made to allow this to dry out before any preventive measures against future penetration commence. If more than slight sulphating has occurred, the remedy must be as recommended for a chimney stack. Rebuilding should be with new material on and including a continuous damp-proof course jointed to and extending over the cover flashing turn in, or skirting turn in, right through the wall thickness. Where only slight surface sulphating has occurred and bricks are reasonably non-porous, deep raking out of joints followed by thorough drying out and, finally, repointing, are the measures recommended.

Surface treatments may be possible

If the bricks are porous, the treatment consists of raking out the joints and the application of a non-pore-sealing proofing solution before repointing. It is seldom necessary to proof both sides, particularly where the coping weathers to one side only or where it is evident that driving rain principally causes soaking of one side only. Leaving the less exposed side unproofed, materially assists future drying-out and reduces the risk of continued sulphation. Renderings are unlikely to prove satisfactory unless they are rather open in texture; where they are used, the addition of a gel type waterproofing to the mix, to give greater resistance to penetration, would be preferable to applying a hard dense rendering. Where an old wall can be made generally sound by raking out the joints and flush pointing, a colourless proofing solution or a cement paint (even a stone paint)—preferably of two-coat application to ensure complete coverage—will give protection against penetration for a limited time. Tar applied hot, or a bitumastic emulsion, gives protection equal to paints but, obviously, would not be suitable where appearance matters. Usually, the more rough and porous the surface generally, the better these coverings perform. At best, they are all relatively temporary remedies and would need renewal every few years.

Where appearance is most important without change of colour or texture, the colourless metallic liquid and silicone proofings renewed from time to time would appear to be the best answer. If change in appearance is not important, then the cement and stone paints are useful. It must be remembered however, that most of the cement and stone paints, ordinary paints, tars, and bitumastic coverings, seal pore ends; whilst they prevent further ingress to water, they also prohibit evaporation if it enters from another point.

Where driving rain penetrates from the outside of a parapet wall and downwards past the flashings and is not materially assisted by soakage from the inner side of the parapet wall, the surface treatments must be carried downwards past the level of the wall ceiling junction to a point which must be determined in each individual case; the whole wall is usually at fault, however, with this type of penetration so the entire area will require treatment. The only other alternative is the rebuilding of the entire portion of the affected wall to cavity construction.

Solid roofs may bridge cavities

Bridging by the solid roof construction where cavity construction exists is usually indicated if a strip of dampness at the ceiling/wall junction level persists after remedial treatment to a parapet above, where the outer surface was most exposed to a flat roof. The outside cladding skin of the wall should be cut away and rebuilt to continue a cavity upwards to the underside of the newly inserted horizontal damp-proof course. This cavity need not, providing that it is kept scrupulously clean of debris and mortar droppings, be more than an inch wide. A vertical damp-proof course dropping from cover flashing level on the inside of the parapet wall to the bottom of the bridging level externally—such as is fixed to a bridging lintel to an opening—would also serve. This too would avoid oversailing the rebuilt outer skin of the wall to form the cavity. Where bridging by a roof edge permits this type of penetration across a cavity, it is also a "cold" bridge, and condensation internally may be materially adding to the damp condition. No amount of internal waterproofing or insulative treatment alone can really be regarded as the remedy to such penetrations if they are at all severe. Stripping plasters and replastering with waterproof renderings, applying foil membranes, metallic paints, etc., may, as

FIG. 69.

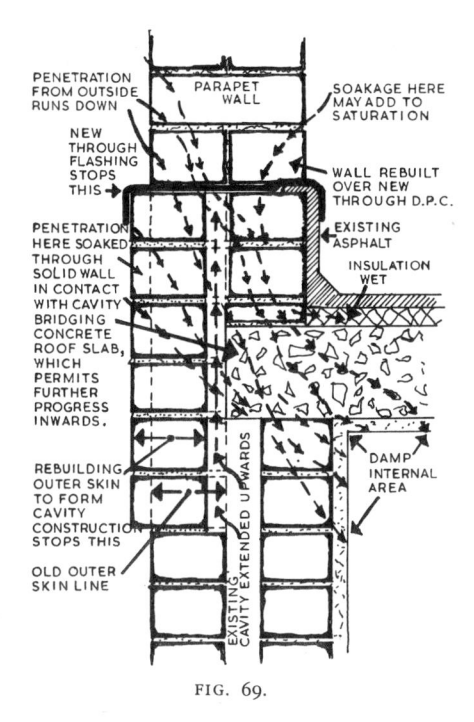

noted for penetrations from chimneys, serve for a short or even quite a long time, but where condensation internally is adding materially to the surface dampness they have little insulative value and this is likely to continue. Unless the penetration is stopped, or very considerably restricted, these treatments will either be by-passed or erupt from the wall quite quickly.

Canopies and balconies may assist soakage

External projections, concrete porch canopies, balconies etc.—flat roofed extensions abutting taller walls—may all give similar trouble if their cantilevers bridge cavities or if run around penetration behind flashings occurs. This can result from rain driven directly on to the wall surface above being held by deflected wind on to the vertical wall surface immediately above the flashing, or from its damp condition being reinforced by splashings from the roof surface. This type of penetration may be intermittent, perhaps occurring only once in five years or so when an exceptionally long storm occurs and water is driven by persistent winds from one particular direction.

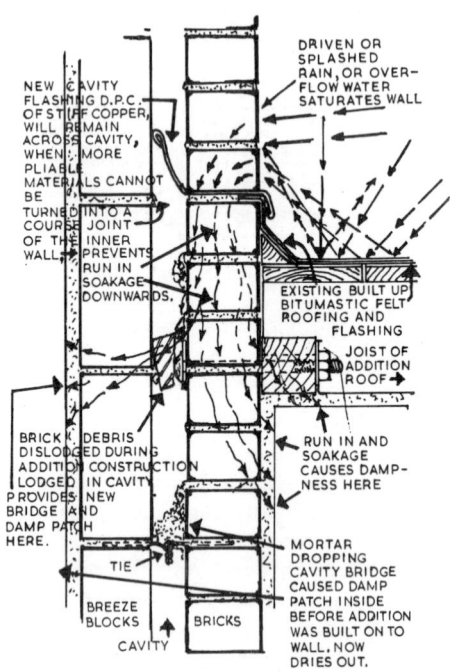

FIG. 70.

If cavity construction exists at such a point and the bridging is not covered by a cavity damp-proof course, as for a lintel, then one should be inserted as a permanent remedy.

Casual and slight dampness may develop to severe conditions

Where the penetration occurs only once in several years, a band of colourless non-pore-sealing liquid proofing applied about eighteen inches high above flashing level every five years usually provides a satisfactory answer. Repeated penetrations at much more frequent intervals, however, ultimately produce "run-in paths" through porous constructions resulting in penetration occurring from much less intense or persistent rain and wind until conditions of relatively permanent dampness exist, especially in construction susceptible to sulphate attack or the production of hydroscopic material within these paths on to the inner surface.

Isolated severe patch penetrations anywhere on an external wall may build up from slight localized penetration in the same way: one very porous brick or stone; one very underburned brick; a cavity tie with a mortar dropping bridge or a fallen brickbat lodged across; a short length of mortar jointing into which a clay pellet has accidentally been incorporated; some sand which salts or animal droppings or urine has affected; even joints not weather pointed; or—the most obvious as well as most usual example—small areas of joints where pointing has eroded or been burst-off. Concentrated delivery of run-off water from a projection or attachment on to a wall patch when it rains, may be the cause of the material unit or joint failure. Such causes resulting from blocked, overflowing or leaking gutters and rainwater downpipes, can usually be readily detected and remedied; but one so often sees cascades of algae, moss—even luxuriant vegetation—behind and down either side of downpipes which must have been leaking or overflowing for months or even years. Once so soaked, the affected walls may never properly dry out if they become hydroscopic. Internally the affected wall will remain capable of absorbing condensed atmospheric moisture entering through external or internal pores, even where these have been treated with a proofing solution that can "breathe". Alternatively, if the outside has been rendered or treated with a pore filling wax, vapour entering from inside will not be able to pass through and must at some time condense and be trapped.

Treating areas affected by run-off

The best treatments after repairing the cause of the run-off, are as follows: externally—cleaning down surfaces, raking out the joints (allowing as much drying time as possible and shielding from rain if necessary), and finally repointing. Internally, depending upon the severity and length of time of penetration—cleaning down, stripping decorations, fungicidal washing or dusting, plaster removal if hydroscopic or perished, or applying a covering in the form of a vapourproof membrane and an insulating layer, before the final redecoration. External and internal treatments should both be carried rather beyond the extent of the areas obviously affected: leaving the outside untreated, except for repointing, permits maximum drying-out. Other causes of cascades of dampness are overflows from warning pipes to water closet flushing cisterns and main storage tanks. A persistent drip blown back on to the wall below or splashing from a lower projection (see fig. 70) commences the production of damp patches which may prove to be permanent: these should not be ignored. Overflowing hopper heads on domestic waste pipes from baths and basins, too, can cause similar troubles.

Fixing of gutters and downpipes needs thought

Quite recently, a wall to a first floor room was observed which was very damp at an external angle from floor to ceiling. The cause was a nozzle outlet to an eaves gutter discharging into a hopper head. This was fitted so closely, as well as being out of centre to the nozzle, that splashing over its edge always occurred in heavy rain. The wall behind was rendered over old flint and brick walling. The splashed water was caught behind the hopper in a patch of rendering which was damaged, cracked and loosened—probably when the pipe nails were driven in. The trapped water was soaking downwards and inwards. If the hopper had been kept a few inches lower and the nozzle had been centred over it, the splashing would not have occurred and the broken rendering would then not have mattered. Pipe nails driven into mortar joints, particularly if these are of hard mortar, may split the joint and permit water to enter.

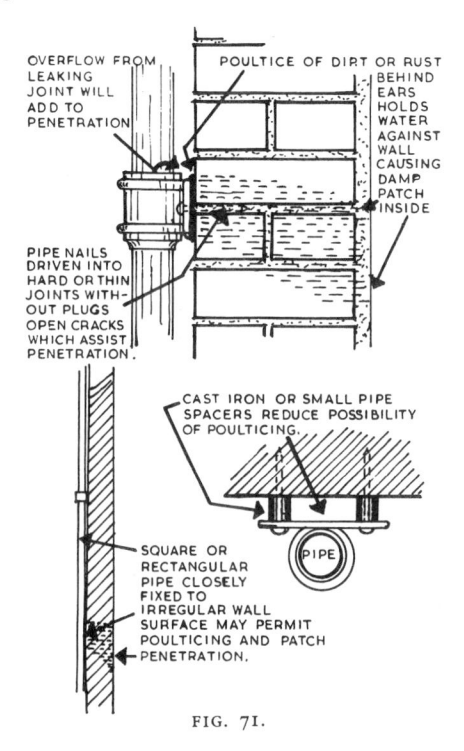

FIG. 71.

Rust expansion and poulticing

Drilling and correct plugging before nailing or screwing with hot dip galvanized nails or black japanned or brass screws, would be less likely to open up a penetrative path to water thrown on to the wall. Cast iron and steel nails are used for pipe fixings because not only are they stiffer against bending when driven directly into joints but, being crystalline by nature, they are less affected by rust than are rolled, punched or wrought mild steel or wrought iron nails. Less rust means less possibility of expansion and burst joints. Spaced off ears, see fig. 71, also reduce poulticing-shelf effect against the wall, which is produced when dirt lodges behind and fills the unevenness between the back of the cast on ears, or tacks, and the wall. If dirt does not fill this space, rust could.

Rectangular downpipes and flat backed gutters can cause trouble

The author feels some doubt about the new closely fitting back to the wall-face P.V.C. rectangular pipes. If there is an uneven wall-face they could easily touch, or almost touch, the wall at intervals and here trapped falling or windblown debris can be caught and lodge to form poultices (see fig. 71), retaining patches of rain against the wall. Penetration into the wall might be offset if the pipes gain sufficient solar heat and conduct it to their shaded rear to evaporate the trapped water. This is not a new problem; rectangular lead and cast iron pipes, closely fitted to walls, have caused similar troubles in the past. O'Gee and other flat-backed gutters, too, in cast iron, zinc or P.V.C. closely screwed back to fascias or resting upon continuous corbels of brick or stone may cause similar soakage problems—particularly if they become blocked and overflow. Both pipes and gutter in P.V.C. have one advantage over the older materials: their easy removal and replacement. All specifications covering maintenance work, whether pointing walls or repainting woodwork, should incorporate a clause requiring that flat-backed pipes or gutters should be taken down to facilitate repointing or painting behind them. Before re-fixing, these pipes and gutters should also be repainted if this is necessary. Gutters which cannot be removed from corbels require regular cleaning-out with wire brushes followed by soft brushing and drying; finally two coats of bitumastic paint should be applied inside to keep them thoroughly watertight. Leaks cannot be readily detected, and considerable damage may be done before they become evident. Rainwater downpipes closely fitted into outside recesses in walls invite troubles of this kind, unless they are constructed to sanitary pipework standards; the tendency to trouble being more likely if they are rectangular in section.

Examine attachments for run-in sources

When investigating causes and sources of penetrative dampness not affecting general wall surfaces, all exterior attachments, projections, and their immediate surrounding areas should be closely scrutinized. Cold asphaltic repairing mastics from cans, suitable for knife or trowel application, and many of the more modern tube packed bitumastic or rubber, resin and oil-bonded caulking mastics if well forced into cleaned-out cracks and crevices will very effectively remedy run-in into most building materials. They usually need replacement every few years because nearly all of them harden, shrink and crack with exposure. One of the non-hardening resinous tapes, which are sold in rolls of various widths, will have a very useful effective life as a preventative measure against run-in leakages. These tapes should be well rubbed on to cleaned surfaces to span cracks and open joints, particularly of glass, hard gloss painted surfaces and metals. Edges of narrow flashings, glazing bar covers etc. which persistently lift or become dirt-filled, or joints which mastics cannot span satisfactorily due to excessive movements or into which they cannot be caulked, can often be kept weathertight for considerable periods with this material. It should not, however, be used across the flow on surfaces having very little slope, or it may cause the formation of a dirt poultice. On glass this might not be other than a nuisance, but on metals or somewhat absorptive material and paints its presence can assist degradation or penetration.

Severe dampness over window openings

Areas of dampness, too persistent or severe to result from condensation, located over window openings to cavity walls indicate the absence or ineffectiveness of an overhead damp-proof course. If absent, the only reliable remedy is to cut out six inches of wall above the frame and insert one as shown in all textbooks on building construction. Very often a course is present, but is ineffective through mortar droppings piled upon it and bridging the cavity. The situation will normally be remedied by the removal of at least half of the brickwork of the width of the opening, thorough cleaning-out, and careful replacement of the brickwork to avoid the re-creation of a bridge. Internal repair may or may not be necessary; drying-out may suffice. With solid walls, the indication is that water is running-in over the top edge of the frame. Remedies here are, the provision of a throating where possible—cut into the lintel or arch soffit externally; or a

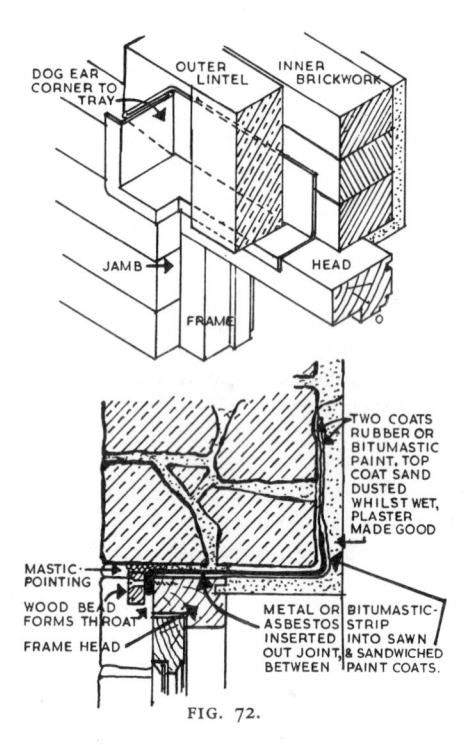

FIG. 72.

weather drip cut into a joint above and dressed down to half-an-inch or so below the bottom outer edge. A less visible repair can sometimes be made by raking out the joint vertically behind the arch or lintel, where these form the facework, and inserting upwards into this a damp-proof riser lapping the frame and secured thereto by suitable nailing or a fixing bead, or turned-out below the arch over a weathered or throated bead fixed to the frame. Repointing should be finished with a mastic.

In cases where no vertical joint exists above the frame and behind the wall facework, such as where brickwork is built directly off the frame head, over which there is not a damp-proof course, one should be inserted. This will involve cutting out and rebuilding the wall thickness for at least six inches above the frame head, building in a "tray" damp-proof course over the frame and up into the replaced work above, either behind a half-brick or a similar thickness of other walling material as would be done for an over lintel course to a cavity wall opening. To be safe, it should also extend a few inches beyond each jamb and be dog-eared to give a return outwards.

Removal of brickwork is not always necessary

Where cutting out of the wall itself over such an opening cannot be carried out, or is undesirable, then a compromise could provide the cure. Rake out the mortar joint immediately above the wood frame head right through to the inner soffit, cut away the internal damp stained plaster to this and the wall face, brush down, coat the inner wall surfaces with a good layer of chlorinated rubber or bitumastic paint, make up and pass over the frame head a strip of non-ferrous sheet metal or prepared bitumastic/asbestos sheet which can be turned down one inch over the frame outside and carried back under the inside soffit a few inches—or if it is only a few inches wide, back and turned up the inside wall face as far as necessary, but well bedded in the paint previously applied. The flashing underneath should then be sealed, sandwich style, under a second coat of paint. Prepare the second paint coat for plastering by dashing fine sand over its still wet surface and, when it is set, replaster using preferably a softish or insulative mix. Re-pointing of the overframe joint should be finished externally with mastic. A wood bead screwed through the flashing strip fixes this and also provides a throating. (See fig. 72). A bitumastic or rubber paint saturated wood slip forced into the overframe joint over the flashing, and leaving about half-an-inch for mastic finish pointing, could also be used instead of mortar filling.

34: Jamb, sill, and isolated patches

WHERE there is no general penetrative dampness but there are patches thereof to window or door jambs set in solid walls, it is indicative of driven rain coming in through cracks between the frame and reveal. Shrinkage of the timber of the frame or moisture movement of the wall may have opened the crack in the mortar pointing. If the crack is not more than an eighth of an inch wide, this can sometimes be adequately dealt with when repainting the frame, providing filling is properly carried out with white lead and that the normal paint is carried over the pointing. Wider cracks should be cut out and repointed, preferably with mastic. With less important work, readily painted resinous tapes could be used to bridge the gap; leaks past the abutment of steel frames, too, respond better to mastics or tape than to solid setting mortar pointing. Where there is no crack in the pointing to the frame and the wall is of cavity construction, access is probably through porous jamb material. If the frame is in a recess or to a jamb of a cavity wall, it is possible to rake out behind the reveal or across the cavity filling and insert as deep a damp-proof course as is possible—similar to that suggested on page 314 for a window head. Where the cavity filling damp-proof course has been omitted, this is the complete and only lasting remedy.

In solid walls it may be necessary to treat the internal reveal or jamb in a similar manner to that shown in fig. 72, p. 314, if drying out does not follow this treatment.

Remedial work should not be hurried

When dealing with this type of defect, it is often necessary to work in stages and to assess the effect of each before proceeding further; sometimes the following stage is not necessary. Each case needs individual attention—even one which appears to be so alike another.

Rendering to outer reveals appears to be a way of "killing two birds with one stone", when there is the possibility of an open joint to the frame and also porous jamb material. It should be remembered, however, that the fact that the penetration only exists to the jamb (even possibly only to one side of an opening) means that driven rain is concentrated into the joint and on to the reveal surface; it is possibly driven sideways off the glazing or impervious painted frame. Otherwise, there would be general penetration over the adjoining walls. Care is needed as unless it is possible to guarantee a permanent and perfectly watertight joint between the frame and the proposed rendering, the watertightness of the rendering will often add to the concentration of the driven water at the junction. If rendering the reveal or coating it with a repellent solution is considered, then a secure and lasting mastic joint must be provided at the junction. When rendering, place a narrow width timber rule against the frame and work up to it; when the rule is withdrawn, there is a satisfactory straight-sided joint into which mastic pointing can be knifed or gunned to produce watertightness, and a neat appearance will be achieved. The following alternative method is the practice adopted for new work. If the frame can be removed or the work can be done *in situ*, a groove is cut into the frame corresponding, at the side farthest from the reveal edge, with the face line of the proposed rendering so that a tongue of the rendering is worked into it to form a weatherstop.

Internal patches at ends of sills

Patches of dampness, roughly three quadrants of a circle in shape, at the ends of inner window boards or sills usually result from run-in and run-down from reveal cracks or open joints. The moisture soaks in off frame sill horns upon which, in cavity construction, jamb closures are often built and upon which, where these closures are of slates spanning the cavity, mortar droppings are nearly always left and a moisture bridge is thereby formed. In solid walls, driven rain at the foot of the frame and sill creeps in between the tenons and around the sill horn through inlets formed as a result of shrinkage arising when wet pointing dries out. Initial remedial works should be to thoroughly clean out the frame–sill and jamb reveal–sill junctions. If no open joint can be readily seen, it is worth testing by placing a thin flat feeler gauge blade, or a thin knife blade, flat upon the sill surfaces and attempting to push the blade into the joint. It is surprising how often this can be done. Also, when such dampness has been present for only quite a short time internally it is not unusual to find the sill horn (if softwood) or the frame tenons alone (if sill only is hardwood) decayed by wet rot.

Hardwoods need sealing

Where the timber is sound, thorough drying and caulking of open joints with mastic sealed with paint may prevent further ingress of water. One difficulty is the reluctance of hardwoods to accept paint. Oak and mahogany need a lead primer: white lead in three parts turpentine to one part linseed oil—known in the trade as "sharp" colour; a little red lead will dry it off more quickly. Teak requires sealing with knotting or varnish before application of a coat of sharp colour. Aluminium primers, too, are very useful where the timber will be exposed to hot sun conditions—particularly where the binder has a resin-alcohol base. Pinchin Johnson and Associates Ltd. now produce a water-emulsion primer called PJA Primer/Undercoat (water based) which can be applied over damp surfaces; this is said not to require knotting pre-preparation. This is possibly an improvement upon the older established practice of using a couple of coats of washable water paint to "kill" the oily sap which bleeds from teak and discolours oil paints. P.J.A. also claim that a variation of this primer (PJA sealer for bituminous surfaces (bleed seal)) can be used over creosoted woodwork and weathered bitumastic painted surfaces.

A carefully cut and rubbed in resinous tape covering to the mastic pointing, half on to the frame and half over the sill, will give quite a good foundation to a paint seal.

Where decay is found, it will be necessary to cut out all affected woodwork and piece in properly with new sound timber jointed to the existing structure at all connections and abutments with thick sharp priming paint. It will be necessary to cut out at least a half-brick from the foot of the external jamb; it is provident to cut out two courses so that a damp-course tray or cloak can be inserted around the end of the repaired sill, thus ensuring that no future inward damp penetration will occur. Removal of this amount of jamb brickwork will also enable any lodged bridging mortar over the horn in a cavity wall to be removed. Internal work can be as required according to the severity of salting and staining. Extension of and turning up at the ends of a metal sill weathering as shown in figure 66 (p. 287), where this too was necessary, into a shallow rebate cut into frame and dressing up and into a raked out jamb reveal joint, would seal the frame–sill joint.

Absence of waterbar protection

Where wooden sills have been simply bedded on to stone, tiled or brick sub-sills without a waterbar being inserted, there is usually enough shrinkage space between the two to allow the insertion, from the outside, of a thin copper or aluminium sheet metal strip. The stooling to reveal joint should be raked out so that this strip can be introduced for the full length of the wood sill. If a half-brick is removed, as suggested earlier, at each end then this strip underflashing can also be turned up at either end to form the tray around the sill ends. The internal window board will need removal so that when the metal strip has been pushed through, it can be turned up, bedded in paint or mastic, and nailed to the inside of the wood sill. If a groove exists in the sill, to house a

tongue at the rear edge of the window board, the
ing can be turned into this and the tongue of
eased to refit the narrowed groove. It will th
necessary to nail the underflashing. This remed
be applied where a wooden sill has been set on
studding without waterbar protection. Here, however, it
will probably be necessary to cut through nails or screws
holding the sill to the studding. An "eclipse" saw, which
will cut wood or metal, is very useful for this: it will also
widen the sill-studding head joint gap to take the underflashing, if this is necessary. Here, the external finish to the
window apron will usually be tile hanging, or rendering on
lathing. The pushed-in underflashing can then either be a
substitute for the existing apron flashing or, if this is nailed
flat to and on top of the stud head, can be dressed down over
to weather it externally. Internally, the new flashing is
turned up behind the sill and secured by screwing to the sill
through the flashing, a rounded bed mould, or narrow
window board.

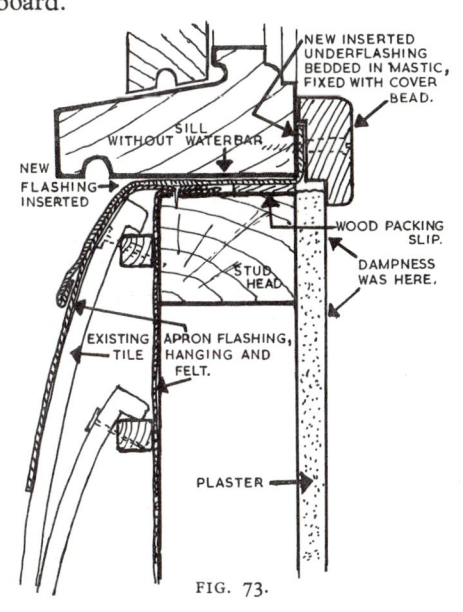

FIG. 73.

Isolated patches on walls

Roughly circular damp patches—isolated, and upon external walls—result from spot run-in in solid walls or point cavity bridging in cavity walls. The point of external entry through solid walls must be found and stopped, unless the patch is so small and only just damp at the internal plaster surface that it is possible to mask-treat it—remembering to carry the masking to at least the patch diameter beyond its entire perimeter. The point of entry should be sought horizontally from the inside patch level or higher: e.g. an open perpend, a porous brick or stone, or a hole or crack, etc. With cavity walls its cause is nearly always a dropped mortar bridge on a tie or a piece of debris, a brickbat, or a piece of wood lodged across the cavity. Occasionally, a run-in drip soaks into the inner skin from a leak higher up from a projection on the inside surface of the outer wall skin, or from seals crossing the cavity head wetted from a roof leak which has run down on to a strip tie, or a projection from the inner skin wall.

Cavity inspection may be necessary

Inspection is the only way to ascertain the conditions in a cavity. If there is only one isolated patch, then it is best to cut out one brick, as near as possible to the patch centre, from the outside wall skin. Working from outside saves plaster and decoration disturbance inside; but if for some reason it is more convenient to work from inside, then there is no objection. Removal of the bridge is the only remedy which will prevent further penetration. There is sometimes surprise when, on opening up a cavity, no bridge is found on the exposed tie or on any of those surrounding and, furthermore, there may be no tie at all nearby. This is because the cutting-out process may have dislodged the bridging material from the tie or from its lodgement. Although the actual bridging is not there, the appearance of the surface of the other skin wall will confirm whether or not the correct point has been disclosed: where there has been a bridge, this wall will either be damp, or show damp discolouration or efflorescence, and probably also a mortar stained patch where the bridge has been detached. Whilst the hole is open the opportunity should be taken to inspect the cavity thoroughly. A small mirror held at 45° across the cavity will reflect light and increase sight range, thereby facilitating the location of the relodged dropped mortar or debris and possibly other bridges, etc. A suitably bent raking tool may be used to dislodge articles within raking range, including any pieces of brick, etc., which may have been dislodged during entry or, indeed, in the process of the investigation of the cavity. The unintentional dislodgement of brickwork is difficult to avoid in these cases, and it is very important to ensure that any debris so added is also completely removed. If at all possible, always cut through a vertical joint (a perpend) and try to saw around the brick you wish to remove, along its top to cut the frog mortar, and then down the other perpend. Chop into the joint below with an electrician's bolster chisel, which is thinner than a bricklayer's, lever the brick up to loosen, and prise it out with two thin blades, or small pointing trowels, used simultaneously as levers at each end. If the brick becomes lodged, saw through the cuts again until sufficient clearance is gained: in this way only dust drops into the cavity.

If it is desired to inspect a greater area of cavity, a larger area of outside skin must be cut out; enlarging a hole is less difficult than removing the first brick. With the use of a larger mirror and, if necessary, an electric torch, or by putting your head right inside the hole it may be possible to see clearly.

Quoin access is useful

If it is desired to inspect a whole cavity, one or two quoin bricks should be removed to give a clear view over the entire length to the flank as well as the front. The removal of lodged material is not easy unless it is only lightly lodged, which mortar droppings seldom are. This is where corner or quoin access is preferable to entry through the centre of a face. From corner access, a long length of light steel tube (electrical conduit is ideal) or other probe can be used with some force—even hammered—to dislodge debris. It may have to be manoeuvred several times before the debris descends to below horizontal damp-proof course level where it will do no further harm. It is sometimes possible to hook the end of the probe, and when the debris is loosened to remove it with such an instrument. Whichever method is adopted, the debris must either be removed completely or dropped to below damp-proof course level. Clearing a cavity of one or two bridges can prove quite an expensive job, or it could be quite simple and inexpensive—it is impossible to forecast which before the cavity is opened and clearance attempted. Where attention is needed below sill level, useful access to cavities can often be gained by removal of an internal window board or sill. The removal of jamb closures is seldom profitable, unless its plasterwork needs renovation or major plastering and redecoration work is also contemplated. The removal of a frame or cutting out a means of access to a cavity for any reason whatsoever should be used as an opportunity to inspect the cavity and, as far as is practicable, to remove any potential cause of future bridge penetration. Corner inspection or mirror-reflected viewing with sufficient light, particularly during or just after rain, may also enable drip points overhead to be located so that they can be eradicated by probes if they are projections, or traced into roofs if this appears to be the source. In walls where general penetration through the outer cavity skin occurs or where massive condensation arises on its inner surface, these drips—even miniature cascades of water —may be seen to drop from the ends of over-lintel or frame head damp-proof courses. The cause would be cured here by opening up at the lintel end, reshaping the overhang so that it returns the collected water back on to the outer leaf surface, clearing obstructed weep holes (open vertical joints) and providing new ones where these have been omitted, through the outer leaf just above the damp-proof course. Weep holes are only really necessary where it is reasonably certain that a considerable amount of water will stream down the inner surface of the outer wall leaf.

Causes may be unusual

An unusual cause of a damp patch which appeared upon a house wall about two years after modernization work was completed proved, on cavity inspection, to be a length of P.V.C. covered electric cable dropped from the roof space down the cavity and taken into a wall of a room below. The cable touched the outer skin, looped down below its point of entry through the inner wall skin, and lodged on to a cavity tie which held it against the inner skin. Rain penetrated cracked rendering and soaked through outer brickwork, ran on to and down the cable surface, was absorbed into the inner skin breeze blocks through which it penetrated and finally showed on the inner plastered surface. The contact point of the cable with the outer skin was several feet above the damp patch: the rendering crack nearly a foot above that. The surface of the outer wall was examined minutely, over quite a considerable area level with and above the damp patch, for signs of possible water entry; but, prior to opening the cavity, none was found. Once the cause had been traced, the remedy was simple. The cable was pulled back taut into the loft and secured so that it no longer bridged the cavity: the damp patch dried out. The external rendering crack was caulked with mastic; this was to stop further soakage of the outer skin although that will no doubt recur at some future date. It had probably existed before the inside damp patch occurred, but had caused no internal nuisance.

The tracing of isolated patch penetrations, particularly where run-in and down occurs, is often a long—sometimes costly—and usually tedious process. One always hesitates to advise cutting away, but this so often is the only possible means and, after much surface searching and thought, finally has to be undertaken.

Remedies for solid walls

Solid walls where patch dampness occurs respond to pointing repair, cutting out, and rebedding new non-porous material in place of porous or otherwise defective units. On unimportant work, spalled or porous bricks or stones can be cut back an inch or so and plastic replacement of the surface made with cement mortar. Rendering, too, can be properly hacked off taking care to remove all loose work surrounding missing or cracked sections. The edges left should then be prepared, as suggested in the notes on plastic stone repairs (p. 296), to secure a good key for the patch followed by re-rendering in two coats. The outer coat to be a weaker mix than the inner: but neither stronger than the existing.

Similarly, roughcasts and pebbledashings, texturing, and like surfaces which are found to be defective and suspected or known to be the cause of rain penetration, can be repaired. One should be prepared, however, to deal with sulphated brickwork below, as recommended for chimney or breast work, as this may have been the cause, or have played its part towards, the defects of the coating. All of the considerations and suggested remedies with regard to sulphated chimney brickwork, will apply to any other work affected to similar degrees but arising from other causes. In all cases, one thing is certain; the ingress of water to, or its passage through, the renewed or repaired work must be stopped. If sulphating has already occurred or one cannot be certain that interstitial condense of vapours will not take place within the materials then, once the material is dry, all its surfaces should be sealed with a moisture- and vapour-proof acid-resisting membrane—application of at least two coats of bitumastic paint can serve this purpose. Reference is again recommended to National Building Studies Bulletin No. 10, published by Her Majesty's Stationery Office, entitled *External Rendered Surfaces for Walls*.

Making patch repairs less obvious

If repairs are contemplated to external renderings of any kind for any reason, it must be realized before commencing that it will not be possible to leave the repair matching the existing work. On new or recently completed work, it is often possible to detect batching differences, one day's application from the next, and even scaffold drop deviations. Both plain renderings and textured or dashed finishes all show the slightest difference in the sand colour, the amount of cement or lime, of mixing content, and of application technique. Although the differences may be less obvious with textured or dashed finishes they are, nevertheless, noticeable. Consequently many builders, when asked to quote for such repair work, point this out to prospective clients and suggest colouring the whole when the repairs are completed: painting on plain work, cement or stone painting upon textured or dashed work. The use of clear liquids in these cases does not have the desired effect. Protected lime washes, exterior quality distempers, and emulsion-type paints, are useful where they are suitable and, to some extent, they are less likely to seal pores than are ordinary oil paints, cement washes, and modern stone paints.

To paint or not to paint?

Where renderings are already generally impervious but are cracked and run-in is occurring, wide cracks should be brushed out with a wire brush and stopped; lesser cracks should be soft brushed out; in both cases followed by the application of two coats of a modern stone paint. These measures will often secure the surfaces against penetration for a long time—several years in fact. These paints will bridge the lesser cracks and they remain elastic to a certain degree. Generally with ordinary paints, the harder and more glossy the surface when dry, the less it is likely to bridge cracks during application. Any paint applied to either the inside or the outside of a wall must, to a degree, inhibit diffusion of moisture vapour through the wall from the inside and also hinder, if not prohibit, evaporation at the outer surface. Broadly speaking, if the problem is very largely penetration from outside—paint; if the trouble arises through condensation inside—do not paint. It is almost as simple as that. Which action to take should be evident if the wall is already rendered to a hard outer surface finish, has cracked, and shows patch internal dampness which can be related to cracked areas: more general internal dampness should guide one away from pore filling and towards proofings "which can breathe".

Finally, before distempering or otherwise coating any material other than timber, glass or metal, remember that once a paint of any kind that will key to the groundwork has been applied, it is almost impossible to remove all visible traces thereof; it is even less likely that any pore filling can be removed. The only materials which can possibly be restored to anything near their original surface state are soft stone, timber, and brick which have their colour and texture evenly distributed throughout the material thickness and can be rubbed back to resurface after stripping the coating. When dealing with property under leasehold covenants or restrictive repairing or maintenance agreements, ensure that whatever it is proposed to apply will not have to be removed at a later date. Also make quite sure that if the appearance of the building is to be materially altered through the work envisaged, that both the appropriate agreement and planning approval are obtained before any application work commences.

Patches on internal walls

Patch dampness occurring to internal walls—other than to chimney breasts or walls backing flues or where signs indicate rising capillary trouble—usually results from rundown from roof leaks or abutments, or from leaking service pipes or fittings. Incidentally, it is well to remember that where dampness is caused by rising capillary movement, this can show at considerable height above ground level. Drips from condense on tanks, pipes, etc., may run down internally within walls or partitions, even hollow stanchion or column casings; when their free passage downwards is blocked, they pool and soak through.

The author was told by an architect of repute that in a

quite important building, a wet patch to a stanchion—forming part of an internal wall and situated several storeys below a roof level tank room—became increasingly evident a few months after the work had been completed. It was known that no water service ran up the building within reasonable range of this point but, when opened up, the casing showed that water was running down from above. Since the tank room was roughly overhead at this point, the tank—a cast steel sectional one, works coated with bitumastic inside—was emptied and inspected. No trace of a hole or leaking joint could be found: however, the tank side was too close to the wall on the leak side to permit external inspection from the tank room. When the tank was refilled and the stanchion casing adjacent thereto was cut away, a pin-hole leak was discovered in one of the sections near to the tank base. The jet issuing from the hole was so fine that it could not be seen; evidence of the leakage was, however, seen when a piece of paper became wet when placed in the path of the water. It must have been spraying into a hollow or hole in the stanchion casing, penetrating, and then running in and down the steel until it reached an obstruction where it pooled and soaked out. Whilst this can be a "million to one" chance, it can happen and it is necessary to know how to trace such a cause.

Suspect any cause

When investigating dampness, anything and everything must be suspected until, in each case, the possibility can be eliminated. The author has seen presumed rising dampness traced to as fine a pinpoint leak as occurred in the above tank but, in this second case, it was found in a lead, underfloor, service pipe.

A sound rule in these cases, therefore, is to search around the damp patch level for pipes etc. entering the wall. If one does enter and appears to proceed in the direction of the patch, but is dry where exposed above that point, the patch should be opened up. It may be necessary to expose back upwards to find the leak. If no pipe enters the construction from within the surrounding rooms, examine the roof and underfloor spaces; if still without success and the wall is a party structure, then a search should be made in the adjoining property. Examine walls for pipe chases or ducts concealed by decorations. It should also be remembered that water can enter and flow through an electrical conduit and run out at another point without causing an electrical short circuit; thus it can become a path for water which can cause patch dampness through a leak or by concentration of condensation—as seen above with the P.V.C. cable in the cavity wall.

The strangest instance of which the author has knowledge occurred in his own house. A damp stain of about four inches in diameter appeared on a ceiling below a hot water storage cylinder cupboard in the room above. It was not directly under the cylinder and no pipes serving it entered the floor of the cupboard on that side of the cylinder; furthermore, the floor was dry as were all the surfaces of the pipes and cylinder even when it was cold. Nevertheless, there was a damp stained patch which investigations proved could only have come from some source between the ceiling and floor above. It appeared in early spring but did not spread and it was not, therefore, considered to be in need of urgent attention. Before any further investigations were made, it dried out to leave only the faintest discolouration of the distemper of the ceiling. However, the following spring it recurred. A board was removed and above the stain, resting on the ceiling of the room below was a nest of field mice: the stain wetness was of their production and certainly did not arise from any other source. They were cleared out and their re-entry stopped; no further "dampness" has occurred.

Roof leaks at abutments and verges

Where the roof overhead is either flat or pitched, patches found on ceilings adjacent to a wall, or on walls themselves, in top floor rooms can result from open abutment joints between the roof covering and a parapet wall or a run-in under a defective verge. Tracing and caulking a crack to a flat roof covering abutments is, as a rule, not difficult providing that the possibility is anticipated of capillary entry and progress through the finest of cracks and open joints. Cold asphaltic mastics are extremely useful here on almost any material covering. With pitched roofs, however, soakers and apron flashings may be at fault and quite often the actual site of the penetration can be traced to run-down on wall surfaces within the roof space. Defective soakers and flashings can be replaced with new; minor leaks can be caulked. Where cement and sand angle fillets have been used in place of soakers or flashings, the repair will be as for defective renderings. If, however, loose lengths of cement fillet have to be replaced, flashings and/or soakers could be substituted; but if the cement is re-run, a better appearance and more lasting weathertightness is obtained by placing the cement mortar into the angle; but, instead of trowelling-off the fillet surface, bed into it cut-to-width slate or tile slips to form the surface. This gives a result similar to a tile sill or projection weathering and will not crack, craze, or leave the wall so readily as often occurs with cement alone. Before placing the cement mortar the joints of the wall with which it will key should be well raked out, the roof coverings well brushed down, and both damped.

Isolated damp patches, or even bands, occasionally show intermittently for short periods to the plastered or painted internal surfaces of outside walls. Bands could be from a string or band course of walling material more or less absorbent or dense than the wall generally. If the more absorbent nature can be seen or detected outside, proofing of this area is an answer. If considerably more dense nature is exhibited, one of two things may be happening. Internal condensation may be occurring upon the more heat absorptive inner surface so produced or, if the bricks or other material units are non-absorptive—such as in the case with some blue engineering, glazed, or Southwater type bricks, glazed faience blocks or possibly granite or slate blocks—surface run-off water from outside may be soaking into the porous mortar joints, or into capillary joint cracks resulting from thermal movements of the dense material, to reach the inner surfaces. This occurs because the possibility of external re-evaporation is less attractive than internal, and any other dispersal or run-down path is blocked by the surrounding dense material.

In this case the remedy is to render weathertight the joints to the band or larger area. Good weatherstruck pointing with a hard mortar is possible here; but if there is any possibility of imperfect adherence to the units, mastic may give better results.

Sweating brickwork in underfloor spaces

Horizontal damp-proof courses composed of a few courses of blue brickwork below a floor plate and through an external wall thickness often show "sweating" on the inside and sometimes beads of white or cream-coloured "perspiration" dripping down the surface. This is from a similar cause or causes: the coloured drops being salts or efflorescence from the mortar or, if the bricks are in contact with outside earth, possibly salts therefrom carried in through the joints in solution. Condensed underfloor moisture not only adds to the sweat, but is in fact encouraged by the deliquescent deposits therefrom. Very little damage, if any, will be done by this, especially if it is intermittent, unless salt crystals grow over the surfaces and extend to bridge to timbers. If this occurs the dangers are obvious—possible fungi growth. Additional underfloor through ventilation will usually constitute a cure; spraying with a fungicide will inhibit the growth of deposited fungi spores. Otherwise the provision of an inner or outer cavity could cure such a surface defect if it became necessary to do so. Often where this type of dampness occurs the oversite concrete is too porous, and proofing this would materially assist by reducing the amount of readily evaporable moisture at the surface.

Underfloor air entering from a warm sunny elevation and taking up evaporated moisture from site concrete or soil will produce condense when contacting dense cool surfaces of shaded sleeper walls or those to cooler external elevations. Draught proofing of timber ground floors, close carpeting, covering open jointed boarding with hardboard sheets, laying impervious sheet or glued down tile coverings on insulative underlays will, whilst being admirable improvements from the heat loss reduction point of view, increase the possibility of such condense. Above floors, an odd isolated occasional condensational damp patch could result from one hard, dense, non-absorptive brick having been built into the inner wall surface by accident or design; in the latter case, to save ordering and waiting for a few additional ordinary bricks or where salvaged bricks of mixed types are being reused. Treat this like a cavity cold bridge.

There is a product, known as "Eff-or-less", a spirit-based liquid, which the manufacturers claim will neutralize efflorescent salts within the pores of materials: it is intended for internal use. The instructions for use state: brush-off or sandpaper the dry visible surface salts, and apply one coat of liquid (thirty-five yards super to the gallon coverage per two coats) plus one fifteen minutes later. It is colourless and said to penetrate four to six inches into the material and the manufacturers claim it cures efflorescence. Demonstrations certainly appear to support this claim, but only time can prove for how long it is effective or if there are any side effects which would not become evident perhaps for some time. This appears to offer a possible alternative to stripping off internal affected plaster, or using leaching or masking treatments before redecoration. The fact that it is suggested that surface deposits should be brushed off or removed with sandpaper, indicates that a dry surface condition is necessary for application. If this is so, then the query arises as to whether it would in fact penetrate to between four and six inches if the pores are moisture filled (which they very probably will be on older plastered surfaces) where surface deposits are sufficient to be brushed off. Spirits do not readily diffuse into aqueous solutions, unless an emulsion is formed with water before application.

35: External claddings and surface coatings

WHEN whole external wall areas are constructed with surfaces which are not sufficiently resistant to rain penetration or other wind-driven droplets of water, or have developed porosity with age, then two courses of treatment other than rebuilding are available. Cladding can be added to shed the water driven on to the wall before it reaches the porous surface. This cladding need not, as we have seen earlier, be itself entirely non-porous if it either covers an impervious, sandwiched membrane or has a sufficient cavity between its rear and the wall it is protecting. Reference back will show the possible needs of either, according to the effect desired.

Where claddings are inappropriate, or cannot be applied, some form of brush, trowel or sprayed waterproof or repellent coating will be the best protection. Where there is no objection to change of appearance, there is choice from all kinds of renderings, both cement and cement/lime bonded, or of resinous or bituminous bonded types, as well as of almost any kind of surface texture and colour. If there is an objection to altered appearance, the only treatment available is the use of clear colourless repellent solutions or impregnants.

It is not possible to advise upon or discuss all and every one of these two kinds of coatings. Every job will need individual consideration, but the following guides should be followed.

The surface to which the coating is applied must accept it without further deterioration, crumbling, injurious reaction to either itself or the applied coating, or detachment from its general mass. Thus a strong *in situ* coat which will adhere firmly to a backing and have any appreciable shrinkage in setting, must never be applied over soft, friable, or loosely held back, surfaces. If the surface varies then, except to very small patches, the majority backing must be satisfactory. With paints having reasonable elasticity, one expects satisfactory adherence if about twenty per cent of the backing provides an efficient key, but thicker coatings require much more; further, in both cases, it must be evenly and generally disposed. As we have stated earlier, in general, the softest and most elastic coat which will achieve the required effect is best.

All coatings are best if not overworked at their surface with smoothing or spreading tools. This tends to pack down the top surface and produce exactly the opposite result to the one required—i.e. a softer top than interior or backing. This is where spraying of plasters and renderings or other thick coating is advantageous when compared with trowel application. Brush texturing after trowelling on, too, helps in this respect. Brush application tends to incorporate air into the thickness generally and to reduce density.

Hard, dense surfaces over porous or softer backings always craze and crack upon setting or with age. A cracked or crazed surface coating is worse than useless as protection against driven water or run-off. So if possible the least dense material of any class should be chosen and applied with the minimum amount of tooling. But ensure that coverage is one hundred per cent complete. This is why so many manufacturers and advisors stipulate: "at least two coats": defects of coverage or surface continuity in the first application are sealed by the second coat. Any gap, however small, will receive a more concentrated supply of water from run-off than that area of surface would otherwise have to resist; the remainder being more resistant. The effect would only be to convert general, and perhaps not too severe, internal dampness to severe patch dampness at least. If any wall is subject to surface movement, wet *in situ* coatings which set rigid cannot be used. In any case all open cracks, hollows, and deep depressions, should, before any coating is applied, be filled with material of roughly equal density and porosity to that of the general backing surface. If this is not done, the unequal coating thickness necessary nearly always causes cracking or distortion over or around such defects. "Dubbing out", as plasterers term such filling of depressions, is good practice in any *in situ* coatings. Lining or marking out to resemble stone blocks etc. on smooth, hardfaced coatings only invites cracking in straight lines instead of in crazy patterns: water penetrates either. If crazed or line cracking occurs, allow the backing to dry out thoroughly and then stop and paint the whole with as elastic a paint as is practicable. Where drying-out of cracks cannot be guaranteed, the use of emulsified water paints where these are suitable for outside use is more appropriate as these paints do not usually set to a very dense skin; a water/bitumen emulsion can also be used. Their water content enables them to penetrate the moisture-filled cracks which would have a repellent effect upon oil or spirit vehicles. Furthermore, these types of paint are seldom one hundred per cent impermeable and permit a degree of re-evaporation to trapped water.

Where coating of sufficient thickness cannot be applied, impregnation with waxes in solvents, or as aqueous emulsions, can sometimes be used. Providing some depth of penetration is achieved, this provides protection for considerable periods: only wax exposed at the surface becomes degraded in a year or two. Soft stones and those which as claddings have a tendency to curl are sometimes protected in this way. If wax is used, however, the pores are sealed and completely prevent any possibility of diffusion of water vapour through them if it is present from previous penetration or can reach the inside from another source. Siliconate-latex treatments also offer an alternative here, without pore sealing. They also resist wind-forced water entry.

Metallic and silicone repellent solutions which are brush or spray applied in accordance with the manufacturers' directions, simply prevent the spreading of drops of water alighting upon a surface; they thus do not penetrate, but run off. Very heavy and sustained wind could, however, drive through such coatings any water trapped in hollows or run-in width cracks. This is why "those that breathe" are better propositions than "sealers": in all cases, all hole filling should be carried out before application of the solutions.

If repointing is to be in porous-soft material, to be compatible with the structural units, lime mortar for instance, then this too should be done before applying the solution. Dense, water-proof pointing is best done after application as suggested in chapter 33—surface treatments may be possible.

Coatings must be complete for the same reason as noted for thick *in situ* work. Most manufacturers introduce a fading (fugitive) dye into otherwise clear solutions, to facilitate recognition of complete coverage, and normally recommend two coats. Very few, if any, have a life of more than a few years but they are not expensive. Tars, black bitumastic paints, ordinary cement paints, and tallow protected limewashes are cheap and useful, where they are suitable. Most clear colourless repellent coatings can be overcoated with maintenance applications of similar material later when they need renewal, so too can most cement paints, tar, bitumastics, lime washes etc. after wire or stiff bristle brushing-down and filling obvious hollows or flaked-off areas. Annual or bi-annual treatments with cheaper materials, particularly where they restore brightness or contrast where this is desired, is widespread and satisfactory practice for domestic, farm, and small commercial premises.

Appendix 1: Thomson weir

A Thomson weir, referred to in Vol. 1, p. 64, consists of a dam placed across the flow of freely flowing water. For temporary incidental use as suggested here, it can be a piece of board of suitable width, 6 or 9 in., with a vee notch having an internal angle of 90° cut into it from its top edge (see fig. 74). For our purpose, it would be fixed half way along a trial hole or slit trench, and we should have to bale, if the flow were slow, or pump if it were faster, the overflow water from the down stream side of the weir, so as to permit free, even flow through the vee until a settled depth became evident. Then, either from markings on the weir board, or with a dip measure, held into the bottom of the vee, the flow depth in inches can be read off.

The quantity of water flowing over the weir will be:

Depth in inches	Gallons per minute
$\frac{1}{4}$	0·06
$\frac{1}{2}$	0·34
$\frac{3}{4}$	0·89
1	1·87
$1\frac{1}{4}$	3·26
$1\frac{1}{2}$	5·15
$1\frac{3}{4}$	7·60
2	10·60
$2\frac{1}{4}$	14·20
$2\frac{1}{2}$	18·44
$2\frac{3}{4}$	23·42
3	29·18

FIG. 74.

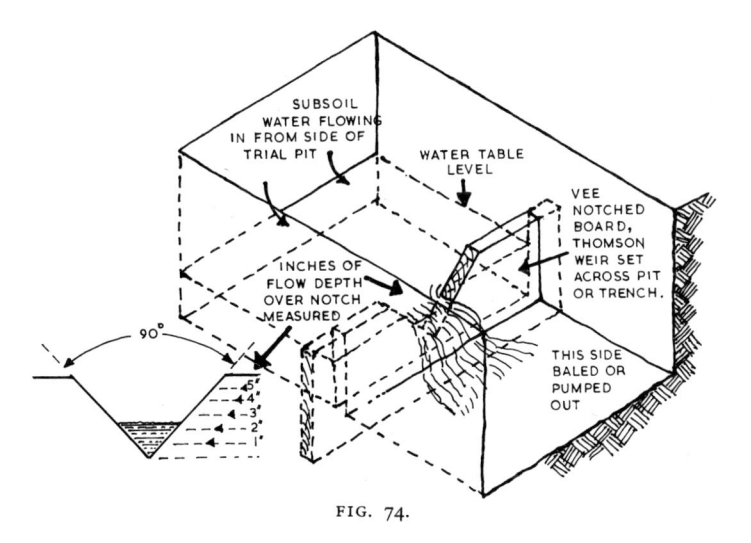

Appendix 2: Wet and dry bulb thermometers. Hygrometers.

WET and dry bulb thermometers consist of two ordinary thermometers, divided to the Fahrenheit scale at present in

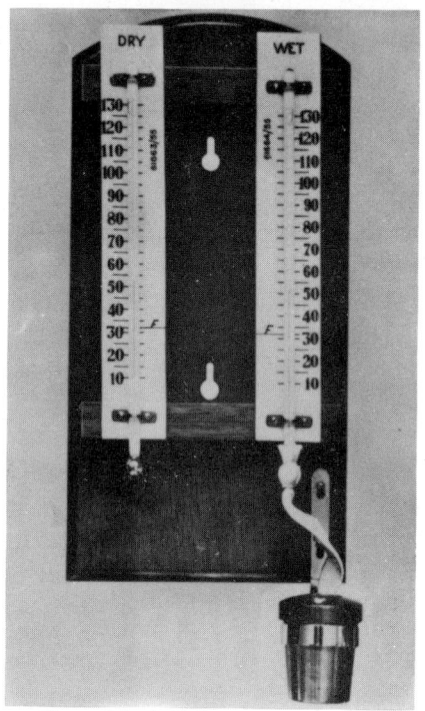

FIG. 75. *Wet and dry bulb thermometers, wall mounted type.*
(Courtesy Griffin & George Ltd.)

this country, mounted side by side on a frame. One has its bulb free, whilst the other has the bulb sheathed in a degreased cotton covering, which dips into a water filled trough, from which water drawn up by capillary action can evaporate to the air surrounding the bulb.

The dry bulb records air temperature, heat lost or gained by it being by radiation and convection only, whereas the wetted bulb records these losses or gain from radiation, convection and evaporation. This means that the dry reading is usually higher than the wet. In excessively humid weather conditions this tendency could be reversed.

Tables 1 and 2, are necessary to ascertain relative humidity of air to be tested, although you may find that some hygro-

TABLE 1. Dew Point Computation.
Using Wet and Dry Bulb Thermometers.

Dry Bulb Thermometer °F	Factor	Dry Bulb Thermometer °F	Factor
25	6·53	50	2·06
26	6·08	51	2·04
27	5·61	52	2·02
28	5·12	53	2·00
29	4·63	54	1·98
30	4·15	55	1·96
31	3·70	56	1·94
32	3·32	57	1·92
33	3·01	58	1·90
34	2·77	59	1·89
35	2·60	60	1·88
36	2·50	61	1·87
37	2·42	62	1·86
38	2·36	63	1·85
39	2·32	64	1·83
40	2·29	65	1·82
41	2·26	66	1·81
42	2·23	67	1·80
43	2·20	68	1·79
44	2·18	69	1·78
45	2·16	70	1·77*
46	2·14	71	1·76
47	2·12	72	1·75
48	2·10	73	1·74
49	2·08	74	1·73

Dry Bulb Thermometer °F	Factor	Dry Bulb Thermometer °F	Factor
75	1·72	86	1·65
76	1·71	87	1·645
77	1·70	88	1·64
78	1·69	89	1·635
79	1·685	90	1·63
80	1·68	91	1·625
81	1·675	92	1·62
82	1·67	93	1·61
83	1·665	94	1·60
84	1·66	95	1·595
85	1·655	96	1·59

TABLE 2. For Computing Relative Humidity from Wet and Dry Bulb Thermometers. Maximum weight of water vapour per cubic foot which air can hold invisibly at Dew Point. (7,000 grains = 1 lb.)

Dew Point Temperature °F	Water Vapour per cubic foot Grains Weight	Dew Point Temperature °F	Water Vapour per cubic foot Grains Weight
14	1·00	58	5·39
16	1·09	60	5·77
18	1·19	62	6·17
20	1·30	64	6·59
22	1·42	66	7·04
24	1·51	68	7·51
26	1·68	70	8·01 [*2]
28	1·82	72	8·54
30	1·97	74	9·10
32	2·13	76	9·69
34	2·30	78	10·31
36	2·48	80	10·98
38	2·66	82	11·67
40	2·86	84	12·40
42	3·08	86	13·17
44	3·32	88	13·98
46	3·56	90	14·85
48	3·82	92	15·74
50	4·10	94	16·69
52	4·39	96	17·68
54	4·71	98	18·73
56	5·04	100	19·84
57·61	5·32 [*1]		

DAMPNESS IN BUILDINGS 343

meters have scales attached to enable assessments of conditions to be made without calculations. These do not usually show relative humidity as a percentage, but can do so.

To use the hygrometer, expose it in the air to be tested; some instruments are mounted so that they can be swung around like a football supporter's or old fashioned watchman's rattle (see fig. 76). This enables more sensitive tem-

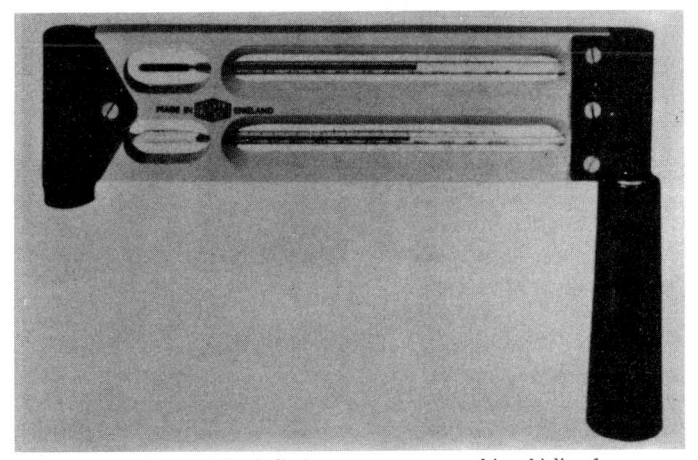

FIG. 76. *Wet and dry bulb thermometers mounted in whirling frame.*
(Courtesy Griffin & George Ltd.)

perature readings to be made in less time than would be possible if the instrument were just hung in rooms where little air movement exists. Read off the dry and wet temperatures and subtract the latter from the former. Now multiply this temperature difference by the factor from Table 1 for the dry bulb reading.

The product is then subtracted from the dry bulb temperature reading, to give the dew point temperature for the air being tested. Table 2 is now consulted, and against this calculated temperature will be found the amount of water vapour which this air is actually holding invisibly.

To find relative humidity, or the percentage of saturation, which this condition shows, further reference is made to Table 2, and read off the amount of vapour which can be

FIG. 77. *Hygrometer giving direct relative humidity reading.*
(Courtesy Griffin & George Ltd.)

held by air at DRY BULB TEMPERATURE, but which the air being tested does not hold in full. If we now,

$$\frac{\text{Calculated temperature moisture content}}{\text{Actual dry bulb temperature possible moisture}} \times 100$$

we get relative humidity for the air being tested.

Example: Dry bulb reading, 70°F. Wet bulb reading, 63°F.
thus, 70° minus 63° equals, 7°
factor for 70°F, from Table 1, is 1·77,★
which multiplied by 7° × 1·77 equals 12·39.
Subtract this from dry bulb reading, 70°F.
gives, 70° minus 12·39, equals, 57·61.
From Table 2, we get, interpolated between
56° and 58°,★[1] 5·32 grains of water vapour actually held.
Relative humidity, or percentage of saturation.
Consult, Table 2, dry bulb temperature, 70°F.
equals, possible moisture, 8·01 grains.★[2]

thus we get $\frac{5\cdot 32}{8\cdot 01} \times 100$ equals, 65·17% saturated.

Thus this air at this temperature could take up a further 2·69 grains of vapour and hold it invisibly.

★, ★1 and ★2 are indicated on the Tables for ready reference from the example.

Appendix 3: The Kata thermometer.

THE Kata thermometer measures heat loss in air by radiation and convection, at a temperature similar to that maintained by a human body. Readings and calculations will give the

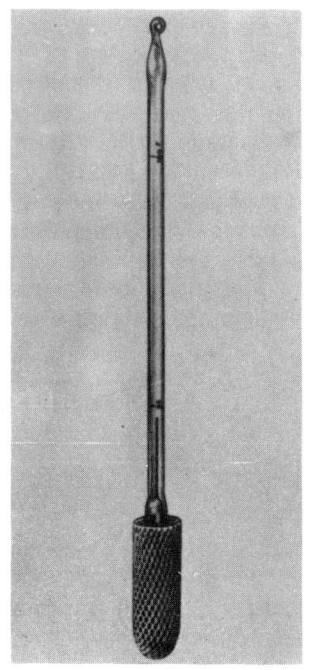

FIG. 78. *Kata thermometer with sac.*
(Courtesy Griffin & George Ltd.)

cooling power of the air being tested, in millicalories cm^2/sec. (One calorie is the amount of heat required to raise the temperature of one gram of water 1° Centigrade. A millicalorie is one-thousandth of this amount.) (Human body temperature is normally 98·4°F.)

Each instrument has a factor marking etched upon its stem. This factor is relevant only to the instrument upon which it is marked. Dry and wet readings are taken as with the wet and dry bulb thermometers but with rather more preparation, and not in degrees of temperature—they are taken as a time, in seconds.

Dry readings are taken by suspending the instrument in air on a thread, with the bulb first immersed in water at a temperature of about 150°F., until the fluid rises into but does not fill the top bulb. Then the water container is removed, the bulb dried of surplus water, and timed in seconds with a stop watch, to show how long the liquid takes to fall from the 100° marking down to 95°—the only temperature markings shown on the stem. This procedure is repeated four times, and an average of the last three is calculated. The first reading is ignored; it is a warming-up trial run. The calculated average time is then divided into the "factor".

Wet readings are taken in the same way as for the dry but with a silk sheath, dried down so that no water actually drips from it, kept around the bulb when it is withdrawn from the water container: the averaging and calculations are then carried out.

For comfort the dry Kata should show a cooling power of around 6 in winter and 5 in summer. The wet should show not less than 18, which means that relative humidity is between 65% and 70% of saturation.

Thus the Kata thermometer is designed to deal with human habitation conditions.

It can additionally be used as an anemometer (for measuring wind velocity), the dry average timing being used together with an ordinary Fahrenheit thermometer dry reading, with which air velocity in feet per minute can be read off by reference to a chart (fig. 79).

KATA THERMOMETER CHART.

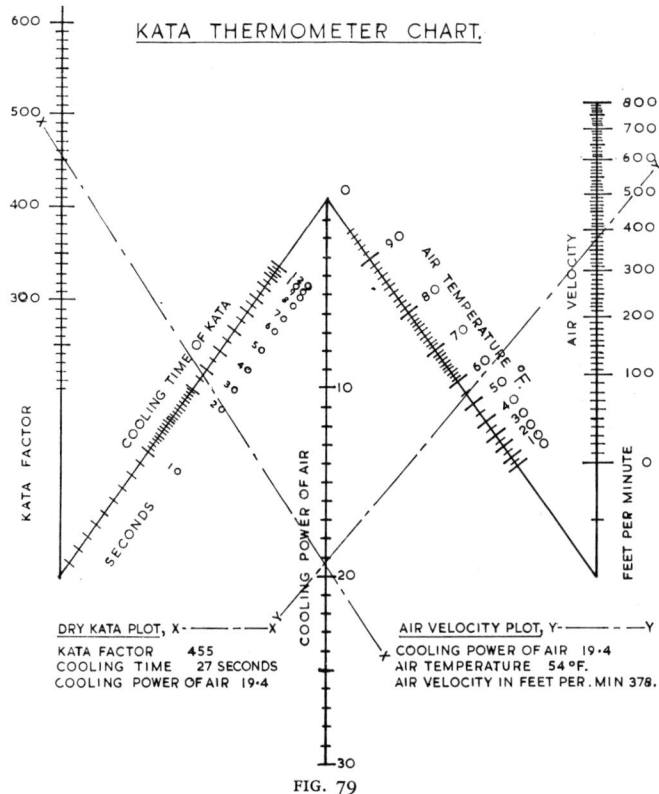

FIG. 79

Reading example: Time in seconds of four readings,
  63·9 (ignored)
  62·25
  61·75
  62·66

Total 186·66 divided by 3 equals 62·11 seconds, divided into factor, shall we say, 378, gives 6·086, which is very slightly too much for comfort; one would feel an occasional chilly feeling in such air.

An anemometer example is shown on the chart.

Index

Acids produced from combustion, 258–9, 260
Air, bricks, 187, 255
 cavities, conductivity of, 201
 convectional movement of, 222, 228, 230, 240, 249–50, 255
 dew point temperature of, 189–90, 207
 dirt in, 227
 humidity of, 180, 189, 190, 191, 220, 256
 in buildings, 195, 196
 in water, 182, 183
 locks, 183
 saturated, 189–90, 191, 192, 195
Algae, 309
Aluminium, 261
 liners, 267
 primer, 319
Asbestos, cement sheets, 207
 conductivity of, 201
 fibre as paint filler, 244, 246, 252
 sprayed, 245
Asphalt, 207, 287, 288
 mastic, 292, 313
 roofs, 211, 286
 surface temperature of, 209

Balconies, 307
Boilers, supplementary air inlets to, 270–71
Brickwork, 202
 conductivity of, 201, 207
 sulphate saturated, 276–7
 sulphation from, 266
 sweating, 332
 "U" values of, 197, 198
 with sulphated joints, 261, 277
Bricks, blue engineering, 331
 glazed, 331
 quoin, 323, 324
 Southwater type, 331
 sulphated, 265, 326

Bridging, dampness caused by, 322–3
 precautions against, 251–2, 308
British Standard Code of Practice, The (CP 341.300.307:1956), 197
Building Research Station Digests, No. 21, 245
 No. 58 (*Mortars for Jointing*), 245, 304
 No. 60, 267
 No. 65 (*The Selection of Clay Building Bricks*), 304
 No. 123 (*Sulphate Attack on Brickwork*), 304
Buildings, deterioration of, 259
 new materials for, 196
 preheating of, 226

Calcium bicarbonate, 258
 carbonate, 258, 259
 oxide, 260
 sulphate, 260, 261, 292
Canopies, 307
Capillarity, 216
 inward pull theory of, 180
 surface skin theory of, 180
Capillary penetration, 280, 281, 283, 286, 289
Carbon dioxide, 258, 259
Carbonic acid, 258
Cavity clearing, 323–4
 inspection, 322–3
Ceilings, anti-condensation paint for, 246
 condense on, 235
 insulation of, 238–9
 prevention of condensation on, 237
 sulphating on, 272–3
 surface resistances of, 200
Cement, 297, 298
 as rendering, 216
 mortars, 261, 266
 Portland, 260, 298
 "Roman", 298

Cement (*contd.*)
   slab—wood wool, conductivity of, 219
Chimneys, 262, 263, 271
   pots, 272
   remedies for sulphated, 264–5, 266
Cladding, external, 213–8, 284, 334
   anti-frost shields, 215
   battens for, 214, 215
   cedar boarding, 216
   galvanized steel, 215
   tile brick, 214
   tile/slate, 213, 214
   timber, 214, 215
   underfelting of, 215
   weatherboarding, 213
   windshields, 215
Clean Air Act, 1954, 259
Coatings, surface, 334–7
Combustion processes, 257–8
Concrete, ballast, conductivity of, 201
   condensation on walls made of, 224
   foamed, conductivity of, 219
   lightweight, conductivity of, 201
   liners for flues, 268–9
   precast, 207
Condensate, 191
Condensation, 179–85, 307, 331
   "bloom" caused by, 193
   effect of temperature on, 188
   encouraged by draught proofing, 234
   grooves and channels, 250–51
   in domestic flues, 253, 257–63
   in kitchens, 242, 245
   in W.C.s, 243, 244
   misting caused by, 193–4, 249
   modern causes of, 225–6
   moulds caused by, 193, 222
   occurrence of, 192–3, 194, 210, 211
   on cold bridges, 251
   prevention of, 187, 196, 213, 218, 237, 242, 245, 249, 264–78
   remedies for, 264–78
   surfaces and, 188–9, 243–4
Condense, 207, 211, 213, 219, 283, 332
   and fungi, 231
   on cold surfaces, 243–4

Condense (*contd.*)
   on walls, 222, 249
   structural hazards of, 247–8
Copings, penetration through, 303, 304
Cork, as paint filler, 244, 245
   board, conductivity of, 219
   loose granulated, conductivity of, 219
   slabs, conductivity of, 200
Cottage, Devonshire cob, 199
Course, damp-proof, 306, 308, 314, 315, 332
Crystallization, 260–61, 264, 276

Dadoes, insulated, 218
Dampness, aggravated by heating, 254–5
   aggravated by structural additions, 255–6
   caused by absence of throatings, 286
   caused by acids produced from combustion, 258–60
   caused by bridging, 322, 325
   caused by field mice, 330
   caused by run-in, 313
   condensational. *See* Dampness, penetrating
   development of, 309
   effect of relative humidity on, 191
   ground. *See* Dampness, rising
   inspecting for, 329–30
   penetrating, 213, 250, 279–89, 303, 306
   rising, 179, 213, 218, 249, 250
De-greasing units, 247
De-humidifiers, 246–7
Diffusion, 196, 231
Dirt, and condensation, 227–8
   over radiators, 228–9
Distempers, exterior, 327
Double glazing units, 179
Downpipes, fixing of, 310–11
   P.V.C. rectangular, 312
   rainwater, 313
Drainage, joint, 284
   ledge, 283–4
   of large weathered areas, 284

Draught proofing and condensation, 234, 332

Ebonite, expanded, conductivity of, 219
Efflorescence, 258, 260–61, 276, 277, 300, 304, 332, 333
"Eff-or-less" liquid, 333
Evaporation, 180, 182, 185, 186–7
  caused by paraffin oil heaters, 226
  caused by washing machines and spin dryers, 226
  definition of, 182
  from human beings, 192
  prevention of, 187
  rate of, 186
  re-evaporation, 219, 220, 246
  source of, 179
  temperature and, 182, 188
Extractor hoods, 243

Faience blocks, 331
Fans, 256
  effectiveness of, 242
  use of, 249
Fibre boards, conductivity of, 219
Fibreglass, 218, 236, 298, 299
  conductivity of, 219
Fish and chip ranges, hazards of, 247–8
Floors, surface resistances of, 200
Flues, domestic, 259
  Building Regulations for, 266, 269, 271
  cool flues on outside walls, 273–4
  concrete liners for, 268–9
  condensation in, 253, 257–63, 269, 274
  flexible metal liners for, 266–8
  porous linings in, 274–5
  rain in, 275
  soot doors in, 269–70
  sulphating in, 266, 268, 275
  ventilation from, 274
Foils, aluminium, 223, 235, 236, 277, 278
  lead, 223, 278
Fuels, chemical results of combustion

Fuels (contd.)
  of, 253–4, 257–8
  combustion processes of, 257
  condense from, 273
Fungi, 231, 332
  fungicidal paste, 231, 278
  precautions against, 231

Gases, behaviour of, 196, 257
  effect of temperature on evaporation of, 188
  molecular activity in, 181, 182
Gels, 192, 254, 281
  distempers, 254, 255
  gelatinous binders, 254
  paperhangers paste, 254
  Silica gel, 192
Glass, 207
  conductivity of, 201
  temperature drop in windows of, 199
  "U" values for, 197
Glass wool quilt, conductivity of, 201
Goldsize, 278
Granite blocks, 331
Gutters, fixing of, 310–11
  flat-backed, 312

Hardboard, conductivity of, 201
Hardwoods, difficulty of painting, 319
Heat build-up, 220–21
  flow, direction of, 205
  input, 221
  losses, 204, 205–6, 220–21, 235
  resistance, calculation of, 202–4
Heating, central, 243
  electric, 221, 225, 234, 249, 250
  gas, 254
  "H" values and, 197–8
  hot water radiator, 221
  inseparable from ventilation, 197
Hopper heads, 310, 311
Humidity, calculation of relative, 191
Hygrometers, 338–44

"Inertol Dinaphon V. 33" paint, 246
Insulation, 209–11, 215
  cladding and, 215, 216, 217

Insulation (*contd*.)
  layers, 233–4
  linings and, 218–20, 234
  of ceilings, 238–9
  of tanks, 244
Insulators, 218, 229
  plasterboard, 236
  plastic, 245

Jamb, door, damp patches round, 317
  remedial work on, 318, 320
Joints, eroded, 309
  open, 300, 319, 324

Kapok quilting, conductivity of, 219

Lichens, 281
Lime, 216
Limestones, 297
Linings, for flues, 260, 266–9
  insulative, 218–20
Liquids, deliquescent, 192
  effect of temperature on evaporation of, 188
  molecular activity in, 181, 182

Magnesium oxide, 260
  sulphate, 260, 292
Mahogany, 319
Mastics, 313, 315, 317, 318, 320, 332
Materials, conductivity of, 200–201
  effects of ageing of, 280
  incompatible, 292–3
Mineral wools, 218
  conductivity of, 219
Ministry of Public Works and Buildings, Advisory Leaflet No. 57, 245
Misting, of shop windows, 249
  prevention of, 248–9
Moisture vapour, absorption of, 192
Molecular activity, 181, 184, 185, 227
Mortars, 261, 298, 332
  lime, 299
  sulphate resistant, 292
  sulphated, 265–6, 300
Mosses, 281, 288, 309

National Building Studies, Bulletin No. 10 (*External Rendered Finishes to Walls*), 217, 277, 326

Oak, 319
Oil, linseed, 216
Osmosis, 196

Paints, action of spalling on, 261
  aluminium, 278
  anti-condense, 218, 244–5, 246, 251, 278
  bitumastic, 252, 261, 277, 312, 315, 326, 337
  cement, 305, 306, 337
  chlorinated rubber, 223, 252, 315
  emulsion, 327
  leaflets on, 245
  red lead, 278, 291, 319
  stone, 298, 305, 306, 327
  throatings blocked by, 286
  to paint or not to paint, 327–8
  water-thinned, 238
  white lead, 319
Pattern staining, 229
Perspiration, 192
Pipes, as possible causes of dampness, 329–30
  correct fixing of, 311–12
  leaks in, 313
Plaster of Paris, 299
Plasterboard, 239
  conductivity of, 201
  foil backed, 238, 277
Plastering, wet, conductivity of, 201
Poly vinyl chloride, expanded, conductivity of, 219
Polystyrene, expanded, 196, 207, 218, 239–41, 245, 246, 251, 278
  conductivity of, 200, 219
  self-extinguishing, 239, 240
  sheeting, 218
  underlinings, 238, 239
Polyurethane, 218, 245
  freon blown, conductivity of, 219
  varnish, 216
  water blown, conductivity of, 219

Poulticing, 312
Primers, 319
  P.J.A. Primer/Undercoat, 319
  P.J.A. sealer, 320
Proofings, 213, 305, 309
Protozoa, 281

Radiators, heating, 249
  cause of dirt over, 228
Rain, damage caused by, 279, 280, 306, 308, 317, 318
Renderings, 216, 217, 261, 280, 305, 318, 327
  difficulty of matching repairs to, 327
Roofs, aluminium recommended for, 261
  bridging caused by, 306
  condense in, 236
  insulation of, 234–5
  leaks in, 330–32
  surface resistances of, 199
Rust expansion, 311–12

Salts, deliquescent, 222
Sandstones, 295, 297
Sawdust, conductivity of, 201
Sheeting, bitumen-impregnated, 223
Silicon esters, 293
Silicone-latex, 293
Siliconate, metallic, 293
Sills, bedding of, 302, 320
  dampness at ends of, 318–19
  repair of, 291, 292, 293, 300
Slate blocks, 331
Slates, 292, 293
Smoke abatement, 259
Snow, 280
Soakage, 280, 312
  through canopies and balconies, 307
Sodium sulphate, 260
Solids, effect of temperature on condensation on, 188
  molecular activity in, 180
Spalling, 261–3, 293
Steel, corrugated, 207

Stonework, acid attacks on, 292
  degradation of, 291–2
  P.C. 100 repair process to, 298–9
  plastic repairs to, 296–8, 299
  re-cutting of, 294–6
  restoration of, 296
  'stucco'' repairs to, 298
  with sulphated joints, 261
Straw board, compressed, conductivity of, 219
Sulphoaluminate, 260
Sulphur dioxide, 258, 259
Sulphuric acid, 192, 258, 260
Sulphurous acid, 258
Surfaces, 188, 194
  condensation on, 193, 207, 223, 243–4
  corrugated, 199, 200
  masking of, 278
  pebbledashed, 326
  prone to condensation, 194
  resistance to heat transmittance of, 188–9, 197
  resistant to condensation, 194
  roughcast, 326
  spalling of, 261–3
  textured, 326
"Synthaprufe", 277

Tapes, non-hardening resinous, 313, 317, 320
Tars, 305, 306, 337
Teak, 319
Temperature, 188, 198, 205, 209, 239
  effect of insulation on, 209–11
  effect on the body of, 254
  interstitial, 209
  surface, 207–9
Thermal resistance, formula for calculating, 202–4
Thermometers, "Kata", 191, 345–7
  wet and dry bulb, 191, 340–42, 343, 344
Thomson weir, 338
Throatings, 284, 285, 290, 295, 314
  decay caused by lack of, 286–9
  repair of, 291

Throatings (*contd.*)
   stone degradation caused by erosion of, 291–2
Tiles, clay, 292, 293
Timber, conductivity of, 200
Titanium tetra-chloride, 244
Town Planning, effect of, 215, 218

"U" values, 197–8, 201, 204, 208, 215, 221, 237
Underflashing, 300, 301, 320, 321
Urea formaldehyde, foamed, 205, 206
   conductivity of, 201, 219
Urea resin, 299

Vapour barriers, 237, 238
   density, 186, 196
Ventilation, 186, 242–52, 332
   as a counter to condensation, 193, 237, 242
   extractor hoods in, 243
   fans in, 242
   inseparable from heating, 197
Vermiculite, loose exfoliated, 236, 239
   conductivity of, 219
Vitriol, oil of. *See* Sulphuric Acid.

Wallpapers, underlining of, 238
   vinyl coated, 231, 255, 278
Walls, cladding of, 216
   dampness in, 196, 215, 317, 318–319
   dampness over, 313–5
   flue condense patches on, 276–7
   heat loss and, 198

Walls (*contd.*)
   isolated damp patches on, 322, 325, 326, 331
   patches on internal, 328–9
   penetrating dampness in, 279–89
   sulphating on, 272–3
   surface resistances of, 199–200
   vegetation on, 309
Washes, protected lime, 327, 337
Water, free surface energy of, 180, 181, 182
   locks, 183
   measures against penetration of, 212
   penetrating capabilities of, 279–80
Water vapour, cooling of, 179
   in exhaled breath, 192
Waterbar, 320, 321
Waterproofing solutions, clear, 293–294
Wax impregnation, 336
Weather flashings, 273, 315
   aluminium, 261
   by-passed by dampness, 304, 307
Weep holes, 324
Windows, decay of sill of, 287–8
   repair of sills of, 291, 292, 293, 300
   temperature drop of, 199
Winds, horizontal pressures of, 283
   penetration caused by, 281–2, 284, 285, 304, 336
Wood wool slab, conductivity of, 200
Woodwork, dealing with decay to, 320